How the Troubles Came to Northern Ireland

Peter Rose

First published in hardcover 2000

First published in paperback 2001 by
PALGRAVE
Houndmills, Basingstoke, Hampshire RG21 6XS and
175 Fifth Avenue, New York, N. Y. 10010
Companies and representatives throughout the world

PALGRAVE is the new global academic imprint of
St. Martin's Press LLC Scholarly and Reference Division and
Palgrave Publishers Ltd (formerly Macmillan Press Ltd).

ISBN 0–333–75346–1 hardback (*outside North America*)
ISBN 0–312–22434–6 hardback (*in North America*)
ISBN 0–333–94941–2 paperback (*worldwide*)

This book is printed on paper suitable for recycling and
made from fully managed and sustained forest sources.

A catalogue record for this book is available
from the British Library.

The Library of Congress has cataloged the hardcover edition as follows:
Rose, Peter, 1938–
    How the troubles came to Northern Ireland / Peter Rose.
        p. cm.
    Includes bibliographical references and index.
    ISBN 0–312–22434–6 (cloth)
     1. Ulster (Northern Ireland and Ireland)—History. 2. Political
    violence—Northern Ireland—History—20th century.
    3. Wilson, Harold, Sir, 1916——Views on Ireland. 4. Ireland–
    –Foreign relations—Great Britain. 5. Great Britain—Foreign
    relations—Ireland. 6. Northern Ireland—History. I. Title.
    DA990.U46R637 1999
    941.6082'3—dc21
                                                        99–25772
                                                        CIP

10   9   8   7   6   5   4   3   2   1
10   09 08 07 06 05 04 03 02 01

Printed in Great Britain by Antony Rowe Ltd, Chippenham, Wiltshire

To the memory of Richard Francis

Contents

Foreword to the Paperback Edition   ix

General Editor's Preface   xi

Author's Preface   xiii

Acknowledgements   xvii

List of Abbreviations   xviii

Chronology   xix

Introduction   1

1   'Leave it to Terence': the Labour Government, October 1964–March 1966   11

2   The 'Crucially Difficult Year', April–August 1966   31

3   Putting off the Evil Day, September 1966–May 1967   58

4   The Phoney Peace, May 1967–March 1968   79

5   The Road to Londonderry, April–October 1968   99

6   'History is against Us', November 1968–April 1969   118

7   To the Top of the Agenda, May–August 1969   150

8   Conclusions   171

Notes   180

Bibliography   204

Index   209

Foreword to the Paperback Edition

Sadly all that has happened since the hardback edition of this book was published a year ago has shown that Northern Ireland remains the United Kingdom's most intractable problem since the Second World War. The Good Friday Agreement is as shaky as ever and the bombs have come back to mainland Britain. Therefore I would claim that the justification for an attempt to explain the origins of 'The Troubles' remains as strong as ever. This paperback edition has given me the opportunity to consult the government papers for 1969 – the last year considered by this book – which were not available at the time of writing. Gratifyingly those documents that were released in January 2000 largely confirm my own findings. However, as I suggested in the original book, some files were likely to be withheld. So I was hardly surprised to find, for example, that the Cabinet minutes for the period after the troops went in during August 1969 did not include ministers' discussions on the Ulster crisis. Instead the researcher reads:

> The Cabinet discussed the situation in Northern Ireland and conclusions reached were separately recorded and circulated only to the Queen, the Prime Minister and those ministers who had to take action.

What is available provides valuable corroboration for the sources I used not least the published and unpublished diaries of Richard Crossman. It was fashionable to accuse Crossman of inaccuracy and irresponsibility. For example I quoted James Callaghan saying 25 years later: 'Well, of course you have to take anything Dick says with a pinch of salt.' But Crossman turns out to have been a good reporter.

What also comes out clearly from the new documents is the totally inadequate intelligence about Northern Ireland available to the government and the Army during those crucial months in 1969 before the troops went in. This I argued contributed significantly to the government's fatal hesitation that year. A revealing minute from the Joint Intelligence Committee who had been considering the worsening situation in the July admits: 'We can only keep our fingers crossed and hope for the best.'

Another important revelation concerned the infamous Apprentice Boys' March on 12 August 1969 which in effect sparked off the whole of The Troubles. Whether or not to allow the march split the Cabinet and the Prime Minister, Harold Wilson, claimed later in his memoirs that he had wanted to ban the march but had reluctantly allowed 'unwiser counsels' to prevail. This was clearly a reference to the Home Secretary James Callaghan who had agreed that the march go ahead. That this was not merely hindsight is confirmed by a memorandum from Callaghan on his decision to be found in the Prime Minister's files. In the margin is a scribbled note in green ink initialled by Wilson expressing his concerns about allowing the march.

Finally the documents confirm my findings that detailed contingency plans for intervention in Northern Ireland were well advanced by the summer of 1969 despite the Cabinet's reluctance to take any such step. My principle informant was Sir John Chilcot, former Permanent Secretary at the Northern Ireland Office, who as a young civil servant in the 1960s had prepared a 'war book' on possible intervention. He told me of these secret preparations which he rightly said would be revealed for the first time in 2000. Sure enough a Callaghan memorandum to the Cabinet in May 1969 reports that at the beginning of the year a contingency plan was drawn up including a draft Bill for direct rule from London. What is entirely new, however, is a remarkable warning from Callaghan to his Cabinet colleagues. In the event of an insurrection in Northern Ireland military rule may have to be brought in including trying civilians by Court Martial!

PETER ROSE
London

General Editor's Preface

Between 1880 and 1921 Ireland was a running sore in British politics. The constitutional settlement of 1921, however, for all its flaws, brought this period to an end. As chronicled in the first book to appear in this series, *The Northern Ireland Question in British Politics*, the British political classes, much to their relief, were then able by and large to ignore Ireland, both North and South, for much of the next 50 years. British governments of both parties essentially left the Unionist statelet that had been created in 1921 to its own devices. That statelet, meanwhile, sought to secure itself against what it saw as a disloyal – and substantial – minority. The mechanism enshrined in the 1920 Government of Ireland Act to ensure a reasonable representation of that minority, the single transferable vote, was removed for local elections and all but the university seats in the lower house in the 1920s. There was gerrymandering of boundaries and restrictions on the local government franchise. In addition, although by no means uniquely in post-war Europe, housing allocation was used to maximise the representation of the politically loyal.

Such measures, however, far from ensuring the survival of the Unionist statelet, seem to have contributed to its downfall. Stormont nevertheless saw off the IRA border campaign of 1956–62, not least with the co-operation of the Irish *garda*. But internal consent was failing. The 1960s saw a gathering and increasingly vociferous campaign for civil rights for the minority Nationalist community. As Peter Rose shows, by the mid-1960s the Prime Minister of Northern Ireland, Terence O'Neill, was already deeply pessimistic about the chances of successfully managing the situation. The Unionist statelet was falling apart and the Unionists themselves were internally divided over how to respond to the civil rights movement. The Wilson government elected in Britain in 1964, however, did little in the face of this steadily deteriorating situation.

This is the first book to examine British policy towards Northern Ireland at this critical juncture. Using newly released papers and extensive interviews with both politicians and civil servants concerned with the development of policy towards Northern Ireland, it explores the British responses to the gathering crisis. For the first time it shows how well aware the British were of the problem. Not only was there an active group of Labour backbenchers, the Campaign for

Democracy in Ulster, constantly trying to draw attention to the issue. Wilson himself promised to address the problem of civil rights abuses in Northern Ireland during the 1964 election campaign. In the event, however, his government proved no more willing than its predecessors to intervene in Northern Ireland. This arms-length principle might have been convenient, if nothing else, if the Unionist statelet had remained stable. But it did not. As a result the Wilson government was in the end forced to intervene, deploying troops in aid of the civil power in 1969.

Their reluctance to take this move is understandable; as subsequent history has shown, putting the troops in was a lot easier than getting them out again. The question Peter Rose has sought to address is whether this expedient could have been avoided by judicious and more limited intervention at an earlier stage, before the problems in Northern Ireland reached critical point. Indeed, would the British, by such means, have succeeded in continuing to keep Northern Ireland off the domestic political agenda? This is, of course, a counterfactual question – we cannot know whether such intervention would have been effective. What he does show, however, for the first time, is the extent to which such intervention was contemplated. Nevertheless, down to 1969 the Wilson government never really had the courage of its convictions, continuing to leave it to O'Neill to tackle a situation which he was not equipped to deal with. Whether a different policy would have been more successful is unknowable, though that does not mean that the question should not be asked. After all, what we do know is that the consequences of the flare-up in Northern Ireland by the end of the 1960s were years of civil strife and unrest and the deaths of more than 3000 pople.

PETER CATTERALL

Author's Preface

The burden of this book is the Labour government's Northern Ireland policy from October 1964 to August 1969. The idea for the book arose out of discussions with two people personally involved in the events which followed the decision to send troops to Northern Ireland in August 1969. They were Kevin McNamara, MP, later shadow Northern Ireland Secretary, and Sir Richard Francis, Controller of BBC Northern Ireland in the early 1970s. Both pointed out that no research had been done on the failure of the Wilson government to develop a policy to meet the deteriorating situation in the province, something which was clearly discernible from 1966 onwards. Both believed that research would show that a successful intervention in some form by the British government at an earlier stage would have been possible and might have prevented the rise of the Provisional Irish Republican Army and the tragedy that unfolded thereafter.

Time spent on filling this research gap was easy to justify. The breakdown in law and order in the province, following the collapse of the Labour government's policy of non-intervention led to the loss of more than 3000 lives and nearly wiped out a Conservative Cabinet. The cost to the taxpayer of combating terrorism for nearly 30 years has been immense. The 'Troubles' consistently diverted ministers and officials from the normal conduct of business in a mature democracy. There was also the Ulster factor at Westminster which first reared its head soon after Harold Wilson came to power in 1964. His government, which barely had a majority, could have been brought down by the Ulster Unionist MPs voting with their Tory allies. Finally, we now know that the Wilson government was confronted by the Irish question early on. Papers released in January 1997 show that the government was planning to send troops to Northern Ireland to deal with an IRA bombing campaign which intelligence reports predicted would mark the fiftieth anniversary of the Easter Rising in April 1966. These revelations make it all the more remarkable that Wilson and his ministers paid so little attention to Ulster until serious violence erupted in October 1968.

The focus of my research was entirely on Westminster and Whitehall. Much had already been written about events in Northern Ireland, including the role of the Stormont government. The political parties and the pressure groups which arose in Ulster in the 1960s such as the Northern Ireland Civil Rights Association (NICRA) and People's Democracy (PD) are beyond the scope of this survey and have in many cases been the subject of thorough academic research. Much has also been written about the Northern Ireland Labour Party which in any case was in decline by the time of the 1964 General Election.[1] The one exception to this general rule is the Ulster Unionist Party at Westminster, which drew considerable hostility from Labour MPs, not least Harold Wilson himself.

In addition, the examination of the role of Dublin during these years is somewhat limited. By the 1970s, of course, the Republic was a key factor in the attempts by successive British governments to resolve the crisis. But until the violence of August 1969 Dublin did not really impinge on the Wilson government's thinking. Relations with the Republic had improved and the Irish government seemed happy enough to shadow London's policy of non-intervention in the province.

Research into government policy during the 1960s faced serious difficulties. Because of the 30-year rule no official documents were available for much of the period under examination. This meant that it was essential to interview the major players, the senior politicians and civil servants of the day. However, several of them had died or were too frail to interview. These, alas, included the Prime Minister of the time himself, Harold Wilson, Michael Stewart, the Foreign Secretary, and George Brown, Deputy Prime Minister until 1968. Fortunately this deficiency was at least partly made up by wide use of the primary sources available. These included: national newspapers, the weeklies, and the Ulster press, particularly the estimable *Belfast Telegraph*.[2] A detailed analysis of *Hansard* for the years 1964–69 proved invaluable. I also consulted archives not subject to the 30-year rule including the records of the Campaign for Democracy in Ulster, the principle pressure group for reform at Westminster, the Society of Labour Lawyers [who took up discrimination in Ulster very early on], the Labour Party and the Conservative Party.

Crucial information came from a seminar on Northern Ireland policy in the late 1960s which I organised in conjunction with the Institute of Contemporary British History (ICBH). The chief witness was the Home Secretary of the time, James Callaghan. His evidence, and that of several other witnesses, provided some of the most illuminating material in the course of my research. I am grateful to the ICBH, and its director, Dr Peter Catterall, for giving me this opportunity.

The secondary sources were meagre. Memoirs and ministerial

diaries were consulted but the subject has held little interest for historians and politicians. An exception is Richard Crossman, who gives revealing, if highly personalised, insights into Wilson's thinking as the situation in Northern Ireland worsened. Wilson's own memoirs, much criticised and self-serving though they were, contained brief but significant references to his Northern Ireland policy. The remainder of the diaries, monographs, memoirs and so on consulted proved disappointing. The politicians wrote largely about the momentous events of the time seemingly unaware of what was happening in Northern Ireland, something which itself is a significant factor.

The aim of the book, in short, has been to answer one central question: why did the government not act sooner? It is taken as read that the only people capable of bringing reform to Ulster were Labour ministers elected in October 1964 and returned 18 months later with a majority of 97. The full weight of the 'establishment' in Britain may have been against intervention and certainly the traditional advice of the civil service was always cautious. The media, with a couple of honourable exceptions, were not interested. (I was a lobby correspondent at Westminster from 1966 onwards and I was as unaware as the rest of my colleagues of the growing crisis in Ulster.) However, what are ministers for if not to act? Wilson came to power sympathetic to the idea of Irish unity, and having made promises to Ulster civil rights workers that a Labour government would tackle Catholic grievances.[3]

Five years later little had been achieved. I have attempted to establish whether or not the government was guilty, as some have argued, of moral failure in not acting decisively earlier. But whatever else I hope I can claim that a research gap has been filled.

STRUCTURE OF THE BOOK

The Introduction is concerned largely with the development of Labour's Irish policy from the later 1930s, when the party supported the return of the Treaty ports to Eire, to the guarantee given by the Labour Prime Minister, Clement Attlee, to the Protestants of Northern Ireland after Dublin's decision in 1948 to set up a Republic. In general, the subject is treated chronologically. Chapter 1 deals with the election in 1964 of a Labour government committed to reform in Northern Ireland but with a tiny majority. The constitutional question and the convention that Ulster matters could not be discussed at

Westminster are analysed and the new papers revealing that the government was warned of a major IRA campaign in the spring of 1966 are examined in detail. Chapter 2 is concerned with the first five months of Wilson's second administration when there was a growing demand from Labour backbench MPs for intervention in Northern Ireland and when sectarian violence returned to the province. Chapter 3 examines the pivotal period in the first half of 1967 when the government received a series of warnings about Catholic unrest. Chapter 4 covers the period between May 1967 and March the following year when the government's policy of non-intervention was consolidated, first by Roy Jenkins and then by his successor as Home Secretary, James Callaghan. Chapter 5, covering the period from April to October 1968, charts a sharp change in the political atmosphere, from the optimism arising out of Captain Terence O'Neill's fifth anniversary as Prime Minister of Northern Ireland to the explosion of violence in Londonderry. Chapter 6 deals with the collapse of O'Neillism and the demise of the Labour government's policy of non-intervention. Chapter 7 examines the period between O'Neill's resignation in April 1969 and the decision to intervene by sending troops to Ulster to contain the outbreak of serious violence in the province in August. The Conclusion summarises and evaluates the evidence thrown up by the research which, it is suggested, demonstrates that there was a real chance that earlier intervention by the government might have prevented the rise of the Provisional IRA without provoking an unmanageable Protestant backlash. It is not possible to prove that such a course would have worked but many share the view that it might have done.

Acknowledgements

I gratefully acknowledge help given by the following: the staff of the Public Records Office at Kew, when I was researching government documents; the staff of the Public Record Office Northern Ireland when I was examining the files of the Campaign for Democracy in Ulster; the staff of the Institute of Contemporary British History; Stephen Bird at the National Museum of Labour History, Manchester; Dr Angela Raspin, former Head of the Archive Department at the British Library of Political and Economic Science. I should also like to thank Sir Kenneth Bloomfield, Sir John Chilcot, Sir Frank Cooper, Professor John Griffith, and Roy Lilley for providing me with indispensable information. I am particularly indebted to the following for all the help and consideration they gave me in the completion of the thesis on which this book is based: Kevin McNamara, MP, Professor Paul Bew, Professor Peter Hennessy, Professor John Ramsden, Dr Sarah Palmer, Professor John Miller and Dr Peter Catterall. Finally, thanks are due to my wife Susan Rose for all her help with the project from proofreading to much-needed moral support.

In addition I am grateful for permission to quote from the unpublished diaries of Crossman, CDU files (PRONI), Society of Labour Lawyers' files (the B.L.P.E.S. LSE) and the Macmillan diaries.

List of Abbreviations

CDU   Campaign for Democracy in Ulster
CSJ   Campaign for Social Justice [in Northern Ireland]
DEA   Department of Economic Affairs
ICBH   Institute of Contemporary British History
ICJ   International Commission of Jurists
IRA   Irish Republican Army
NCCL   National Council for Civil Liberties
NEC   National Executive Committee [of the Labour Party]
NICRA   Northern Ireland Civil Rights Association
NILP   Northern Ireland Labour Party
PD   People's Democracy
PIRA   Provisional Irish Republican Army
PLP   Parliamentary Labour Party
PPS   Parliamentary Private Secretary
PRO   Public Record Office
RUC   Royal Ulster Constabulary
SLL   Society of Labour Lawyers
UVF   Ulster Volunteer Force

Chronology

1921	*May*: George V inaugurates Northern Ireland Parliament.
1948	*December*: Irish Premier J.A. Costello announces that Eire is to become a Republic and leave the Commonwealth.
1949	*June*: British government passes Ireland Act which guarantees that Northern Ireland will remain within UK unless its parliament decides otherwise.
1963	*March*: 'Liberal' Terence O'Neill succeeds Lord Brookeborough as PM of Northern Ireland.
1964	*October*: Labour win the British General Election. Harold Wilson is the new Prime Minister and pledges to improve civil rights for Northern Ireland's Catholics.
1965	*January*: historic meeting between Irish Prime Minister Sean Lemass and Northern Ireland premier O'Neill. *June*: Campaign for Democracy in Ulster (CDU) founded in London.
1966	*June*: sectarian violence in Northern Ireland. UVF commit three murders. Ian Paisley convicted of unlawful assembly and sent to prison.
1967	*April*: Northern Ireland Civil Rights Association (NICRA) formed.
1968	*October*: RUC clash with civil rights marchers in Londonderry. [Television coverage worldwide.] People's Democracy (PD) radical leftist group formed at Queen's University, Belfast. *November*: British government forces Stormont to bring in reforms; subsequent reforms regarded as inadequate by civil rights movement. *December*: O'Neill's televised 'Crossroads' speech appealing for reconciliation.
1969	*January*: 'Battle of Burntollet Bridge'. PD march attacked by Protestants. *February*: General Election in Ulster fails to strengthen

O'Neill's position. He resigns in April and is succeeded by James Chichester-Clark.

August: outbreak of violence in Londonderry followed by riots in Belfast. Wilson sends troops to Northern Ireland to prevent civil war. Irish Prime Minister Jack Lynch threatens to intervene. The Troubles and decades of slaughter begin.

Introduction

When Harold Wilson came to power in 1964 he was committed to changing Labour's Irish policy, something which had been set in stone since the Second World War. Ireland's neutrality and later her decision to leave the Commonwealth and establish a Republic led Labour's leaders to distrust Dublin as much as their Conservative opponents did. However, before the war Labour had adopted a more benign stance towards Ireland and her leader, Eamonn de Valera. This was demonstrated when, in April 1938, the Government of Neville Chamberlain agreed that the three Atlantic naval ports, the so-called Treaty ports retained by Britain because they were seen as vital to her defence since 1921, should be handed over to Eire. This deal, which was supposed to usher in an era of friendship and co-operation between Britain and Ireland, was welcomed by Labour leaders who congratulated Chamberlain on his success. Labour at that time considered de Valera's approach reasonable. He had not taken the South out of the Commonwealth and they were sympathetic to his vision of a united Ireland.

During the first year of the war, Labour leaders remained well-disposed towards Dublin; this is shown by a remarkable letter Ernest Bevin wrote to Churchill on 18 June 1940 shortly after he joined his coalition government. [He entered the war cabinet in September, 1940.][1] In it Bevin, who was to be responsible as Foreign Secretary for Britain's foreign policy for the five years after the war, argued strongly that in exchange for co-operation over defence Eire should be offered a new constitution on the basis of a united Ireland at the end of the war. Another of Labour's leading figures, Herbert Morrison, had begun the war with 'instinctive prejudices against Unionists'.[2] Morrison, as Home Secretary in the War Cabinet, was responsible for Northern Ireland and he visited the province each year. However, he soon changed his mind, impressed by the passionate loyalty of the Ulster Protestants. In a speech given in 1943 he said that the differing relationship between Britain and the two parts of Ireland during the war was bound to have a permanently modifying effect on many people's opinions in Britain. Morrison was no longer concerned with the lack of social justice or political democracy in

Ulster and after the war he continued to keep a protective eye on Ulster's interests in the Labour Cabinet.[3]

Morrison's experience, and prejudice, clearly influenced the attitude of the new Labour government after 1945. Ministers who were about to begin a major programme of decolonisation might have been expected to be sympathetic to nationalist aspirations in Ireland and the rigid right-wing stance of the Unionist administration can have hardly been to their taste. That nothing was done to disturb the Protestant hegemony can be attributed, at least partly, to the intervention of Morrison. As Lord President he had no direct responsibility for Irish policy, North or South. However, his views were highly respected by Lord Addison, who as Dominions Secretary,[4] was responsible for Irish policy. In 1946 following a private visit to de Valera, Morrison wrote a memorandum for the Cabinet in which he advocated total support for Partition whatever the consequences for Britain's relationship with Eire.[5] Addison had already warned the Cabinet that the British people would not take kindly to any attempt to embrace Dublin at this stage because of Eire's neutrality and he advocated continuing the policy of distant relations with Dublin.[6] Addison also made it clear that for strategic [by which he clearly meant military] as well as political reasons Partition could not be on the agenda. A year later the Cabinet had before them an account of a long meeting Morrison had held with de Valera, on 12 September 1946. Commending Morrison's uncompromising attitude, Addison told his colleagues that any suggestion that the Government was prepared to consider Partition was certain to lead to serious trouble, adding, 'We must be careful not to find ourselves on a slippery slope'.[7]

For the remainder of Labour's period in office, according to the historian of the Attlee government, Kenneth Morgan, nothing whatever was done to overhaul the system of government in Northern Ireland for all its proven gerrymandering by the Protestant Unionist ascendancy.[8] Thirty backbench Labour MPs set up the 'Friends of Ireland' group to campaign for equal rights for Catholics in Ulster, a forerunner of the Campaign for Democracy in Ulster (CDU) which was formed during the first Wilson administration. Indeed some of the older members of the CDU had been involved in the earlier campaign. However, the 'Friends of Ireland' were largely ignored by their own government. A distaste for involvement in Ulster, wrote Paul Bew, 'was accompanied by a general reluctance, on the part of the English ruling class to appear to take sides against a Northern government which was seen as having "done its bit" during the war in contrast to the government in the South...."[9] For its part, the Unionist regime in Belfast had greeted the election of a Labour government intent on a massive programme of nationalisation with considerable suspicion. Would there not follow, inevitably, clashes between the two governments which might endanger the union?[10] Indeed, Dominion status was briefly considered as a means of escaping socialist planning. However, fear of losing huge agricultural subsidies to Ulster farmers and other benefits voted by the Imperial Parliament persuaded Stormont against such an option.[11] Twenty years later the Wilson government was to consider withholding subsidies to persuade Belfast to speed up reform.[12]

When Labour came to power in 1945 Eire was still a member of the Commonwealth. However, in September, 1948 the new Prime Minister of Eire, John Costello, announced his intention to repeal the External Relations Act making it clear this meant the South would leave the Commonwealth and set up a republic. Writing in 1971, the Irish historian F.S.L. Lyons, said it would not have been surprising if some alarm and disapproval had not been voiced or even expressed in some kind of retaliatory action. That this proved not to be the case may have been due in part to the good offices of the other British Dominions.[13] The papers released since Lyons wrote those words[14] show that Labour ministers did voice alarm and disapproval at Dublin's decision but recognised that retaliatory action would be futile.[15] Under pressure from the Dominions (as Lyons had suggested) they accepted Ireland's exit from the Commonwealth while at the same time allowing the new republic the same privileges regarding trade and citizenship as before. Their main preoccupation was to assuage Northern Ireland's fears that secession by the South threatened Partition.

From the very start of the crisis Labour ministers were determined that the economic and constitutional status of the North would not be adversely affected. Between September 1948 and March 1949, at a series of meetings, the Cabinet discussed at great length what the British reaction to the Costello announcement should be. In view of the events that occurred in Northern Ireland 20 years later, it is significant that some Labour politicians who were involved in these discussions held senior office in Wilson's 1960's governments. This, after all, was their introduction to the seemingly intractable problems of Anglo-Irish relations. Wilson, President of the Board of Trade, attended most of the Cabinet meetings which discussed the Dublin *démarche* though there is no record in the Cabinet minutes of what part, if any, he played. The meetings were also attended by Sir Frank Soskice, Solicitor General, who became Home Secretary with responsibility for Northern Ireland in 1964 and Patrick Gordon Walker, under-secretary at the Commonwealth Relations Office, who held several offices under Wilson including Foreign Secretary. At the outset the Cabinet received a warning from the Secretary of State for Commonwealth Relations, Philip Noel-Baker, that the Dublin decision had raised 'grave problems' for both Britain and the Commonwealth. Noel-Baker was too old for office by the time Wilson came to power but he was one of the most influential elder statesmen in the Parliamentary Labour Party.

The Cabinet papers covering many of the debates which preceded the decision to bring in the Ireland Bill (described below) have been published by the historian, Ronald Hyam. In his introduction Hyam comments that a notable feature of the way Ireland was handled was the determination to be friendly and practical. Noel-Baker was anxious to do everything they could to meet de Valera on revision of the British nationality law, avoiding forms of words which needlessly embarrassed him [a change from Morrisonian disdain of the 'Long Fellow'] or were distasteful to Irish nationalists. When the Irish Government had first proposed leaving the Commonwealth there was, said Hyam, a good deal of misgiving in London. Eire seemed to put formal independence before the reunification of Ireland. Although in fact Partition was not negotiable, if only for strategic reasons, and the Labour government feared they would find it awkward to have to support Partition positively and give Ulster the vigorous protection which would almost certainly be demanded. Attlee was all for putting the implications squarely to the Irish and being as co-operative as possible.[16]

British ministers held two secret meetings in Paris with Commonwealth leaders who sympathised with Dublin's position. During this process the Prime Minister of Northern Ireland, Sir Basil Brooke, spent the night of 20 November at Chequers.[17] Two days later Attlee revealed that he had given the Northern Ireland leader an assurance that the constitutional position of the province would be safeguarded which assurance he had agreed Sir Basil could make public.[18] At a Cabinet meeting three days later [attended incidentally by several non-Cabinet members including George Brown, Michael Stewart and Christopher Mayhew, all of whom served in Wilson's government] it was decided that the Prime Minister should tell the

House of Commons of the outcome of the secret meetings at Chequers and in Paris.[19] On 15 December, Bevin, Foreign Secretary and the most influential figure in the Labour government, made his first intervention on Ireland's secession. He was concerned lest the change in the constitutional status of Eire should have the effect of creating in Great Britain an Irish vote which would be embarrassing to him in his conduct of foreign policy and he was anxious that the Foreign Office should not undertake any responsibility for Irish business. Attlee assured him that Irish business would be left to the Commonwealth Relations Office.[20]

While the Cabinet was keeping on good terms with Dublin, Labour ministers were also giving cast-iron guarantees to Belfast. On 6 January 1949 talks were held between British and Stormont ministers. Attlee's team included Patrick Gordon Walker.[21] At the Cabinet meeting six days later the Prime Minister revealed that the legislation to deal with Dublin's decision (which became the Ireland Act 1949) would include the guarantee that Northern Ireland would not cease to be part of the UK except with the consent of the Parliament of Northern Ireland.[22] Just how hard the Labour government's position had become on Partition is indicated by the report of a special working party of officials contained in a memorandum to the Cabinet from Attlee. This declared that it would never be to Great Britain's advantage that Northern Ireland should form part of a territory outside HM's jurisdiction. 'Indeed it seems unlikely that Great Britain would be able to agree to this even if the people of Northern Ireland desired it.'[23] There was, however, one member of the government who strongly opposed Attlee's guarantee to Ulster, Lord Pakenham, Minister for Civil Aviation and the holder of an Irish peerage who was later to be a member of Harold Wilson's Cabinet. Pakenham said that in two northern counties there was a majority in favour of ending Partition and if the issue ever came before an international court the view might be expressed that these counties should be transferred to Eire. The right solution lay in the political unity of Ireland and the strategic unity of Ireland and the UK.[24] [Twenty years later, as Lord Longford, and Leader of the House of Lords, he was unsuccessfully trying to alert Wilson and other Cabinet members to the dangers of failing to redress the grievances of Northern Ireland's Catholics.]

Senior Labour ministers, however, never wavered in their determination not to alarm the Unionists. When the Ireland Bill was published on 3 May 1949 the Irish Foreign Minister, Sean MacBride, protested to Bevin and Noel-Baker about the guarantee to the North. Bevin's reply was uncompromising. Without the help of the North, Hitler would have unquestionably won the submarine war and the UK would have been defeated. That would have brought Hitler to Dublin and they would have made the Irish their slaves. Bevin added that the Irish had made any move about Partition even more difficult by leaving the Commonwealth and refusing to join NATO.[25]

Throughout this period ministers also had to take account of King George VI's views. That the King was taking a close interest in the Irish crisis is revealed in notes prepared by officials for Attlee for his regular weekly meetings with the Monarch. As early as 10 September 1948, the memorandum listing subjects suitable for discussion referred to the forthcoming meeting of Commonwealth Prime Ministers and suggested, 'The Prime Minister might also tell the King how it is proposed to handle the question of representation of Eire at the meeting.' On 7 October, the note suggested that Attlee might refer to Costello's statement about the repeal of the External Relations Act and 'indicate what steps HM's Government were taking in the matter'. On 25 November, it was proposed that when Attlee saw the King the following day he should give him a brief summary of the position of the UK and other Commonwealth countries vis-à-vis Eire.

These regular, and apparently detailed briefings continued until after the Second Reading of the Ireland Bill on 11 May 1949. Attlee was advised that when he saw the King five days later, 'His Majesty may wish to have a first hand account of the debate ... and to be informed in more detail of the Government's attitude towards recent statements which have been made in the Dail about Partition.'[26] One issue that troubled the King was the question of change in the Royal Style and Titles that would be necessary once Eire became a republic. In a letter to the King on 12 January 1949, Attlee explained that using the name 'Ulster' instead of Northern Ireland had been very carefully considered but rejected because this would certainly have provoked unfriendly feelings between the Irish peoples. A note from Sir Alan Lascelles, the King's private secretary, to Laurence Helsby, Attlee's Principal Private Secretary, the following day made it clear that Attlee had convinced the King. It said that, 'His Majesty fully appreciates the reasons why the name "Ulster" was not adopted.'[27]

The King might have been satisfied but the views of Attlee, Bevin and other senior ministers did not receive the unanimous endorsement of Labour backbenchers. Indeed the hostile reaction towards the Ireland Bill of a large section of the Parliamentary Labour Party (PLP) marked the beginning of a concern among Labour back-benchers for the rights of the Northern Catholics which resulted 15 years later in the formation of the CDU. Moving the Second Reading of the Ireland Bill on 11 May 1949 Attlee explained that the government recognised the right of the Parliament of Northern Ireland to decide on behalf of the people of Northern Ireland to stay in or leave the UK and Commonwealth.[28] At a Cabinet meeting the following day ministers were informed that a small number of Government supporters had abstained from voting on the Second Reading. They were anxious about the fairness of the electoral arrangements in Northern Ireland. Doubts were expressed about the wisdom of leaving the powers of veto in the hands of a Parliament which might not fairly reflect the people's will. The suggestion was made that after the Bill was passed the UK government might investigate whether Stormont did reflect fairly the views of the electors. However, the minutes record that it was the general view of ministers that the UK government would be ill-advised to intervene in a matter which fell wholly in the jurisdiction of Stormont.[29] This determination that Westminster should not intervene to reform the voting system in the province was maintained by Wilson's administration until the violent events in Londonderry on 5 October 1968.[30]

The size of the backbench rebellion, one of the biggest of Attlee's administration, that now followed alarmed the government. During the Committee Stage of the Bill on 16 May, most speakers from the government benches attacked the guarantee to the Northern Ireland Parliament with its entrenched Protestant Unionist majority. In an attempt to head off a major revolt, the Lord President of the Council, Morrison, said that the issue was exceedingly serious and the future of the country was somewhat involved in it. The result, however, was a damaging rebellion against government policy. According to an analysis in *The Times* on 18 May 'one third of Government back-benchers did not vote in defiance of a three-line-whip'.[31] The revolt had been reported prominently in *The Times* the previous day under the headline 'Labour Votes Against Government' and the news-paper's political correspondent wrote that the anti-government vote would have been even greater but for a cogent speech by Morrison.[32] The following day *The Times* suggested that no disciplinary action would be taken against the rebels other than a mild rebuke by party leaders.[33] This clearly underestimated the fury of Attlee and Bevin. On 19 May the leading report in *The Times* reported that Attlee had sacked four Parliamentary Private Secretaries who had voted against their own government. They included Robert Mellish who was to be Government Chief Whip in 1969, the year the troops were sent in to Northern Ireland. (A fifth PPS resigned anticipating Attlee's action.) Attlee told the ministers whom these PPSs served that they had committed a serious breach of party discipline. However, it is clear than many Labour backbenchers felt that Attlee's purge was unwarranted.[34] Large though the revolt had been the rebels were not united in their reasons for opposing the guarantee to Stormont. Professor Bew has pointed out that the main division was between those who took a traditional nationalist line and collaborated with the Anti-Partition League and a larger group who were simply concerned that 'British' standards of democracy and justice did not exist in Northern Ireland.[35] The CDU was the natural descendant of this second group because few of them were pressing for an end to Partition.

This was the last time that a Labour government found itself involved in the affairs of Northern Ireland until the campaign for civil rights in the province in the late 1960s. It is now clear that the surprising degree of support for an Ulster administration which was at the other end of the spectrum, in political and economic terms, from the Labour Party was based on strategic considerations and not on admiration for Protestant Unionism. Stormont did not commend itself to at least one member of that Cabinet, Harold Wilson, who had had first-hand experience of it during the war. At the time, Wilson, a young wartime temporary civil servant, was joint secretary of the British War Cabinet's Manpower Requirements Committee. During a visit to Ulster he was appalled by the way the province 'signally failed to achieve an impressive popular mobilisation for the anti-fascist struggle.'[36] He prepared a detailed report on the province's war effort. In it he wrote: 'Ulster far from becoming an important centre of munitions production has become a depressed area.... Northern Ireland's contribution to the economic war effort has been negligible ... there is little or no economic co-ordination between Great Britain and Northern Ireland.'[37]

The Ireland Act was the high point of Labour 'Unionism'. From the loss of the 1951 General Election until Labour's return to power in 1964, both right and left of the party moved towards a position sympathetic to the nationalists. Writing in the *Daily Herald* in June 1953, Michael Foot, a future Labour leader (though not a minister until 1974), sounded a warning about the violence to come in Northern Ireland. Headed: 'Ulster: the bomb on our doorstep', the article outlined religious discrimination in the province and calculated that election malpractice in Ulster disenfranchised 300 000 people. It was time, wrote Foot, to ask questions 'about this forgotten island where Britain still retains a foothold of responsibility. We should not wait for bomb outrages to shake us from our sloth'.[38] Speaking in the House of Commons from Labour's Front Bench on 6 July 1953 Aneurin Bevan said the time had come to end the representation of Ulster at Westminster.[39]

In 1954 two leading right-wingers also began to have second thoughts about Labour's Irish policy. In his diaries, Patrick Gordon Walker, who was to become, very briefly, Foreign Secretary in the first Wilson administration, wonders whether he ought to come out against Partition in Ireland which was morally wrong and put Britain in the wrong. He put the argument to George Brown, who appears to have agreed but said that trade union leaders would have to be consulted. Gordon Walker then spoke to the Irish Foreign Minister, Liam Cosgrave, stressing that a condition of ending Partition would be that the South entered NATO. Cosgrave said he was sure there would be no difficulty.[40]

CONCLUSION

During the 25 years before the election of the Wilson government in 1964, Labour's thinking on Northern Ireland was dictated by external events rather than by any considered policy for the whole of Ireland. Ireland only came high on the political agenda – for both Labour and Conservative ministers – when issues such as the Treaty Ports, Dublin's role in the Second World War, or Costello's announcement that Eire would quit the Commonwealth came to the fore. At such times Westminster and Whitehall were temporarily compelled to face up to the unfinished business of the Government of Ireland Act, 1920. At first Labour leaders were sympathetic to de Valera and enthusiastically backed the return of the Treaty Ports to Eire. However, as has been shown, this benign view was soon transformed by the experience of the war years in the North and South of Ireland. By the time the Attlee government was in office leading figures including Bevin and Morrison were hostile to Dublin. Eire's decision to leave the Commonwealth hardened this view and led to a Labour government giving Ulster Unionists the guarantee that they could remain part of the United Kingdom for as long as they wished.

This was the end of active policy-making towards Ireland by either government for many years. Once the Ireland Act was in place the issue returned to the back-burner where it remained during Labour's long years in opposition. The leadership, certainly until men like Callaghan, Gordon Walker and Brown were in senior positions, remained unwilling to disturb the *status quo* and even consider reform, let alone Partition. Their attitude was still governed by the 'treacherous Dev' image to which Morrison had subscribed.

1 'Leave it to Terence': the Labour Government, October 1964–March 1966

A convention is a hardened constitutional practice ...
Professor John Griffith[1]

This chapter deals with Labour's Northern Ireland policy in the run-up to the general election in October 1964 and the development of that policy during the brief administration, which ended with the General Election of March 1966. The attitude of the Labour leader, Harold Wilson, is considered both in opposition and in government and the early attempts of backbench Labour MPs to raise Catholic grievances in the Commons are analysed. They were prevented from doing so by the convention that Northern Ireland issues – including discrimination – could not be raised at Westminster. The origin of this convention, and the question of whether it could or could not have been breached, are discussed in detail. Evidence newly released under the 30-year rule – mentioned above – of the threat of a major IRA bombing campaign to mark the 50th anniversary of the Easter Rising is examined and the chapter ends with a hint of constitutional change – a secret proposal by Wilson to curb the powers of Ulster MPs at Westminster.

Between the Ireland Act of 1949 and the advent of a Labour government in 1964, Ireland, North and South, was given a low priority by the Labour Party. In part, this was, no doubt, due to the absence of political unrest or violence in the province during those years. The IRA campaign of 1956–62 had failed to arouse Catholic support and had been easily suppressed by the local security forces. A reading of the minutes of the Labour Party National Executive Committee for those years[2] makes it clear that the party was content to leave Ulster politics to the Northern Ireland Labour Party (NILP). Though not affiliated the NILP did receive a small annual subsidy from the British party.[3]

An important exception to Labour's apparent lack of interest in

Northern Ireland was a brief visit to the province in 1954 by a party of senior Labour MPs led by James Callaghan who was to be responsible for Northern Ireland as Home Secretary 13 years later. Callaghan was accompanied by Alf Robens and Arthur Bottomley, both Opposition Front Bench spokesmen. The main purpose of the visit was to investigate the hardship caused by the high level of unemployment. Sir Charles Brett, a leading member of the NILP, regarded the visit as significant because the local party felt that they now had 'friends' at Westminster. In the early 1960s Brett and David Bleakley, NILP treasurer, met Hugh Gaitskell, the Labour leader, and formed 'useful relations'.[4] Callaghan reported on his Northern Ireland visit to the Commons on 31 January 1955. Speaking from the Opposition Front Bench [he was the party's spokesman on colonial affairs] he said:

> We have done what we could to bring the plight of the people of Northern Ireland to the attention of this House and however inconvenient it may be to Ulster Unionists opposite. I promise them that we shall bring it up here again and again until they rise and make certain that their own government in Stormont and at Westminster solve this tragic problem.[5]

Many years later Callaghan recalled that during the visit to Ulster the Labour delegation had also been appalled by discrimination against Catholics in the allocation of housing. He wrote:

> we had been particularly incensed by the blatant discrimination shown in the building and letting of houses by the local authorities. Some of them hardly troubled to deny that they built housing estates only in Protestant areas and had little or no intention of relieving overcrowded slum conditions for Catholic families. When I became Home Secretary several years later the position had improved very little and I applied strong pressure to the Stormont Government to remove their housing powers from the local authorities....[6]

Labour's interest in Northern Ireland revived in 1964, the year that the Campaign for Social Justice in Northern Ireland (CSJ) was launched in Belfast.[7] Harold Wilson, who had succeeded Gaitskell as Labour leader after the latter's death the previous year, was considered sympathetic to Irish Catholics.[8] A large proportion of his voters in his Huyton constituency were of Irish Catholic origin. However, it went far deeper than a constituency concern. Wilson's former press secretary and close confidant, Joe Haines, has given this insight into Wilson's feelings towards Ireland and the Irish.

> Remember that the 1921 settlement for somebody like Harold wasn't all that far away. It happened in his lifetime. As he grew up it was part of his consciousness.... He had the traditional attitude of the Left that Ireland should be united under Dublin. He held that fairly constantly throughout his life. In 1974 he really would have done something about it had he had a big majority.[9]

In July 1964 Wilson wrote to Patricia McCluskey, one of the founders of the CSJ. He promised to introduce new and impartial procedures for the allocation of houses and to set up joint tribunals to consider particular cases of alleged discrimination in public appointments.[10] In a second letter a month before the General Election Wilson wrote:

> I agree with you as to the importance of the issues with which your campaign is concerned and I can assure you that a Labour government would do everything in its power to see that infringements of justice are efficiently dealt with.[11]

The CSJ regarded Wilson's messages as a major coup. Pat McCluskey said some years later that Wilson 'wrote just before the election saying that if he were returned he would settle things out for us'. She added that the CSJ 'used that letter and published it as often as we could on Harold [*sic*] all over England'.[12]

However, the actual policy statement with which Labour went into the election made no such specific promises. This statement 'Signposts to the New Ulster' was drawn up by the Northern Ireland Labour Party in conjunction with the Home Policy Sub Committee of the British Labour Party's National Executive Committee. It promised that electoral laws in Northern Ireland would be brought in to line with the remainder of the UK but gave no commitment for early action on specific Catholic grievances.[13]

In Northern Ireland the Unionist administration was already considering the consequences of a Labour victory. Roy Lilley, then a political journalist with the *Belfast Telegraph*, recalled:

> [Terence] O'Neill was exceedingly nervous about the implications of this for Northern Ireland at that time.... He went out of his way to make contact with, and try to cultivate, Harold Wilson in this period.... O'Neill saw the likelihood of Wilson coming and felt that

this would signal a change in the British Government's attitude to Northern Ireland, that it would not necessarily be a back-burner issue anymore.[14]

According to Lilley the two men had a 'couple of lunches or a dinner' but he did not know who had organised these meetings.

This was when Wilson was still Leader of the Opposition but we knew, obviously, that Parliament couldn't run beyond 1964.... Wilson, to O'Neill's surprise, seemed very sympathetic towards him which is not to say that he wasn't laying down markers and giving indications that there had to be change....[15]

Backbench MPs had a rare opportunity to demand reform in Northern Ireland during a Commons debate that took place in July 1964,[16] only three months before Labour came to power. One of them was Hugh Delargy (Labour, Thurrock) a veteran critic of Protestant hegemony in Ulster. Educated at the Gregorian University, Rome, he had been chairman of the Anti-Partition of Ireland League. In 1975 he recalled taking part in Anti-Partition meetings throughout Britain with de Valera.[17] Delargy told MPs that a deputation of Nationalists had recently met MPs at Westminster to protest about discrimination against Catholics. 'This happens nowhere else in the UK and everybody must confess that it is a sad state of affairs.' The Liberal MP Eric Lubbock (Orpington) spoke of a *prima facie* case of discrimination in employment and housing and of gerrymandering the electoral areas at local government level. However, the Conservative Home Secretary, Henry Brooke, adhered to the traditional Government response to charges of discrimination in Ulster when he wound up the debate. He said:

it has been held by successive governments in the UK, regardless of party, that the reserve powers in the Government of Ireland Act do not enable the UK Government to intervene in matters which, under Section 4, are the sole responsibility of the Northern Ireland Parliament and Government.

Though a new government was in power three months later, Brooke's interpretation of the limited rights of Westminster to intervene in Ulster's domestic affairs prevailed, with rare exceptions, until the dramatic events in Londonderry in October 1968 (Chapter 5).

Significantly, evidence that all was not well in Ulster surfaced only days before Harold Wilson got to Downing Street. The worst communal violence seen in Belfast for 30 years erupted during the General Election campaign though both the press and television made little of it in mainland Britain, being preoccupied with the political confrontation between Labour and Conservatives who appeared to be running neck and neck as polling day approached. The origin of the violence lay in the complex situation that prevailed in the constituency of West Belfast. The Ulster historian, Jonathan Bardon, explained:

> there were four candidates: Harry Diamond, Republican Labour; Jim Kilfedder, Unionist; Billy Boyd, Northern Ireland Labour; and Liam McMillen, Republican. The Unionist Party feared a Labour victory at Westminster – Harold Wilson promised action against discrimination if he became Prime Minister – and was anxious that Boyd could attract enough Protestant votes to ensure the election of Diamond.[18]

Ian Paisley, the extremist Protestant leader, now became involved. On 27 September he threatened to remove a small Irish tricolour in the window of the Republican headquarters in Divis Street if the police did not remove it first. Next day the RUC removed the flag sparking off a confrontation with local people which led to intense rioting.[19] *The Times*, on an inside page, reported:

> Disturbances broke out again last night on a more serious scale in West Belfast. One policeman was injured seriously. Crowds threw home-made fire bombs at two police vehicles and 13 police officers were taken to hospital. The rioting, the worst in the city for a quarter of a century, went on for hours ... the scene according to bystanders was reminiscent of the Troubles of 50 years ago....[20]

The riots continued for three nights and on 3 October *The Times* wrote in a leading article 'the display of violence will disappoint those optimists who thought religious and nationalist antagonism were dying away in Ulster ... the General Election contest has opened up old wounds....'[21] However, Kilfedder, the Unionist candidate who was returned for West Belfast did not share this pessimism. For his victory he thanked Paisley, without whom, he said, it would not have been possible.[22]

Wilson became Prime Minister on 16 October 1964 after Labour had won the General Election by a majority of only five. [This was reduced to three after Patrick Gordon Walker, Wilson's Foreign Secretary, who had lost his Smethwick seat in the General Election, was defeated at the Leyton by-election in January 1965.] Early in his term, the new Prime Minister encouraged the view that his government's approach to Ireland, North and South, would differ from previous Tory and Labour administrations. He decided to return to Ireland the remains of Roger Casement, who was hanged for treason in 1916. However, it is significant that the Cabinet was anxious not to offend Stormont which was bitterly opposed to acceding to Casement's wish to be buried in Northern Ireland.[23] Wilson wrote later: 'There was no doubt that this action, followed by the much closer trade relations ... did a great deal to improve friendship between the two countries.'[24] Wilson was also to return to Dublin the Irish flag which had been raised above the GPO during the Easter Rising. Thanking Wilson, the Irish Prime Minister, Sean Lemass, said: '... the British government intend this as a gesture to the Irish people and it is a further contribution by them for the building of good will and better relations between the two communities'.[25] The 'closer trade relations' referred to by Wilson was in fact a free trade area agreement with the Irish Republic. That ministers believed that the agreement would yield more that mere economic benefits is made clear by a memorandum written towards the end of the negotiations by Arthur Bottomley, the Commonwealth Relations Secretary. The agreement, said Bottomley, looked a 'fair economic bargain to both sides'. But, he added:

> It would also have a political importance. The disappearance of the old leaders in the Republic and the increasing prosperity there have introduced a new realism into Irish politics. There is a readiness to put less emphasis on the issue of Partition and, particularly among the growing middle classes and the business leaders, to accept the economic interdependence of the Republic and Britain.... Indeed, an agreement could place our political relationship with the Republic on a better footing than ever in the past.[26]

It seemed a far cry from the hostility of the Attlee years or the trade wars of the 1930s!

As early as March 1965 Wilson proposed a possible meeting in London between the premiers of Ulster and the Republic. The suggestion was made at the St Patrick Day's Banquet at the London Irish Club when he referred to the recent meeting in Belfast between Lemass and O'Neill.

All of us recognise that even before your next St Patrick's Day banquet if we maintain this momentum things can be better. If we can turn our backs on the past and our faces to the future I believe, speaking of the two islands, there is nothing we cannot do together.[27]

The speech however, infuriated O'Neill, who said that it would have been only courteous if the British Prime Minister had given him an indication of what he intended to say. He would have asked Wilson what useful purpose a tripartite meeting would serve and he said he emphasised 'with all the force at my command that our constitutional heritage ... is our most precious possession and will be maintained by all the means at our disposal'.[28] The political correspondent of *The Times* suggested that O'Neill's strong reaction was the result of a misreading of Wilson's remarks by Unionist MPs. 'He is not proposing any new initiative on constitutional or political matters.... He thought it reasonable that he should propose ... a social gathering in London so that he could chat with the two premiers about the progress being made in establishing greater co-operation between Northern Ireland and Eire.'[29]

Wilson's first administration lasted only 17 months. He had been forced to trim his programme by the smallness of his overall majority and the economic situation. However, in the words of one observer 'through all the ups and downs he handled public relations superbly ... and on platform and television screen he appeared, pipe in hand, as the avuncular, reliable statesman ... who could be trusted with the nation's affairs'.[30] There is little evidence that during this time he seriously considered Catholic grievances despite the assurances he had given to leading civil rights workers in Ulster before polling day. Sir Oliver Wright, who was Wilson's private secretary at 10 Downing Street at the time, said:

> Whatever the letters written to these various characters may have said ... and I think it is very important that they were written when he was in Opposition, when you are actually sitting at the Cabinet table in Number 10 the world looks very different, and the world is very different.[31]

Wright did not consider that the gestures Wilson made to Dublin were the signal of the start of a great reform movement. 'I cannot remember in my time with Wilson in Number 10 that Ireland ever really rated very high in Wilson's preoccupations.'[32]

However, government papers released under the 30-year rule in January 1997 reveal that – contrary to Wright's recall – Ireland did rate 'very high in Wilson's preoccupations' if only briefly. We now know that ministers thought they were facing a major IRA campaign of violence both in Ulster and mainland Britain to mark the 50th anniversary of the Easter Rising. In December 1965 the Northern Ireland Prime Minister, Terence O'Neill, raised the matter of the threat with the Home Secretary, Sir Frank Soskice. In a letter he said: 'As you already know from correspondence and from my recent meeting with you, we have been advised by the RUC that preparations are on foot for an early resumption of IRA activities in Northern Ireland'. O'Neill suggested to Soskice that the assistance of the Irish government should be sought in 'effectively suppressing clandestine illegal activities in the Republic and in dealing with terrorists who sought refuge there after committing acts of violence in Northern Ireland.' An opportunity to seek this help would come when the Irish Prime Minister, Sean Lemass, visited London the following year. O'Neill added: 'Perhaps the most serious aspect of the present situation is that all year the IRA have been holding regular training sessions and camps at a number of locations in the Republic.' Instructions at these sessions, he said, had included lectures on the use of explosives and advice on attacks on government buildings. He then gave a list of the 34 camps adding, 'it will be seen how widespread this activity has been particularly so close to the border'. He warned that a resumption of terrorism mounted from the Republic 'would be a serious setback' to his efforts to cement a more friendly relationship with the Republic. And he warned the British government: '... Amongst the information coming to the RUC have been references to the perpetration of IRA outrages in England as well as in Northern Ireland.'[33]

Soskice suggested to the Prime Minister that when he (Wilson) saw Lemass he should say that 'you are sure that his Government will keep an eye on all this and do what they can to prevent the IRA causing mischief in Northern Ireland'.[34] During lunch Lemass told Wilson that on the whole he thought reports about the IRA tended to be exaggerated but that this did not mean he was taking them lightly and if there were attempts to mark the Easter Rising with lawlessness the authorities in the Republic would do all they could to prevent this.[35]

However, three months later – only six weeks before the anniversary of the Rising – the British government was, if anything, more alarmed. On 4 March Soskice went to 10 Downing Street to tell Wilson that according to the latest intelligence, extremists on both sides of the border were likely to be active. For the first time he suggested that it might be necessary to use British troops stationed in Northern Ireland to help the RUC.[36] By now the Ministry of Defence was getting heavily involved. A meeting of the Chiefs of Staff Committee agreed that their primary concern was the threat to military installations and the requirement for aid to the civil power. However, it was decided that intelligence gathering on the IRA in Northern Ireland could still be left to the RUC Special Branch and not to recommend that MI5 should go in.[37] [This proved to be a significant and probably ultimately disastrous decision because intelligence remained the responsibility of the RUC until August 1969 when the troops finally did go in.] At this point, the Cabinet Secretary, Sir Burke Trend, decided to warn Wilson that he might get the blame if the IRA threat was not successfully contained. He told the Prime Minister that there was a real risk of trouble 'of sizeable proportions in Northern Ireland' and he suggested that Soskice should be asked for a note outlining the preparations taken to meet the threat. This, said Trend, would 'protect the Prime Minister's own position if serious trouble developed and he were subsequently criticised for not having anticipated it'.[38]

The response from Soskice, as he himself admitted, painted a 'gloomy picture'. He told Wilson:

> Information received from both Scotland Yard and the Northern Ireland Government shows that the threat is a real one.... There were some 3,000 trained members or supporters [of the IRA] who could be called out in an emergency.

The Northern Ireland government, said Soskice, feared that the IRA would foment sectarian troubles during the anniversary celebrations 'necessitating the intervention of the police and that the IRA campaign would then be publicised as a people's uprising against the excesses of the Crown forces'. These fears had led to the decision to send to Ulster:

> an additional infantry battalion ostensibly for training. We hope that this move will not attract undue publicity, especially as it is most important to avoid any accusation that by deciding to move

troops to Northern Ireland we have provoked incidents that might not otherwise have occurred.[39]

Three days later the Cabinet approved the preparations to meet the threat.[40]

In the event, there was no serious trouble but the intelligence received by ministers about IRA activity makes it all the more remarkable that the Wilson Cabinet paid so little attention to Northern Ireland until the eruption of violence nearly three years later.

Labour MPs from the outset, however, were determined that the question of reform in Northern Ireland should be debated at Westminster. Early in 1965 a group of them had launched the Campaign for Democracy in Ulster (CDU) under the chairmanship of Paul Rose the young Labour MP for Manchester, Blackley. They were now set on defying the 40-year-old convention that Westminster could not become involved in the domestic affairs of Ulster. The question of religious discrimination in the province, for example, was out of bounds under it. The convention dated from a ruling given by the Speaker of the House of Commons J.H. Whitley, in 1923:

> With regard to those subjects which have been delegated to the Government of Northern Ireland, questions must be asked of Ministers in Northern Ireland and not in this House…. The policy of voting money here in aid of Irish services may be discussed here, but … this right does not cover matters of administration for which a Minister in Northern Ireland is responsible….[41]

This ruling, according to Paul Bew, completed the process, by which Britain insulated herself from the affairs of the Northern Ireland state. 'In so far as this convention was modified, this was on the Unionists' own terms.'[42] Did this mean that the Westminster government had no role to play over allegations of religious discrimination in the province? According to Harry Calvert writing in the late 1960s[43] this question more than any other provoked disagreement as to the propriety of discussing transferred matters. 'An attempt to enact discriminatory legislation by the Northern Ireland Parliament', he wrote, 'would be outside the scope of delegated powers', adding, 'An isolated example of the discriminatory use of transferred administrative powers would not, by itself call for interference from Westminster. But a series might well give rise to the conviction that there was an improper state of things justifying action by the Westminster authorities.'[44]

If Calvert is right, Catholic grievances such as refusal to operate a one man one vote system in local elections, gerrymandering, and unfair pubic housing allocations could not be judged 'isolated examples' but a series justifying – in his words – action by Westminster. However, Calvert pointed out that there had been 'considerable vacillation, as to exactly what the proper attitude towards discussion of ... religious discrimination should be'. While the Speaker had occasionally allowed discussion, 'the government itself has, usually for inadequate reasons, sought to curtail it'. It had been maintained, he said, that transferred matters were the sole responsibility of Stormont 'which begs the question; and that a remedy is available in the courts, assuming erroneously that Parliament is precluded from considering the matter. The Chair has nevertheless, acceded to these propositions'.[45]

Calvert conceded that on other occasions the Speaker had been more tolerant. However, he made the damning allegation that there had been 'a consistent failure to appreciate the distinction between making criticism of the Northern Ireland authorities in respect of individual acts of alleged discrimination, which it is suggested, would not be in order, and raising the question of the effectiveness of Section Five of the 1920 Act to deal with a "state of things"'.[46] Calvert's view was that the convention had very limited authority. He pointed out that UK governments had expressed the view that the scope of ministerial responsibility at Westminster should not be extended and he added:

> In this sense – and in this sense only – can there be said to be a convention, but its scope is somewhat limited.... It is, in summary, merely convention that ministerial responsibility at Westminster will not be assumed in respect of matters which are, at the relevant time, transferred to Northern Ireland.[47]

Calvert's analysis was confirmed 30 years later by Professor John Griffith, Emeritus Professor of Public Law (University of London). He told the author, 'the Table refuses to accept motions and questions put down where the minister has refused to accept responsibility. It is oriented not on subject matter as such but on the extent to which ministers accept responsibility'. Asked whether it was possible that ministers said to the Table Office in the 1960s 'you must not accept these questions', Professor Griffith replied:

> Yes, technically that would be the effect. What they would say is 'We are not responsible. That is for Stormont. Therefore we are not going to answer these questions.' [48]

Once the minister had refused to answer it 'creates a precedent and the Clerks of the Table will continue to refuse questions on that matter once the minister has made his position clear. The ultimate responsibility is that of the Speaker'. There was nobody to arbitrate on the minister's right to make that exclusion, he said. 'This is power without responsibility and it happens now with the Next Steps [Agencies] and Quangoes.' In the case of Northern Ireland 'what happened no doubt with Wilson was that there were a whole lot of things he said he was not going to be involved with and there would not be debates in the House'.[49]

Professor Griffith also refuted the claim of the Unionist regime at Stormont that the convention at Westminster had lasted so long that it was no longer just a convention but had, in effect, the force of law. He said:

> No doubt that is a deliberately confused statement. 'In effect'. Those are the crucial words. 'In effect' it did have the force of law. That was because the convention was being adhered to. What it does not say – by putting in the word 'just' a convention makes it sound something more than a convention. It wasn't.

What actually happened, according to Professor Griffith, happened to conventions all the time where a practice became a convention at the beginning. There was the understanding that things would be conducted in a certain way. That convention, he said, 'gets stronger the more that it is applied and the more it is adhered to. The stronger it gets the more difficult it is to break'. That had nothing to do with 'the great ringing statements in Section 75 that Parliament is supreme over Northern Ireland'.[50] If the government did not bring in legislation the convention held, said Professor Griffith, adding:

> A convention is a hardened constitutional practice…. There are a lot of practices that start off as little babies. They grow and they go on holding their own practices which perhaps start innocently because people adhere to them, but harden into conventions.[51]

Neither practices nor conventions had the force of law, he said.

Section 75 made it absolutely clear that the UK Parliament could legislate for anything it wanted in Northern Ireland. However, he said, 'as a matter of convention it has been the case that ministers have neither introduced Bills nor taken responsibility for matters which fell within Stormont during those years'. If a minister continued not acting 'and the Speaker went on interpreting in the same light then of course people will say we have followed this practice for 50 years. It's a very hard convention. Therefore we will not break it'. But, he added, 'that is very different from saying therefore it cannot be broken'.

Griffith said it was understandable that politicians would argue that one could not set up a subsidiary authority like Stormont and then start interfering with it:

> You have set it up because you don't want it. You have got rid of it so why should you start mucking about with it. Once you have started mucking about with it you have changed your policy.

Nevertheless Griffith had made it clear, that given the will, Harold Wilson, committed to reform in Ulster, could have acted. Why did he not do so? Because said Professor Griffith,

> Here is a man who could have done a, b or c and it would have done him some good and he couldn't do it because of the political constraints. It happens to Prime Ministers all the time. It is a very good example of the enormous limitation in which top people work – Peter Hennessy's argument about overwork at the top.[52]

Ironically, only 18 months before direct rule and with thousands of British troops trying to keep the peace in Ulster, the Chair was still gagging debate. The Speaker told an MP who had been prevented by the Table Office from questioning the Home Secretary about a British subject imprisoned in a Northern Ireland gaol:

> Northern Ireland is neither an independent foreign country nor a colony and many aspects of its administration have been removed by the will of Parliament from the direct control of the UK Government. This situation is inevitably reflected in the rules governing questions.[53]

The first occasion Labour MPs had for challenging the convention came on 22 February 1965 after Labour had been in power for only four months when the Home Secretary, Sir Frank Soskice, opened an adjournment debate on unemployment in the province.[54] The subject could be discussed by the Commons because central government had ultimate responsibility for the economy of the UK as a whole. Sir Frank himself typically made no reference to the case for reform. However, several Labour MPs were determined to raise the subject despite repeated objections from Ulster Unionist MPs. Simon Mahon, Labour MP for Bootle, said that he must talk about discrimination in Northern Ireland. Captain Lawrence Orr, Leader of the Ulster Unionists, objected that this was the province of the Stormont government alone but the Deputy Speaker, Sir Sam Storey, allowed him to continue. Mahon said:

> what I am now putting is the condition in which certain people in Northern Ireland who are subject to our constitution find themselves in because they are not of a particular religious persuasion. I shall not go further with this matter because I do not like the subject. It is intolerable that any man should have to mention it in these days but we shall never get anywhere in these islands unless we can score out these acts of discrimination. We know they are going on.

The Deputy Speaker was less indulgent towards Delargy, who protested against the decision to site the new University of Northern Ireland in Coleraine rather than Londonderry. [The siting of the university at Coleraine, a small Protestant town, instead of Londonderry was a cause of resentment to the Catholic community.][55] He upheld the demands of Ulster Unionist MPs that Delargy could not discuss the issue. The Deputy Speaker also prevented Richard Crawshaw, Labour MP for Liverpool, Toxteth, making allegations of gerrymandering in Londonderry.[56] The most determined attempt to raise discrimination in Northern Ireland came from Paul Rose, the CDU chairman.[57] He said:

> The evidence which I receive week by week points to a manifestation of discrimination in both jobs and housing ... there appears to be a great deal of evidence about the practice of discrimination in the Six Counties ... and a conspiracy of silence seems to hide this evidence from the public....

Rose then warned the Ulster Unionist MPs that in future Labour and Liberal MPs would not allow debate on religious discrimination Northern Ireland to be stifled. However, Rose was infuriated that the case which he and other Labour MPs had tried to make during the debate had been ignored by their own Labour ministers. He wrote bitterly later: 'Not a word came from the two front benches about issues which within five years were to leave the streets smouldering and leave the stench of death on the pavements of Belfast.'[58]

It was certainly true that Wilson appeared unmoved by the arguments of the CDU. His consistent view throughout these years – in public at least – was that Ulster's best hope lay with O'Neill.[59] Shortly after he became Prime Minister, the Northern Ireland premier paid him what was merely a courtesy visit. But on 9 May 1965 after he had been in power for six months O'Neill came to see him again and this time, Wilson recalled, 'we had to get down to realities'.[60] Wilson pointed out that at that time Northern Ireland had not erupted into the troubles that came later,

> but I was anxious that the Ulster Unionist Government under Capt. O'Neill should be encouraged to press on with their programme of ending discrimination in housing allocations and jobs and generally improving the lot of the minority in Northern Ireland. Since coming into office he had, by Northern Ireland standards, carried through a remarkable programme of easement.[61]

This was an incredible statement by Wilson. What 'remarkable programme of easement'? He gave no evidence for such a programme for the simple reason there was none. Three years later MPs belonging to the CDU at their fourth annual meeting at Westminster were in a state of despair over the lack of progress with reform.[62]

The second occasion on which the Commons was permitted to discuss Northern Ireland came on 26 October 1965.[63] Once again the debate was only allowed because the United Kingdom Parliament had ultimate responsibility for the issue under discussion, namely the economy, particularly unemployment. Once againe backbench Labour MPs tried valiantly to shift the argument away from the generalities of the economy to the specifics of Catholic grievances much against the wishes of the Ulster Unionist MPs and the Chair. The debate was also significant for the warning by Labour backbenchers that in future they would flout the Parliamentary convention governing discussion of Northern Ireland affairs. The debate was once again opened by Soskice, and his remarks seem ironic in the light of the letter he received only two months later from O'Neill about the threat of a new IRA bombing campaign which led to his memorandum to Wilson detailing the precautions being taken. After surveying the economic situation he said:

One cannot travel about Northern Ireland and meet people there without feeling that they are buoyed up by a sense of hope and enthusiasm and pride in the performance of their country and its economy.

This remark was so complacent that it would have been reasonable to assume he had been reading from his civil service brief. He was, by general consent, a very ineffective minister. However, there is evidence that he really believed all was well. On his sole visit to Northern Ireland the Labour Home Secretary was quoted by the leading local paper saying of Ulster Unionism

From England we watch it, we admire it and we rejoice in it.[64]

Sir Geoffrey Otton, who was Soskice's private secretary at the Home Office, accompanied him on the visit to Belfast. He recalled going to the office of the Northern Ireland Labour Party, 'an insignificant little room'. Sir Geoffrey said: 'He (Soskice) hadn't the least idea what to do [and] just asked, "is there anything you want?"' 'Soskice', he said, 'was very impressed by O'Neill'.[65]

However, nearly 30 years later Paul Bew suggested that there might be some justification for Soskice's apparently insane view of the province. While there was still mass emigration from the Republic, said Bew, 'Ireland unfree' was able to keep the Irish people at home partly because of the financial benefits of the Union. Both Irish neutrality and the relative economic failure of Irish independence it has been said

are things which are the context for officials who are looking at these issues in the 1960s. Unless you have those in your mind you will never know why Frank Soskice says 'we rejoice in Ulster Unionism'. It appears insanity. It is not quite as insane as it looks.[66]

If Soskice hoped that he could maintain a low key tone to the debate he was soon to be disappointed by his own backbenchers. The attempt to raise civil rights was begun by the Labour MP for Acton, Bernard Floud, who claimed that the philosophy of the Ulster Unionists had been expressed by a former Prime Minister of the province, Lord Craigavon, who had said:, 'All I boast is that we are a Protestant Parliament and a Protestant State.' He was immediately warned by the Deputy Speaker, Sir Sam Storey, that he was out of order. Floud was then continually interrupted until he skilfully avoided further objection from the Chair by referring to a letter which

Harold Wilson had written in September 1964 to the Campaign for Social Justice in Northern Ireland.[67] Floud told the House: 'I do not believe that the PM would have pledged a Labour Government to do everything in their power in these matters if we here had no power to take effective action.' Floud added that he looked forward to hearing from the Home Office Minister who was winding up the debate (George Thomas) what action was 'contemplated to end the scandal of systematic religious discrimination in Northern Ireland'.

However, doubts that Soskice, had any intention taking such action were voiced by Paul Rose who bitterly attacked Sir Frank for 'giving succour and support to the Unionists' when he was the guest of the Unionist Government in Stormont. Rose, who clearly had in mind Soskice's 'rejoice' remark, said: 'I know that one must accept the hospitality of one's hosts and that any harsh words would be out of order but many of his words were interpreted – or misinterpreted – by people in Northern Ireland as giving political support to the existing set-up in Northern Ireland.' Soskice was also criticised by another Labour member, Eric Ogden (Liverpool, West Derby), who pointed out that the Home Secretary had not referred at all to the political situation in Ulster when he opened the debate. He assumed that this was because of 'the convention that we do not intervene or interfere in Northern Ireland affairs'. He suggested that there should now be a 'new convention', and he added: 'Whether or not we are politically responsible in the long run we certainly have a moral right.'

Any hope that Labour backbenchers might have had that George Thomas, under-secretary at the Home Office, might make up for Soskice's complacency when he wound up the debate was unrealised. On the contrary, Thomas emphasised at the outset that the present Labour government had no intention of departing from the policy that Ulster's internal affairs were the responsibility of Stormont alone. He told MPs:

> It is of the utmost importance that we should establish right relationships between the subordinate Parliament and what I might describe as the Imperial Parliament. When we have governments of different political colours in the subordinate Parliament and the Imperial Parliament it is all the more necessary for all to tread carefully to ensure that conventions established over long years are not trampled upon.

Later in his speech Thomas explained why he would not discuss the question of discrimination in Northern Ireland. 'We have followed faithfully the conventions which were observed by the Labour Government of 1945–51 as by the other governments which have come in between.' No Conservative minister could have put the traditional case for non-intervention in Ulster better. Revealingly, he used the term 'Imperial Parliament', the language of the 1920 Act, which by the 1960s had distinct Unionist connotations. For those Labour MPs who recalled Wilson's pledge on the eve of the election just a year before that a Labour government would introduce reform it was a grave disappointment.

During the 1964–66 Parliament the ranks of the CDU were strengthened as a result of a by-election at Hull North in January 1966. The loss of the seat, which was generally anticipated, would have reduced Labour's majority to one. However, Labour won a substantial victory with a swing of 4 per cent from the Conservatives. The victor was Kevin McNamara, a second generation Irish Catholic from Liverpool. Northern Ireland was not an issue during the campaign though McNamara recalled years later that news of the Anglo-Irish trade agreement had been proudly announced shortly before polling day and was not worth a single vote on Humberside.[68] However, one result of the by-election was to send to the Commons a young MP dedicated to civil rights in Ulster and who was to become one of the most active members of the CDU.

A serious anomaly in the constitutional relationship between Westminster and Parliament was revealed during Wilson's first administration. An exchange took place in the Commons which Wilson recorded later as illustrating this 'matter of considerable constitutional importance which was highlighted in the Northern Ireland developments five years later'.[69] On 9 November 1965, Wilson was replying to the debate on the nationalisation of steel. Sir Knox Cunningham, the Ulster Unionist MP for Antrim South (and a former Parliamentary Private Secretary to Harold Macmillan) tried to intervene. Labour MPs called on him to sit down and Wilson told him:

> It really has nothing to do with the hon. and learned Member, because under the White Paper all legislation on steel in Northern Ireland is a matter for the Northern Ireland Parliament.

Sir Knox tried again and was called to order by the Speaker. William Hamilton, Labour MP for Fife West, shouted: 'Send him back to Ireland'.[70]

In his memoirs Wilson referred to the exchange and pointed out that the Conservatives could hold up Labour legislation only because they could command the votes of their 12 Ulster Unionist allies voting on steel policy in Great Britain even though the measure could not affect Northern Ireland ... 12 Ulster Tories had voted to prevent us legislating to outlaw Rachmanism [the unscrupulous exploitation of poor tenants by landlords] even to determine local government boundaries in Northampton when no English Welsh or Scots Member could vote on Rachmanism in Belfast or Derry or on ward boundaries in any local government area in Ulster.[71]

Papers released by the PRO in January 1997 reveal that, at least temporarily, Wilson believed that limiting the powers of Ulster MPs at Westminster was a matter of urgency. In May 1965, during a session of Prime Minister's Questions he had denied that any such change was being contemplated, though he added waspishly, 'What was not envisaged, I am sure, in 1920 was that those who came here with that responsibility for representing Northern Ireland interests should just become hacks supporting the Tory Party.'[72] However, we now know from the papers released by the PRO in 1997 that he was deliberately misleading the Commons and that he had indeed been considering just such action. In January 1966 in a minute to the Lord President, Herbert Bowden, he referred to 'one or two thoughts on points we should be looking at pretty urgently,' and he added:

we ought to make up our minds about the idea I aired last Spring, namely that Northern Ireland MPs should not have the right to vote in the House of Commons on purely domestic matters affecting England Wales, or Great Britain only, where the Stormont Parliament has exclusive jurisdiction on the same subject in relation to Northern Ireland.

Wilson admitted that when he raised the question, the Attorney General 'produced a very serious study of this with weighty arguments against any change'. However, Wilson told Bowden, 'I think we should have a look at the whole subject now and decide our attitude.'[73] A year later, now armed with a majority of nearly 100, Wilson confided to Ian Waller,[74] the political editor of the *Sunday Telegraph*, that he still wanted to restrict the Ulster MPs' right to vote. The result of these talks, on a 'lobby' basis, appeared in an article Waller wrote for the *Catholic Herald* and published on 17 March 1967 – see Chapter 3.

CONCLUSION

Civil rights campaigners in Ulster and their supporters at Westminster who had hoped for early action from the first Labour government for 13 years were disappointed. By the time Wilson went to the country in March 1966 all that had been achieved was a few gestures to Dublin like sending back Casement's bones and a hint by Wilson that Ulster representation at Westminster might be reconsidered. This was the beginning of Wilson's long, and fruitless, dependency on Terence O'Neill to bring in reform. Early attempts by Labour and Liberal backbench MPs to break the convention that Ulster matters – particularly religious discrimination – could not be raised at Westminster were repeatedly thwarted, though, as has been explained, there was no constitutional justification for the gag.

As we now know from the papers released in 1997, between December 1965 and April 1966 the Cabinet was forced to take Ireland seriously because of the new IRA threat. There were several reasons for the Government allowing Ireland to slip right off the agenda once the threat of violence had apparently receded. First, accepting the convention that Ulster was the business of Stormont alone, meant that Whitehall-controlled instruments to engineer change within the province were simply not available. Second, the point made so succinctly by Oliver Wright, pre-election pledges frequently give way to the realities of a Premier's life. Finally, the factor that was to repeat itself throughout Wilson's strife-torn period of government, 'less-urgent' problems like Ireland, were simply crowded out by far more pressing concerns: the sterling crisis, rebellion in Rhodesia, and the need to survive on a tiny majority until the right moment came to go to the Country to call for a fresh mandate.

2 The 'Crucially Difficult Year',[1] April–August 1966

> The loyalist cheers for the Queen tomorrow should not be allowed to soften a very hard line on John Bull's political slum.
>
> *Sunday Times*[2]

This chapter deals at some length with only the first five months of Wilson's second administration, April to August 1966, which proved to be a critical period, both at Westminster and in the Province of Northern Ireland. For the first few weeks, as the new material from the Public Record Office shows, ministers were bracing themselves for an upsurge of IRA violence both in the province and on the mainland which in the end never materialised. On the Government benches there was a growing division between backbenchers, led by the CDU, who demanded some form of intervention and ministers, led by Wilson, equally determined that, though reform was necessary, the right policy was to leave it to O'Neill. By August both sides had taken up entrenched positions. In Ulster sectarian violence had returned in a menacing new form and it was becoming apparent that 'O'Neillism' was not accepted by a large section of the Unionist party.[3] The chapter begins by examining in some detail the role of Gerry Fitt, the new Member for Belfast, West, elected in the March poll, in leading the assault on the convention that Northern Ireland matters could not be raised at Westminster. Wilson's attitude to O'Neill is assessed: did the British Prime Minister really believe O'Neill could deliver reform quickly enough, particularly as Wilson himself said time was running out? These months also saw the sudden – though temporary – interest taken in the worsening situation in Ulster by the press, as Harold Evans, former Editor of the *Sunday Times* acknowledged, after having ignored the province for years. Finally, the inconclusive talks between Wilson and O'Neill and the unique Commons debate two days later, when the convention was seriously tested for the first and last time before the troops went in, are analysed in detail. As will become increasingly clear there was enough evidence during these few months – not least the intelligence reports about the IRA preparations for the anniversary of the Easter

Rising – to support the case for intervention which was to be made with increasing frequency over the next two years, in the end even by O'Neill himself.[4]

Those Labour MPs who were determined that reform should come to Northern Ireland were heartened by the large majority that their party had secured at the General Election. However, the majority itself was less significant for their cause than the fact that one of the new MPs who took his seat on the government side of the House, was the remarkable Irish Catholic Gerry Fitt. Fitt had won West Belfast from a Unionist, describing himself as 'Republican Labour'. The 'impact he made on Westminster was immediate' and the CDU were 'galvanised' by his determination that the Commons would at last hear Catholic grievances.[5] Fitt, who was to become leader of the Social Democrat and Labour Party in 1970, had been a militant Republican and Socialist since leaving the British merchant navy in 1953. While at sea he had educated himself in law and politics and when he was discharged he devoted himself to grassroot politics in his native Dock ward. His 'energy and keen sense of humour soon established him as a personality in local politics' and in 1958 he was returned as an Irish Labour member of Belfast City Council.[6] Four years later he entered Stormont as MP for Dock, a seat he had won from the Unionists. At Westminster, Fitt sat on the Government benches prepared to support the Wilson administration. As one historian of the civil rights movement put it, his

> victory gave added emphasis to the idea that the way to achieve redress of its grievances was for the minority in Northern Ireland to act positively and seek to communicate with potential allies outside, not engage in a fruitless symbolic rejection of the state.[7]

Fitt wasted no time making his maiden speech.[8] He rose during the debate on the Queen's Speech on 25 April and skilfully used the tradition that a maiden speech is not interrupted to taunt Ulster Unionist MPs. The Speaker, Dr Horace King, who had previously ruthlessly suppressed attempts by Labour MPs to raise Northern Ireland matters, allowed him considerable licence. Ulster Unionist MPs were appalled, fearing that the rules of the game were being altered by stealth and to their disadvantage. Their leader, Captain Lawrence Orr (Down, South), complained that Fitt's speech contained 'some of the wildest and most irresponsible assertions I have ever heard in any speech in this House of Commons, let alone a maiden speech'.[9] Yet it was to be two-and-a-half years before the Speaker again allowed such an open attack on the Ulster administration and then only because several prominent figures, including Fitt, were injured in a clash with the police during the Londonderry riot on 5 October 1968.[10]

Fitt began with a forecast that was to prove true but not, however, in the way he hoped:

I feel certain that at the end of this Parliament dramatic changes will have taken place in the North of Ireland ...

Fitt then described attempts which he claimed had been made to destabilise his recent election campaign in Belfast: his telephone had been tapped during the contest and when he was finally declared the victor he had to have police protection to protect him 'from a bigoted sectarian mob'. He added:

At every election at which I have been declared the victor, the bigoted mobs have attempted physically to assault me. Three weeks ago my agents were threatened that if they attempted to enter my opponent's areas ... they would be physically assaulted if they attempted to stand by the ballot box to prevent my opponents from personating votes.

He appealed to all MPs, whatever their party, to ensure that in future candidates in Northern Ireland would 'be free from all threats of physical violence'. However, his main theme – which was one that would be taken up many Labour and Liberal MPs, without success, for the next three years – was the case for amending the Government of Ireland Act 1920 to allow intervention in Ulster by the British government:

No Act is sacrosanct. The changing social conditions over the past 50 years make the Government of Ireland Act completely unworkable. When we realise how every concept of British democracy is being flouted in Northern Ireland we conclude that now, immediately, is the time to amend that Act.

Fitt went on to warn his new colleagues in the Labour Party that his support for the Wilson administration was conditional on their support for reform in Northern Ireland. He claimed to speak not only for progressively-minded people in his constituency but throughout the province. 'I intend to voice their disapproval of the present undemocratic system and the election laws which now exist in Northern Ireland.' He realised, however, that a consequence of this would be a threat to re-election. He predicted that council houses in his constituency would be given to Unionists 'with the intention of unseating me'. Finally, Fitt demanded that ministers set up an inquiry into the Government of Ireland Act, arguing that such a tribunal should take its membership from both sides of the House and he forecast that the result of such an inquiry would be that 'what is now happening in Northern Ireland can no longer be tolerated'.

Anthony Crosland, the Education Secretary, replying for the government, complimented Fitt on his maiden speech, adding: 'We can look forward to exciting confrontations in future.'[11] However, Unionist MPs were infuriated by Fitt's speech. They were only too well aware that Ulster's political and social system would be scrutinized at Westminster as never before. Fitt himself, looking back over 25 years, recalled:

> The Unionists had it all their own way and there was no political spotlight which was ever focussed on Northern Ireland until I came over in 1966, then I began to mobilise a whole lot of people, particularly the Labour Government....[12]

Orr, who spoke later in the debate, disputed Fitt's allegations about lack of democracy and injustice in Northern Ireland and accused him of coming to Westminster 'with the voice of extremism' seeking 'to stir up these things'. Fitt, he argued, should be warned that the House would not tolerate such a performance in future but 'will expect higher standards of accuracy and responsibility from him...'.[13]

The importance of Fitt's election has been fully acknowledged by Roy Lilley, who was the Westminster lobby correspondent of the *Belfast Telegraph*, at the time. Lilley recalled that:

> his arrival at Westminster and his determination to bring Northern Ireland onto the agenda was all part of the mood and the movement of the time. There was a tide beginning to flow and Fitt's arrival made it flow a little further and faster. He was not perceived by Unionists here at the time as anything other than ... the Devil Incarnate but he did add impetus to the whole thing undoubtedly.[14]

Lilley's paper, a staunch supporter of O'Neill's 'liberal' policy, commented sourly in a front page editorial that Fitt was disregarding the convention that Northern Ireland questions should not be raised at Westminster but added: 'there can be no concealing the fact that in

Wilson he has a sympathetic ear'.[15] In fact early evidence that the government was having at least to acknowledge Fitt's presence at Westminster is provided by the documents released in 1997 referred to in Chapter 1. The government was informed that because of the fear of terrorist violence over Easter in 1966 Stormont was planning to detain IRA members. The Army Minister, Gerry Reynolds, warned the Home Office that since nothing had happened over the weekend and that the arrests would coincide with the moving of troops to Northern Ireland there was a danger that the government would be blamed for provoking any violence that occurred. Clearly referring to Fitt, Reynolds added that it was important to mention this so that a satisfactory explanation could be prepared, especially as there was now an Ulster Labour member in the House.[16]

The influence of one backbench MP, however vociferous, should not be exaggerated. While Fitt galvanised the CDU and raised the profile of Northern Ireland in mainland Britain, there is no evidence that Wilson's policy of non-intervention in the province was affected. Wilson was, though, still concerned about the role of Ulster MPs in the House of Commons. On 26 May, four months after he had privately told Herbert Bowden that the matter should be looked at 'pretty urgently',[17] Wilson complained about the conduct of Ulster MPs during Prime Minister's Questions. Fitt had asked Wilson to set up a Royal Commission to investigate the workings of the Government of Ireland Act. When Fitt claimed that it was 'obvious that democracy did not exist', the Speaker, Dr Horace King, cut him short and prevented other Labour MPs from intervening. One of them, Chairman of the Parliamentary Labour Party and former Cabinet Minister, Manny Shinwell, asked, '… if Ulster Members come here and interfere in our affairs cannot we do likewise?' Wilson replied:

> There is the convention which all governments in this House have fully honoured about not dealing with matters which are within the responsibility of the Stormont Parliament. It sometimes means that problems in London, for example, are voted on by Ulster Members here whereas we cannot vote on corresponding issues there. Indeed there could be a change of British government following on a vote on an issue in respect of which we have no rights in Stormont.[18]

Later in the year Wilson returned to this theme, again during Prime Minister's Questions. Kevin McNamara claimed that there was considerable concern among Labour MPs that whereas the MP for Londonderry could ask questions about direct building schemes in Salford, 'we can't ask questions about discrimination in housing matters in his constituency'. Wilson replied:

> There is certainly illogicality here and there have been cases when majorities were smaller than at present when a government could have fallen with a Northern Ireland vote on 'Rachmanism' in London although nothing could be said about housing conditions in Belfast.

In their talks with O'Neill, said Wilson, he and Jenkins, the Home Secretary, 'have been trying to discuss with him some of the questions on which there is anxiety on both sides of the House'.[19]

These replies, Wilson's minute to Herbert Bowden referred to in the previous chapter and his confidential remarks to the Political Editor of the *Sunday Telegraph* Ian Waller the following year (see below), suggest that the Prime Minister was preparing the House for a radical change in the role of Ulster MPs at Westminster, a move that would have serious implications for the constitutional relationship between Northern Ireland and the rest of the United Kingdom. Certainly, Percy Diamond, the experienced London Editor of the *Belfast Telegraph*, was aware of the significance of Wilson's remarks. He noted that Wilson's Commons reply followed his comment of a year before that it had not been anticipated in 1920 [when the Government of Ireland Act was introduced] that Ulster MPs would become 'hacks representing the Tory Party'.[20]

Unravelling the convention had become the main aim of the CDU at this time. Their tactics were twofold. First to put whatever pressure they could upon the Government, principally the Prime Minister, and the Home Secretary, both in and out of the Commons. Here they proved largely unsuccessful as they conceded two years later [see below]. Jenkins particularly was a grave disappointment. He had come into office intent on making a mark as a great reforming Home Secretary and the CDU MPs were convinced that, as the minister responsible for Northern Ireland, a man with his liberal instincts and historical knowledge of Ireland would be receptive to their case.

However, he showed little or no interest in their campaign.[21] Their second line of attack was to use every opportunity to exploit Commons procedure to air Catholic grievances at Westminster. This meant skilful use of the Commons Order Paper and amendments to Bills. In this exercise they were rather more successful. As Fitt pointed out in his BBC interview 25 years later, these activities may not have made much impact on the Commons but they did provide publicity for the cause and were picked up by foreign correspondents.[22] Paul Rose began this ploy with an adjournment debate on the Race Relations Act on 27 May. He said that it was 'high time that the practice of religious discrimination was rooted out and prevented'. But when he added, 'If the bounds of order prevent me from suggesting legislation in this regard to Northern Ireland', he was cut short by the Speaker. However, Rose's move had not been in vain because Maurice Foley, the Home Office Minister, winding up the debate for the government, acknowledged that the Race Relations Act did not extend to 'a number of important fields where discrimination does occur' including Northern Ireland. This brought an angry intervention from the Ulster Unionist MP, Sir Knox Cunningham, who denied that there was discrimination in Northern Ireland.[23]

Fitt was not alone at this time in presenting to mainland Britain a profoundly pessimistic picture of the situation in Ulster. The *Belfast Telegraph*, in an editorial, quoted an article in the *Daily Telegraph* called 'Ghostly Noman's Land of Past Conflicts'. The article claimed that little had changed. The old issues were the new issues. The Protestants remained in control of the Catholics and the Catholics protested.[24] In June Labour backbench MPs discovered a method of bringing before Parliament a full list of Catholic demands without being ruled out of order. The 1966 Finance Bill was at its committee stage and the MPs, led by McNamara, decided to add a series of amendments. MPs who sponsored these amendment included not only the new intake such as McNamara and Fitt, but prominent backbenchers including Ian Mikardo [five years later Chairman of the Labour Party] Bessie Braddock [a member of the Party's NEC] and Harold Walker who was to become a Deputy Speaker. At a seminar held by the Institute of Contemporary British History in 1992 McNamara explained the objectives:

> Each and every one of the particular grievances which were seen in Northern Ireland were raised on the question of the Finance Bill of 1966 because it was the only way we could do it. There was in fact

provision made in that particular Bill for pensions to the senators in Northern Ireland and therefore on that there was a whole host of amendments which I drafted which named every grievance that existed and said that pensions should not be paid until these grievances had been met.[25]

Lord Callaghan, who was a witness at the Seminar, told McNamara:

Kevin, I entirely agree with you about that. I think the way in which you followed [*sic*] was as good as could be but because of the Speaker's convention and the Speaker's rulings, there was frustration by the backbenchers....[26]

Many years later[27] McNamara explained that by tabling their amendments to Clause 48 of the Finance Bill the Labour MPs had been able to put a full programme of reform before Parliament for the first time since the Government of Ireland Act 1920. The amendments called for were as follows:

• Stormont MPs to be elected on the basis of adult suffrage and one vote only per elector. [There was still a business vote for Stormont – although it had been abolished for Westminster elections in 1948. The Stormont business vote was abolished in 1968.]
• Their election to be on the basis of single member constituencies and for electors to be required to vote in only one constituency.
• A Royal Commission into the conduct of Stormont elections.
• The abolition of the business vote, the property qualification and the company vote for local government.
• Local government authorities to be elected on the basis of universal suffrage and one vote only per elector.
• Local authority and other public housing in Northern Ireland to be allocated on the basis of need and not political allegiance.
• Local authority electoral boundaries to be examined by an independent judicial commission.
• Employment in local authorities to be based upon ability and not political allegiance.
• An inquiry into the siting of polling stations for all elections in Northern Ireland.
• An independent inquiry into the reasons for the siting of the proposed new university in Coleraine.
• An independent judicial inquiry into the working of the Special Powers Act and the case for its repeal.[28]
• A public inquiry into the awarding of contracts by the Government

of Northern Ireland.

- Adequate representation of minority political groups on statutory authorities.
- Postal censorship to be abolished.
- An Ombudsman for Northern Ireland to be appointed.
- The Westminster Government to set up an inquiry into the practice of religious discrimination on government sponsored bodies and in housing.[29]

As explained earlier, the focus here is primarily upon Westminster and Whitehall. However, there are times when it is necessary to examine briefly events in the province because of their impact upon the policy makers on the mainland. Such a period was the summer of 1966 and it would be reasonable to argue that 'The Troubles' date from that time and not, as so often suggested, from the introduction of British troops into the province in the summer of 1969. In his memoirs Bloomfield, at the time private secretary to O'Neill, recalls 1966 as 'a crucially difficult year which was to embrace the Malvern Street murders and the emergence of the Ulster Volunteer Force (UVF) murder gang, the commemoration of the fiftieth anniversary of the Battle of the Somme and the Easter Rising, the Paisleyite disturbances outside Church House and that gentleman's subsequent imprisonment....'[30] Ian Paisley, who had been born in Armagh city in 1926, came to prominence at this time as a result of his denunciation of ecumenical trends in the principal Christian churches in Ulster. He drew support from loyalists who feared that O'Neill's bridge building gestures to the nationalist minority were weakening the bulwarks of Unionism. At about the same time the UVF was formed at a meeting in the Standard Bar on the Shankill in Belfast with the aim of bringing down O'Neill and combatting the IRA.

On 25 June three Catholics were shot in Malvern Street in Shankill and one died of his wounds. Three men who had been drinking in the Malvern Arms were arrested soon after and convicted. One of them, Hugh McClean, said to the police, 'I am terribly sorry I ever heard of that man Paisley or decided to follow him.'[31] At the time O'Neill was in France commemorating, ironically, the sacrifices of the original UVF at the Somme. Bloomfield, who was with him, recalled how the Northern Ireland Prime Minister immediately rushed back home and 'plunged into a very late-night [Stormont] Cabinet meeting'. The Stormont government decided to ban the UVF and Bloomfield helped to draft the statement O'Neill made in Stormont the next day,

28 June. In it O'Neill said there could be no connection between the original UVF 'and a sordid conspiracy of criminals prepared to take up arms against unprotected fellow-citizens. No; this organisation now takes its proper place alongside the IRA in the schedule of illegal bodies'.[32]

These events marked the beginning of general concern at Westminster about the deteriorating situation in Northern Ireland. Many Labour MPs, not simply members of the CDU, were alarmed by the sudden outbreak of violence; and whenever Labour MPs tried to raise Northern Ireland in the Commons they were generally backed by the Liberal Chief Whip, Eric Lubbock. Jeremy Thorpe, who was to become Liberal leader the following year, was very concerned about the dangers of communal strife in Ulster and told Harold Wilson personally of the need to act soon and decisively.[33] A meeting of 26 members of the CDU decided to send a deputation to the Home Secretary, Roy Jenkins, and another deputation to Wilson to protest about the difficulties of raising Ulster affairs in the Commons. The *Belfast Telegraph* lobby correspondent, Roy Lilley, wrote:

> Feeling on the Labour benches ... over Northern Ireland has become more focussed than at any time in recent years and supporters of the CDU firmly assert that they will not be content until the British Government shows readiness to take positive action on the Ulster situation which they contend is obviously deteriorating.[34]

Lilley's analysis was confirmed by blunt remarks made by Wilson during Prime Minister's questions in the Commons on 28 June during which he linked Ian Paisley to the 'quasi-Fascist' UVF. Liberal MP Eric Lubbock was able to raise the recent violence in Belfast without being in breach of the convention by raising questions about the Queen's safety during her forthcoming visit to Northern Ireland on 4 July. Lubbock suggested that the Prime Minister should advise the Queen that the visit should be cancelled. He said:

> many people, both in Britain and in Northern Ireland, feel that a visit ... is not wise at a time when disorders are being fomented and murders perpetrated by a gang of neo-Nazis in that part of the Kingdom....

Wilson said the visit would go ahead but he fully supported Lubbock's description of the UVF. Lubbock had not overstated the position. 'It is a quasi-Fascist organisation masquerading behind a clerical cloak.' Fitt then tried to widen the discussion by claiming that 'an explosive situation existed in Northern Ireland today due to the reluctance of the Northern Ireland government to protect the lives of their subjects ... there are Unionist extremists and murder gangs operating in the streets....' However, when he said it was for the Westminster government and not Stormont to intervene he was ruled out of order by the Speaker, Dr Horace King. Wilson ignored Fitt's remarks and instead paid tribute to O'Neill for his 'strong condem-nation' of the UVF.[35] The following day, *The Times*, in a leading article, gave cautious support to MPs demanding reform in Ulster: 'Eric Lubbock, the Liberal chief whip, means well in joining Westminster moves to reform the government of Northern Ireland.' The reformers had a case, said *The Times*, but criticised Lubbock for calling the UVF latter-day Nazis.[36] It is clear from Wilson's remarks in the Commons that the speed with which O'Neill banned the UVF and the trenchant remarks that he made about them impressed him. Whether Wilson really believed O'Neill could deliver reform may never be known but O'Neill's prompt action was a great help to him because it defused somewhat the growing clamour on the Labour backbenches for intervention by the Westminster Government, a policy which Wilson was not yet ready to consider seriously. Wilson's confidence in the Northern Ireland Premier was strengthened by the hardline Unionist opposition to O'Neill that was building up in 1966. But was O'Neill really committed to reform in any case? The leading Irish historian, Roy Foster, wrote 20 years later: 'O'Neill was an unconvincing liberal as well as an inept tactician.... Subsequent events have created the illusion that he stood for introducing civil rights reform for which there is no evidence.'[37]

Foster's scepticism is echoed by Professor Paul Bew who has described the 'pro-Catholic reformism' of O'Neillism as non-existent.[38] It was argued strongly at the London seminar that had O'Neill really wanted to banish sectarianism from Ulster and bring the political system there into line with mainland Britain, he would not have campaigned so virulently as he did against the Northern Ireland Labour Party candidates in the 1965 Stormont election. One witness, Roy Bradford, a former Stormont Cabinet Minister, said that 'Terence was determined to extirpate what there was of the [Northern Ireland] Labour Party.' Bew, also a witness at the seminar, called it 'a classic misjudgement on O'Neill's part'. Bew added:

before he died he (O'Neill) did say to my graduate students that it was a mistake and when he looked back on it he did not know exactly why he had been doing it. He did acknowledge the futility of this whole exercise.[39]

While Wilson and Jenkins continually stated their public faith in O'Neill there is evidence that they privately regarded him as a weak and rather vain man. Roy Hattersley, a defence minister at the time of British intervention three years later recalled:

Yes, there was a lack of confidence in O'Neill because nobody thought of O'Neill as a man of ability. Many people thought he was a step in the right direction at least from Brookeborough [his predecessor as Northern Ireland Prime Minister] that he was not the black Ulster Protestant 'screw-the-Paddies' sort of figure.... But everybody thought O'Neill was a bit of a joke. The story used to be told in the messes of the military that O'Neill was the only guards officer who had been the accompanying officer with a guards band for five years. Apparently, when a band goes on tour it has to take a real officer with it and the real guards officers avoid it at all costs....[40]

Asked why in that case Wilson and Jenkins and later Callaghan thought O'Neill could deliver reform, Hattersley replied:

Well, did they? I can remember having supper with Roy [Jenkins] at that time and Roy making jokes saying to me 'Roy, couldn't you make him a major ... perhaps even a colonel then we would all be able to treat him with more respect.' I don't think Roy had a very high opinion of him.... He happened to be there and it was either doing business with him or have a cataclysm.[41]

A rather different picture of O'Neill is given by an aide who was closer to him in those days than anyone other than his own family, Kenneth Bloomfield, who served officially as his private secretary but unofficially, in Bloomfield's own words, as a 'word-spinner and ideas man'.[42] In his memoirs Bloomfield asks:

Did O'Neill ... have from the outset some grand design to improve relations between the communities in Northern Ireland and between North and South in Ireland? Did he indeed, as some on the right wing of unionism were to imply, have some long-term but covert ambition to blur the distinction between North and South and bring about a united Ireland by stealth? My answer to both of these questions is very firmly negative.... O'Neill remained very fundamentally a Unionist.... In seeking rapprochement rather than confrontation, O'Neill was essentially following his own decent instincts.[43]

Bloomfield then turns to O'Neill's reputation since his resignation (April 1969) which 'has been subjected to mutually contradictory criticism'. According to some of his critics he was a meddler who:

should have left well alone, not raising expectations that he was incapable of satisfying. He was a faint-heart, others suggest; he should have pressed ahead with reform much more boldly, harnessing a great force of good will for him to push aside the objections of obscurantists in his own party.[44]

In an interview[45] Bloomfield expanded on this analysis. If O'Neill had a policy it was to deliver change without replacing the present constitutional system which he recognised was threatened without reform. 'He came in dedicated to economic development not political reform – he came to reform later. He thought reform would strengthen the Union. Keeping the Union was more important than Protestant hegemony.' Asked why, if O'Neill put the cohesion of the Union above eternal Protestant rule, he had tried to destroy the strongly Unionist Northern Ireland Labour Party, Bloomfield replied:

It was because of the moves he had made towards the Catholics. He had to take out an insurance policy with the Unionists by obtaining a big win in the General Election (1965). But where would he get new seats other than from the Labour Party?[46]

Bloomfield had no doubts that O'Neill was serious about political reform:

He hated the injustice to the Catholics. After all he had served in the Irish Guards which was mixed. Some of the Orange[47] excesses he took part in were rites of passage which had to be endured. But he was the wrong man to carry out reforms. Faulkner,[48] the genuine Ulsterman, might have done it. O'Neill had this old fashioned English attitude and accent.[49]

Unlike many Unionists O'Neill had not been wary of Labour coming to power:

He did take Wilson's pro-Catholic line seriously. He was well aware of the vast number of Irish Catholics in his Huyton constituency. Unionist fear of a Labour government had been exaggerated. In fact Northern Ireland has always done better under Labour with their regional economic policies.[50]

For many Labour MPs that summer, however, the issue was not the quality of O'Neill's leadership but the fact that the convention preventing the province's internal affairs being raised at Westminster was still intact after nearly two years of Labour Government. On 1 July the *Belfast Telegraph* carried an article by its London Editor, Percy Diamond, which acknowledged the strength of Labour back-bench concern about events in Northern Ireland, 'highlighted recently by three tragic deaths'. His article included the forecast that the convention would soon be broken. Diamond reported that few backbench MPs had attended the hastily summoned meeting at Westminster presided over by Paul Rose, chairman of the CDU. But he added:

> The fact that the number of MPs sponsoring this campaign rose during the week from 92 to around the 100 mark is an indication of its growing importance. It is capable of exerting pressure on government which cannot lightly be ignored and is known to have sympathies of a number of members of the government who are not sponsors of the campaign. No wonder an Opposition MP observed … that critics of Northern Ireland affairs were now in a stronger position than at any time since the war....[51]

Apart from the demand that the Home Secretary should interest himself directly in the internal affairs of the province in view of the recrudescence of extremist violence, Diamond wrote:

> I see a real prospect of a break being made in the convention that Northern Ireland domestic affairs should not be discussed at Westminster.... It was this subject that Harold Wilson clearly had in mind when he suggested talks between the Home Secretary and Captain O'Neill. With Labour backbencher opinion now so power-fully focussed and because there is certain to be a succession of Parliamentary questions on the proposed talks, there is a strong feeling at Westminster that the discussion cannot be long delayed.[52]

Diamond's conviction that crisis talks were imminent was to be proved right. On 5 August Wilson, O'Neill and Jenkins met at a private lunch at Downing Street to hold what Wilson called the most important discussions on the Northern Ireland situation since he came to power nearly two years before (see below).

To coincide with the Queen's visit to Ulster the *Sunday Times* published an investigation into the growing crisis in the province under the headline 'John Bull's Political Slum'. The article is one of the very few in the British press during those years which made a genuine attempt to warn mainland Britain of the consequences of the failure to tackle Catholic grievance. Three decades later MPs still recall the *Sunday Times* article if only remembering the title.[53] The frankness of its conclusions convinced the CDU that they had at last won a powerful ally in an important section of the serious British press[54] but infuriated the Ulster Unionists. The introduction to the article declared: 'The overture to the Queen's Ulster visit tomorrow has been gunfire, petrol bombs and an upsurge of religious bigotry. The ... investigation plots the underlying sickness that will remain to be cured after the loyal cheers die away'.[55] There was, it said:

a part of Britain where the crude apparatus of political and religious oppression-ballot-rigging job and housing discrimination and an omnipresent threat of violence comfortably coexists with intense loyalty to the Crown. Tomorrow when the Queen visits Northern Ireland, the demonstrations of allegiance will verge on the frenetic. Protestant Ulster has just survived another bloody crisis and is anxious to show where its heart lies.

However the previous week the British public had been confronted with Ulster's endemic brutality and Paisleyism had been denounced as 'neo Nazism' and 'quasi-fascism.' Yet, said the article:

Paisleyism is merely the visible symptom of a deep-seated political malaise for which the Westminster Parliament bears a large measure of responsibility. When the flags are hauled down after the Royal visit, Mr Wilson's government will be confronted with a sharp alternative: whether to use reserve powers to bring elementary social justice to Ulster, or simply allow Britain's most isolated province to work out its own bizarre destiny. During the last 45 years since Partition the latter course has been negligently adopted with what often look like disastrous results.[56]

The article went on to give detailed evidence of gerrymandering in

Londonderry and other parts of the province by the Unionists, of how Catholics were discriminated against over jobs and housing, and of the clear bias by the Stormont government in making decisions in favour of the Protestant community such as the siting of the new University in Protestant-dominated Coleraine. This meant that:

> Catholics believe implicitly, and often hopelessly that these decisions by the Stormont Government are not coincidental. So do a number of British MPs. But one of the most curious aspects of religious discrimination in Ulster is that the Westminster Parliament is prevented by convention from discussing it.

The article then described how the Speaker invariably operated his veto to prevent Ulster's internal affairs being discussed by the Commons and pointed out that this had led to the emergence of the CDU as an organisation dedicated to destroying the convention:

> The CDU has already incurred the venom of the Paisleyites; its chairman, the young Manchester MP Paul Rose, receives messages like: 'Don't come to Ulster again to visit your croppy [*sic*] friend Fitt or the UVF will get you.'

The CDU had told the *Sunday Times* that they believed that a convention was over-ruled by a statute, in this case the Government of Ireland Act 1920 and that they were hopeful of enlisting the support of the Prime Minister when they went to see him shortly. Finally, the article made the prediction that:

> any real liberalisation of the Ulster regime will only come after some vigorous prodding from Westminster. O'Neill may put a brake on Paisley's virulence, but the grass-roots strength of 'Paisleyism' has undoubtedly shaken the Northern Ireland Government, and what little reforming zeal it ever had is in danger of burning out. The loyalist cheers for the Queen tomorrow should not be allowed to soften a very hard line on John Bull's political slum.[57]

The significance of the *Sunday Times* article lies partly in the fact that it was written at all. Its provenance is explained by Harold Evans, Managing Editor at the time,

> The *Sunday Times* having, like the rest of Britain, forgotten about Ulster for a long time, began to take an interest in 1966. We published then during the editorship of Mr C.D. Hamilton, an

examination of discrimination entitled 'John Bull's Political Slum'. The suggestion in that article that reform would never come without 'vigorous prodding from Westminster', attracted deep Protestant fury.[58]

The importance of British press interest in the worsening situation in Northern Ireland was not lost on Dublin. During the Queen's visit to Ulster on 4 July, there were demonstrations and she narrowly avoided injury when a concrete block dropped on the bonnet of her car from the top of a building.[59] The *Irish Times* claimed that an 'ugly situation in the North has been made worse by the incidents on Monday.... Yet if Capt. O'Neill presses on we believe his liberalising trend must prevail'. The editorial continued:

> Monday's incidents, following a period when Northern Ireland has never had such a bad press, raises again the possibility of intervention by the British government.... Can Mr Wilson now sit back and say that the Northern Ireland government has got the situation in hand when influential papers like the *Sunday Times* and the *Daily Telegraph* inform its readers that there is discrimination in Northern Ireland?[60]

A few days later, the *Daily Mirror*'s celebrated columnist, Cassandra [William Connor], compared Paisley to Hitler. But, according to the *Belfast Telegraph*, the article did not appear in the Northern Ireland edition. A *Daily Mirror* spokesman said he could not comment on the reason for the omission.[61] Unfortunately, however, this was to be the last time until the events at Londonderry two years later, that the mainland press as a whole showed any interest in the province.

During his period as Home Secretary, Roy Jenkins was often rumoured to be about to visit the province. He never did so. However, shortly after the violence in Belfast and the Queen's visit, the *Belfast Telegraph*'s London editor, Percy Diamond, predicted a visit before the end of the year. Because Diamond was a member of the press lobby at the Commons and because of the manner in which it was written (use of the phrase 'I understand', etc.) he may well have written the following after a confidential talk with Jenkins:

> Mr Roy Jenkins, the Home Secretary, who is kept closely informed of affairs in Northern Ireland for which he has Cabinet

responsibility, is hopeful, I understand, of paying his promised visit to the province within the next six months. It was sometime ago that he had a warm invitation from Capt. O'Neill but the pressure on his department had been so great in recent months that he has had no opportunity to fit in the visit....[62]

It is ironic that Diamond should have talked of a warm invitation from O'Neill because this certainly was not Jenkins' impression of the Northern Ireland Premier's true feelings. A quarter of a century later later, Jenkins recalled conversations with O'Neill on this subject:

I used to say to him that I ought to come to Northern Ireland. He would say, 'Perhaps in the spring. Perhaps next autumn.' Maybe had I gone I might have got one foot [*sic*] involved. But it would not have prevented 1969. Nobody would have contemplated direct rule before 1969. It [Northern Ireland] was about 12th on my agenda.[63]

Jenkins' lack of interest in Northern Ireland is confirmed in his autobiography in which the problem is barely mentioned in the chapters covering his first period as Home Secretary.[64]

An event which seemed to indicate that the convention, so staunchly upheld by Jenkins, could indeed be breached if the government so wished came later that summer. This was the passing of the highly-controversial Prices and Incomes Act which introduced statutory control of all wage price and dividend increases. As Jonathan Bardon has commented, 'The application of prices and incomes legislation could be seen as interference in areas normally under Stormont's sphere of influence.'[65] Two years later, after the Londonderry violence, Mary Holland wrote that Nationalists pointed to the Prices and Incomes Bill as proof that Westminster was prepared to extend legislation 'to Ulster against the wishes of Stormont'.[66] Asked 25 years later whether this meant that the convention was indeed being waived, Bloomfield replied that he could not recall the Bill in detail. But he said:

The Government of Ireland Act, 1920, did not prevent legislation whatever. It gave a Northern Ireland Parliament power to make laws but did not restrain the powers of the UK Parliament.... It was a convention that government at Westminster would not intrude into the 'transferred' field without the approval of the Northern Ireland Government.[67]

However, unlike their activities on race relations legislation earlier and the attempt to amend the Ombudsman Bill later in the year to make it apply to the province as well as mainland Britain, the CDU MPs do not seem to have taken advantage of the Prices and Incomes Bill to further their protests.

Three weeks later Wilson and Jenkins were due to have what Wilson called 'my most important meeting up to that time with Capt. Terence O'Neill'.[68] Important it may have been but the fact is that Ireland was the last thing on the minds of either the Prime Minister or his Home Secretary. The government was still reeling from a disastrous summer which had started with the Seamen's dispute and ended only two weeks before the planned meeting with O'Neill with the savage deflationary package known as the 'July Cuts'. Jenkins himself was the Minister in Charge of the Emergencies Committee which tried to mitigate the consequences of the Seamen's strike.[69] Wilson wrote in a private diary note 'What really hit us was the Seamen's Strike.'[70] The strike had begun on 16 May and 'after immense pressure on the reserves and on sterling, a settlement was patched up after six damaging weeks'.[71] Wilson had set out to defend his incomes policy by making an example of the seamen but the price was 'the worst sterling crisis the Government had yet suffered'.[72] The savage deflationary package announced on 20 July was a direct result and the government emerged from the whole affair exhausted and discredited. As for Wilson himself:

> In March he had been a miracle worker ... by the end of July he had become an obstacle to progress.... Party morale, noted James Margach [*Sunday Times*] was 'in the most dispirited state for years'. Some spoke of Labour's Suez.... Others compared it to 1931....[73]

One historian has written of the 'air of panic and personal recrimination with which the crisis of sterling had been surrounded'. Wilson's reaction was to retreat 'further into his private circle of advisers and "kitchen cabinet" itself a somewhat motley and frenetic group...'.[74] No wonder then that when Wilson and Jenkins saw O'Neill on 5 August they had in Bagehot's phrase no 'mind in reserve'[75] to apply to a big initiative in the province. We have two versions of that encounter: Wilson's, claiming that O'Neill was warned of the urgency of speedy reform and O'Neill's suggesting that, on the contrary, the

Prime Minister and Home Secretary, did not press him to go more quickly.

First the Wilson version. Writing some five years later, after his defeat in the 1970 election, Wilson recalled that the three men held a private lunch which went on well into the afternoon. Wilson says that O'Neill had already done more for Catholic rights in three years than all his Stormont predecessors in more than 40 years. (What these achievements were Wilson does not explain. Certainly, none of the Catholic grievances mentioned by Wilson when he was Leader of the Opposition had been addressed.) According to Wilson, O'Neill had aroused open hostility from his supporters and many back bench MPs 'to say nothing of a black reactionary group in his Cabinet'. Wilson then says:

> It was essential that the progress be maintained for, as the world learned three years later, time – after so many years had been wasted – was not on our side. The Westminster Parliament, and particularly many of our 1964 and 1966 new entrants was deeply concerned about human rights....

Then Wilson suggests that he warned O'Neill that British taxpayers' money might be withheld if Catholic grievances were not met soon:

> Our members were concerned with the very great increase in financial assistance from the Westminster exchequer to Ulster and without constitutional reform and more liberal policies it was becoming more difficult to justify to MPs and to some members of our Cabinet the large sums they were being asked to vote.[76]

O'Neill, Wilson said, readily took these arguments ... 'but he [O'Neill] gravely underlined the threats to his position and to the reform movement. There must now be a period of consolidation ... or a dangerous and possibly irresistible tide of reaction would set in'. Wilson said that he and Jenkins agreed 'not to press him to go further for the next few months ...'. 'But more time, the most precious commodity in the explosive Northern Ireland situation was being inevitably lost.'[77]

Perhaps the most interesting remark made by Wilson in this account is the hint of financial sanctions. There is nothing in the Cabinet minutes and papers released in 1997 to suggest that the Cabinet did seriously consider such a move during 1966 or whether this was a typical piece of Wilson bluff. A senior civil servant who does not wish to be named, looking back on those years, remarked on Wilson's capacity to come up with schemes, fixes and ploys none of which had been discussed with his Cabinet colleagues let alone civil servants.[78] However, in fairness to Wilson, he was to return to this theme on several occasions during the next three years and O'Neill warned his insubordinate Cabinet colleague, William Craig [Home Affairs Minister 1966–68, sacked by O'Neill, December 1968], that Wilson meant business with his threat to withhold British taxpayers' money from the province.[79]

O'Neill's version of the talks with the British Prime Minister and Home Secretary has no mention of Wilson waving the financial big stick. Wilson, he says, had wondered why he met Sean Lemass against the wishes of the Unionists but both he and Jenkins welcomed these North–South talks. O'Neill makes no mention of Wilson's fears that time was running out but suggests that both Wilson and Jenkins were impressed by the speed of reform.[80]

Confusion about the outcome of the meeting was reflected in the *Belfast Telegraph* report the following day. The first headline read: 'Opposition [in Stormont] expects faster reform' while underneath a second headline read: 'But O'Neill says that he wasn't given timetable at Downing Street.' The report itself spoke of NILP MPs and Nationalist leaders at Stormont being confident that as a result of the Downing Street talks Stormont would indicate its intention to speed up electoral and social reform.[81]

An opportunity for clarification came only two days later when the CDU MPs ingeniously engineered a debate on Northern Ireland in the Commons in the middle of the night. Alice Bacon, Minister of State at the Home Office, who had responsibility for Northern Ireland, was to reply for the government. However, the Labour MPs would have hardly expected enthusiastic support for their cause. Several of them regarded her as virtually a Unionist. As McNamara explained at the London seminar, Bacon had visited Ulster and on her return told them:

how splendidly she was received, what a lovely time she had had at Hillsborough, [the Governor-General's official residence] how the Governor-General couldn't have been better, what a lovely bedroom it was, what views there were from the window, and that was always the way the Home Office … were treated. They were loved, cosseted, the world opened up for them and then they were sent gently back to the UK.[82]

Of all the junior ministers at the Home Office, with responsibility for Northern Ireland during the period being considered, Bacon was probably the least sympathetic to the aims of the CDU. Several of the others, most notably Maurice Foley, made no secret of their sympathy for the civil rights programme.[83] Callaghan said that another, Lord (Victor) Stonham, was dedicated to achieving full civil rights for Catholics.[84] Shirley Williams was not actively hostile, simply not interested.[85] However, in her interpretation of the convention during the debate Alice Bacon was not giving her personal views but clearly stating the position taken by the Home Secretary, Jenkins, her superior, and the government as a whole [no doubt on the advice of the Home Office and civil servants from the Law Officers' Department].

The debate arose during the Consolidated Fund Bill[86] which allows MPs to raise virtually any issue they wish but specifically precludes calls for legislation, a point which was to cause considerable frustration.[87] Fitt opened the debate by quoting Section 75 of the Government of Ireland Act, 1920. Fitt told the Deputy Speaker, Sir Eric Fletcher, that Section 75 gave

> ultimate and over-riding responsibility to the Parliament of the United Kingdom, and as the representative of Belfast, West ... I stand here to demand of the British government that they accept the responsibility which they themselves have written into this Act of 1920.

However, the Deputy Speaker, would not accept this line of argument. He stopped Fitt's flow telling him:

> Section 75 ... does not confer responsibility on Her Majesty's ministers in the United Kingdom over matters within the competence of the Northern Ireland government. My predecessors in this Chair have ruled repeatedly that matters within the competence of the Northern Ireland government, and therefore matters for which Her Majesty's ministers in this House are not responsible, are not subjects for debate in this House.

This ruling sparked off a furious row with Labour MPs determined that for once they would not be silenced. First McNamara asked Sir Eric whether, as vast Exchequer subsidies went from this, the British government, to Northern Ireland they would be allowed to give reasons why these subsidies should not go through and was told that would be in order. Then Elystan Morgan (Cardigan) claimed that the scope of the Consolidated Fund Bill included not only matters of substance but the whole background of policy attaching to it. Again the Deputy Speaker agreed, but he was still not prepared to alter the ruling given to Fitt. This was at once challenged by Michael McGuire (Ince) who argued that if the Home Secretary was satisfied that it was right to intervene directly in the affairs of Northern Ireland he would be the supreme authority delegated with the powers given to him under Section 75. He told Sir Eric:

> Your ruling seemed to me to suggest that he does not have that power but I suggest that Section 75, in anybody's clear interpretation, gives the ministers in this House overriding authority over the Parliament at Stormont.

The Deputy Speaker told him that the confusion was because he had failed to distinguish the position between the United Kingdom Parliament and the United Kingdom government:

> the 1920 Act in Section 75 ... gives this Parliament supreme authority over matters in Northern Ireland and enables the United Kingdom Parliament to legislate on matters affecting Northern Ireland. On the other hand, the responsibility of the United Kingdom government as regards matters in Northern Ireland is limited and Her Majesty's ministers in this country have no responsibility for matters which are within the exclusive jurisdiction of the ministers of the government of Northern Ireland.

That was why MPs could not raise matters for which ministers at Westminster were not responsible.

Fitt now tried to raise accusations of undemocratic practices during elections in Ulster and claimed that people who wished to vote anti-Unionist were not afforded police protection from being attacked by bigoted mobs. The Deputy Speaker again interrupted him saying that unless the Home Office had responsibility for Northern Ireland elections he could not allow him to continue. Alice Bacon, from the government front bench, confirmed that the Home Office did not have such responsibility. The MPs, however, were still not prepared to accept the Deputy Speaker's ruling. Elystan Morgan clearly thought he had discovered a logical reason for allowing Fitt to continue.

> This House is responsible for the expenditure of something like £60 million in Northern Ireland this year. Ministers in this House have to decide how much of the finances which come to their

departments are to be allocated to Northern Ireland. Is it not, therefore, proper to discuss Northern Ireland affairs from the side of the ministers who are in this House and who decide what proportion of their funds should be allocated to that country?

However, the Deputy Speaker could not accept this argument either. Matters which indirectly affected trade or employment had repeatedly been allowed both at Question Time and in debate. 'But the dividing line must be whether or not there is any ministerial responsibility in this House.'

Fitt continued with his speech and was allowed to make a scathing attack on the competence of O'Neill without challenge. But he was again called to order when he claimed that areas of the province which did not support the Unionist party were denied employment. The Deputy Speaker told him that he could not mention matters affecting unemployment that were Stormont's responsibility. Fitt then called on Bacon to note the remarks that been made during the debate and he urged the Deputy Speaker not prevent Northern Ireland affairs being raised in future. Could he:

> in any way help us to rid ourselves of the conventions which exist in this House and which prevent me discussing the welfare of my constituents? I find it rather frustrating when I look to this House for justice for my constituents because I know that any plea I make in the Stormont will certainly fall on deaf ears.

The reply was arguably the nearest to a definitive statement the Commons would ever get on the convention. The Deputy Speaker told him:

> It is perfectly competent for this Parliament to intervene, in any legislative sense, in Northern Ireland. The competence of the sovereignty of the United Kingdom Parliament has been preserved by Section 75 which would therefore, for example, enable this legislature to revoke or amend that Act; but that would involve legislation. It is not permissible, in debating the Consolidated Fund Bill, to introduce matters which involve legislation.

Shortly after 6 am Bacon rose to reply to the debate. She admitted at once that she had difficulty in answering the debate because so many points raised by MPs had been ruled out of order. She then tried to clarify the responsibilities the Westminster government had for Northern Ireland. The Government of Ireland Act had given Stormont power to make laws for the peace, order and good government of Northern Ireland subject to a list of exceptions including international relations, the armed services, coinage and the postal services. Allegations of discrimination by Stormont or local authorities could be tested in the courts. Section 75 of the Act made it clear that the supreme authority of the Parliament, not the government, of the United Kingdom was preserved:

> This means that in no event can there be any question of the United Kingdom Government interfering in transferred matters without legislation....

When this interpretation was challenged by Reg Freeson, Bacon told him:

> To put it as simply as I can ... the Government have powers in those matters reserved to us. We have not powers in those matters that have been transferred to the Northern Ireland Government.

McNamara then asked her whether it would be impossible for the United Kingdom government to appoint a Royal Commission to examine the way in which the present Government of Ireland Act was working. [This was one of the CDU's principal demands.] Bacon conceded that it was possible but it had been decided that it was not the right way to tackle the problem. She said: 'It is perfectly possible for the United Kingdom Government to change the situation, but we should have to think a long time before attacking the problem in that way.' Then she put on record the clearest possible statement that, despite Labour pledges in opposition to bring about reform in Ulster, the present government had no intention of taking any action:

> I should like to remind the House that there has never been an occasion in which legislation on transferred matters has been applied to Northern Ireland against the wishes of the Northern Ireland government. Section 75 of the 1920 Act provides authority for it to be done. It could be done by this Parliament according to Section 75. But it would do great harm to relations between the two governments.... Successive governments have taken the view, however, that so long as Northern Ireland retains its present constitution, it would be wrong for the United Kingdom government and

Parliament to interfere in matters for which responsibility has been delegated to the Northern Ireland government and Parliament.

Alice Bacon rejected the idea that this meant that the government was unconcerned about discrimination in Northern Ireland. 'We are greatly concerned, and we are aware of the disquiet being expressed about the situation there.' However, to those who demanded intervention by the government, she invoked the authority of the Prime Minister who, she said, did not favour such action. '... he prefers the method of informal talks with the Prime Minister of Northern Ireland'.[88]

CONCLUSION

Joe Haines has commented that in both 1964 and 1974 a Labour government pledged to 'solve' the Irish problem was elected without the majority to do so.[89] However, there was a brief period between Labour winning a majority of 97 in March 1966 and the beginning of the Seamen's dispute when Wilson, if he was serious about fulfilling his promises, might have started work on a programme of full civil rights for Northern Ireland. The alibi of a fragile majority was gone and many of the new Labour intake could be expected to demand speedy reform [which they did]. The province itself now had a resolute spokesman at Westminster in the shape of the fast-talking Gerry Fitt. The violence in Belfast during the 1964 general election campaign had been proof enough that the province could boil over at any time. And this had been powerfully reinforced by the intelligence reports that we now know ministers had received in December 1965 warning that the IRA had 3000 trained members who could be 'called out in an emergency'.[90] Nothing, however, was done and within three months the worst sectarian violence for years erupted with the Prime Minister himself talking of a 'quasi-fascist' organisation operating in Ulster. Why did Wilson fail to act earlier? It was not lack of sympathy for the Irish that held him back. As Haines has explained, the Labour Prime Minister remained sincere in his view that Ireland must be 'solved' throughout his political life.[91] It can be argued that his inaction arose from the mistaken view that O'Neill was both serious about the need to address Catholic grievances and could deliver the necessary reforms in the face of fierce opposition from hardline Unionists and without pressure from Westminster.[92]

However, the CDU, now, in effect, led by Fitt, still believed that pressure in the House of Commons could galvanise 'their' government into action. Disillusion over the so-called liberal Home Secretary, Roy Jenkins, had yet to set in. During the summer, as has been shown, they used every device to bring Catholic grievances before Parliament and the British public. The violence of the UVF and the antics of Ian Paisley should have provided the perfect backdrop for their campaign. It was to no avail. Ultimately only the government could put enough pressure on Stormont to bring about the necessary changes but by mid-summer the government was facing grave difficulties elsewhere.

3 Putting off the Evil Day,[1] September 1966 –May 1967

There is still acute concern about many questions affecting the functioning of democracy over there.

Harold Wilson, House of Commons, 27 April 1967[2]

The period covered by this chapter was significant for three separate investigations into the demand for reform in Northern Ireland: a delegation of members of the CDU to the province led by Stanley Orme MP which reported to the Home Secretary, Roy Jenkins; a special survey carried out by *The Times*; and the establishment of a committee of investigation by the Society of Labour Lawyers. At the same time that these inquiries were underway the Prime Minister, Harold Wilson, was privately considering reducing of the powers of the contingent of Ulster MPs at Westminster which, arguably, would have been the first step to major constitutional change since the Government of Ireland Act 1920. Outwardly the Wilson government at first continued to insist that O'Neill should be allowed to carry on with his own policy of amelioration without interference from London. However, by April 1967 an impasse seemed to have been reached with Wilson openly admitting 'acute concern' about the functioning of democracy in the province and O'Neill himself privately recording his growing pessimism.

First, however, this chapter considers the argument of Dr John Oliver, a widely respected former senior civil servant at Stormont, that there was another way out of the impending crisis at that time which the Labour government, tragically, failed to consider. Ulster-born Dr Oliver,[3] believed that the co-operation between civil servants from the Department of Economic Affairs in London and Stormont officials in the mid-1960s provided a model for addressing Catholic grievances in the province. Oliver had a key role in the attempts being made to speed up the economic development of the province. He was responsible for the infrastructure for new industry. Many years later he recalled 'a very good team of chaps' from the Department of Economic Affairs arriving in Ulster:

> We had excellent talks with them.... They were brainy chaps who really knew what they were talking about and we had a great rapport. We took them out and showed them the difficulties and the problems and what we had achieved.... I remember these fellows from the DEA said quite seriously, 'We have nothing to teach you. You have done it all.'[4]

It had been a highly successful operation, said Oliver:

> A pity the same thing did not happen on the political and constitutional side. It is a pity that the Home Office did not send over an equal team to come and talk to chaps like me and Ewart Bell[5] and all the other fellows who were up to their eyes in this stuff and find out what the real problems were. That was a shortcoming.[6]

Oliver had been exhilarated by the way in which the British and Ulster officials had worked together, '... these extremely intelligent fellows arguing with us and saying that's all right but what are you doing about so and so ...'.

They were, said Oliver, all technocrats together. 'It was really very good ... it is a pity that somebody did not do the same thing on local government, local government boundaries, gerrymandering and all the rest of it.' Stormont ministers might have resisted co-operation with the Home Office but 'that would have been a way of doing it. Because so many other things can be done that way. Obviously'.[7]

However, one retired civil servant who held a senior post in Whitehall at the time, is sceptical about Dr Oliver's claim that the 'technocrats' could have achieved a breakthrough over reform: 'The political problems ... were simply not of the same order as the technical issues canvassed with officials of the DEA, a Ministry which was abolished soon after these talks.'[8] Yet, surely this reaction is unnecessarily dismissive. First, the DEA was not the tinpot organisation suggested. Second, reform in Northern Ireland certainly posed different problems from economic development in the province but it was at least possible that highly experienced Home Office officials could have made considerable headway with their Stormont counterparts as Oliver had suggested.

Certainly, in September 1966, the thoughts of HMG could hardly have been further from Northern Ireland. As so often during these turbulent years the Wilson administration was distracted by serious problems elsewhere. The July economic crisis had badly shaken Wilson in a way that had not happened before and for the first time he had felt close to the loss of his Premiership. It was a state of mind from which it took him a long time to recover if he ever did make a full recovery.[9] His government was becoming deeply unpopular, a trend not helped by the devaluation of sterling in November 1967. By-elections, local elections and opinion polls were suggesting that the Tory leader, the previously unpopular Edward Heath, would sweep the country in a general election. Against that background a change of policy over Northern Ireland, which was bound to be controversial and would in any case have been opposed by the Conservatives at this stage,[10] was unlikely.

Yet the possibility that intervention might prove inevitable was beginning to be seriously considered, if not by the Government by those observing the scene at Westminster. *The Times*, in a leading article, warned Unionist MPs at Stormont to back O'Neill's reforms or face intervention by Westminster. It had been a difficult year in Ulster. The commemoration of the Easter rising, *The Times* declared, had

> sent up the national blood pressure in all parts of the island. Mob violence in the streets of Belfast and the extremism of Paisley challenged the Government's attitude.... Unionists do not need to be reminded that there is pressure on the Parliament at Westminster to interest itself in the social conditions of Northern Ireland. Any marked change for the worse in the balance of political forces within the ruling party there would intensify the pressure.[11]

The Times editorial is significant not only for its stern warning to the Ulster Unionist Party right wing. It is one of the first acknowledgements of the role being played at Westminster by the CDU, now stiffened by effective interventions of Gerry Fitt MP.

Evidence that disquiet about events in Ulster was not restricted to Labour and the Liberals was provided the following month by Percy Diamond, London Editor of the *Belfast Telegraph*. In his weekly feature 'Ulster Letter from London'[12] Diamond wrote:

> Never should it be assumed that the Conservative Party is detached or complacent on several Ulster issues which in recent months have received national publicity. Ulster Unionists are finding it as important to study the reactions of their Conservative friends as to meet the criticisms of their political opponents.

The following day one of those Ulster Unionists responded with a remarkable warning of his own. Captain Lawrence Orr, MP, leader of the Ulster Unionist MPs at Westminster, claimed that Harold Wilson intended to 'tinker' with the Constitution of Northern Ireland. The *Belfast Telegraph* considered Orr's comments of sufficient significance for it to be the leading news item on the front page.[13] The headline read: 'Constitutional Change as Sop to Left-wingers? Orr warns Ulster. Don't give Harold Wilson the excuse to interfere'. The report said that Orr 'forecast today that the Labour Government is likely to tinker with the Ulster constitution' and it quoted Orr as saying:

> Harold Wilson might be willing to throw his left wing a sop. The British Prime Minister is out of favour with his left wing and to keep them quiet he might agree to do something about Northern Ireland. The important thing is … that no excuse should be given to Wilson for intervening in our affairs.

Orr was clearly on to something because, as mentioned earlier, there is now evidence from the documents released by the PRO in 1997[14] that Wilson had been contemplating limiting the powers of the Ulster MPs at Westminster for at least 18 months. Orr was also correct in pointing out the low morale of left-wing Labour MPs following the July economic crisis. Some compared the atmosphere to 1931 and 'there was loose talk about a coalition from Tory enemies (who wanted to castrate Labour) and left-wingers (who feared that Wilson might join one)'.[15] Five months later, Ian Waller, a senior political correspondent who was close to Wilson, learned that such a plan was on the Prime Minister's mind.

At the time Waller was political editor of the *Sunday Telegraph*, a Conservative newspaper which could be expected to be a stalwart supporter of the Ulster Unionists. Waller himself was personally sympathetic to Labour[16] and he had a useful rapport with Wilson whom he had known well for some time. However, his article on the Prime Minister's thoughts appeared not in his own paper but in the *Catholic Herald*.[17] It received widespread attention in the province because the *Belfast Telegraph* published large extracts prominently under the headline, 'Irish Unity is Wilson's dream'. Thirty years later Waller explained how he came to write the article.

> Norman St John Stevas and I alternated for some years (each week) writing an article for the *Catholic Herald*. I am not a Catholic. As a matter of fact I am rather anti-Papist but they let me

write what I liked. The article did come from talking to Harold Wilson.[18]

In his article Waller pointed to the presence of the 11 Ulster Unionist members at Westminster 'those faithful slaves of the Conservative Party. Nothing is more calculated to make the hackles rise in the Labour Party than the thought of this rump'. They could never forget that it was this group who almost held the fate of the Labour government in their hands between 1964 and 1966. Waller goes on: 'Indeed one of the most powerful ambitions in the minds of many Labour MPs and ministers is either to eliminate or at least greatly reduce the power of this group.' There was, however,

> another far more important consideration that I know the Prime Minister feels very deeply: the need for a far-reaching constitutional change that would finally end the century old Anglo-Irish quarrel. It would indeed by a feather in Mr Wilson's cap if he could go down in history as the man who re-united Ireland.[19]

Waller then outlined the various steps that the Wilson government had taken to improve relations with the Republic and address Catholic grievances in the North. What was lacking, he said, was that intangible element of respect and goodwill, for which Labour blamed the Ulster Unionist party at Westminster. The crucial question was what the government proposed doing during the next few years about 'this gross absurdity'. Without breaching any confidences, but clearly referring to his confidential talk with Wilson, Waller wrote (again in the *Catholic Herald*):

> Mr Wilson's hope is obviously pegged on solving the Irish issue as a whole, but pending that a great deal of thought is being given to possible constitutional changes that would limit the right of Ulster MPs to speak and vote on issues that are delegated to the Ulster Parliament, and also to define more strictly those functions of the UK government which are also applicable to Northern Ireland, and to restrict the Ulster voting to those issues.

Very little more was heard of plans to curtail the powers of the Ulster Unionists. Waller claimed years later, that this was because 'once Wilson had a large majority they changed their tone and kept their heads down'.[20] There is, however, no evidence that the Unionist MPs kept a low profile as Waller suggested. On the contrary, a reading of Hansard suggests the opposite. It is more likely that

Wilson was not prepared to face the political storm it would create at a time when his government was already facing a series of crises at home and abroad. In the last few weeks of 1966 Roy Jenkins at separate meetings saw representatives of the Northern Ireland Labour Party and the CDU and had lunch with O'Neill. *The Times* carried a leading article paying tribute to the CDU's attempt to break the convention preventing Northern Ireland's internal affairs being raised at Westminster: 'Against the procedural odds a persistent group of Labour MPs struggle to ventilate their allegations of communal discrimination and electoral malpractices.'[21]

Yet despite the events of the previous 12 months and Wilson's anger at the behaviour of Ulster Unionist MPs there is little to suggest from the reaction of ministers whenever Northern Ireland was raised in the Commons that there was a general awareness in government or Whitehall of the mounting political and constitutional problems. Ironically this charge could not be levelled at the Northern Ireland Premier Terence O'Neill. He expressed his doubts in a heartfelt letter to his Stormont aide Kenneth Bloomfield. Writing nearly 30 years later Bloomfield recalled the background to this profoundly pessimistic missive:

> Terence O'Neill, it has to be said, was never an optimist. He had an unusual habit of writing to me at the conclusion of each year, a personal letter in which he would give a summation of the year just past and a forecast of the year to come.[22]

Bloomfield still had such a letter dated 28 December 1966 addressed to him:

> Dear Ken, None of us foresaw the events of the dying year at the end of 1965! Indeed your letter of a year ago spoke of how much stronger my position would be in 1966 after the election! In a sense this was true, though we certainly did not appreciate this point at the end of September [when a number of MPs had attempted to set in motion a putsch to displace O'Neill as party leader]. My forecast for 1967 is that it will be much worse than 1966....[23]

In the event, wrote Bloomfield, 1967 was an unremarkable enough year, but the storm clouds were gathering.

Whether or not O'Neill genuinely intended bringing about fundamental reform is still a matter of controversy. As was pointed out in Chapter 2, Paul Bew is convinced that he was not. However, O'Neill himself, spent some time in his autobiography claiming that had it not been for the hard men of the right in his own party he would have achieved major reform:

> On 1 May 1969 I laid down what had increasingly become totally impossible burdens. I had won the trust of the Catholics as no previous Prime Minister had been able to do, but I was unable to restore to them the rights which small-minded men had removed from them during the first few years of Northern Ireland's existence,[24]

O'Neill had begun with high hopes, particularly as he had evidently built up a good relationship with his opposite number in Downing Street. He recorded that in 1963 he met Harold Wilson, the new Labour leader, at his room in the House of Commons. Notes that he made at the time said: 'I fully expect to dislike him but instead find a lot of charm as well as the expected intelligence.... When I tell him how well we were treated by the last Labour Government, he assures me we shall be equally well treated by the next. In fact I enjoy my interview very much indeed and feel that if he wins we shall get on well – I hope I am right.' This, wrote O'Neill, is how it turned out to be: 'Harold Wilson was detested by many people and quite acceptable to others. I fell into the second category....'[25]

Early successes claimed by O'Neill included the recognition by Stormont of the Northern Ireland Committee of the Irish Congress of Trade Unions. 'Looking back I would say that this was probably one of the most difficult hurdles I surmounted during my Premiership.'[26] He also pointed to his unprecedented meetings with Sean Lemass, Prime Minister of the Republic of Ireland. One immediate and tangible result from this new relationship was the decision by the Nationalist Party for the first time to accept the role of Official Opposition at Stormont.[27] By the end of 1965, he claimed, the election in Northern Ireland 'proved that my policies were acceptable to the vast majority of Protestants and to a growing number of Catholics'.[28] However, the insistence by the Belfast Catholics on celebrating the 50th anniversary of the Dublin rebellion and the reaction by Unionist extremists, O'Neill believed, put paid to any real hope of co-operation between the two communities: 'It was 1966 which made 1968 inevitable and was bound to put the whole future of Northern Ireland in the melting pot.'[29] Reflecting after his resignation as Prime

Minister, O'Neill conceded that the Unionist party would never stand for change. As reform was out, 'I was really reduced to trying to improve relations between North and South and in the North between the two sections of the community.'[30]

A public warning that the storm clouds referred to by Bloomfield were indeed gathering came early in the New Year in a major article in the *Belfast Telegraph*.[31] [In Bloomfield's view the paper and its liberal Editor, Jack Sayers, took a consistent, and courageous line on reform.[32]] The article was headlined 'Attitude in Britain in 1967. Why Ulster still stirs feelings in Whitehall'. It was by Percy Diamond, the London Editor who wrote:

> The British public is less interested in Northern Ireland than perhaps it should be, but it is certainly not hostile. The danger is that it should become impatient over outdated attitudes it cannot comprehend. Harold Wilson … cannot ignore the feeling about Northern Ireland among so large a section of his backbenchers. It is now clear that events are on the march in Northern Ireland and the concern of the British government is to see that 'the momentum of change' in the Home Secretary's words is maintained.

Diamond, shrewd observer though he was, exaggerated backbench influence over Wilson and his government. Wilson and his Home Secretary continued their policy of non-intervention despite Wilson's growing concern about the lack of democracy in the province. Jenkins' passion for reform stopped well short of St George's Channel as he was to make clear later in the year. The truth was that Ulster's Catholics did not have a champion in this crisis-ridden Cabinet [the one possible exception being Lord Longford who was a member of the Cabinet until January 1968 but was generally regarded as something of an eccentric].[33]

The first of the three separate investigations into the charges of discrimination that spring was the visit to Northern Ireland, from 14 to 16 April, by a delegation of Labour MPs from the CDU led by Stan Orme who was to become a cabinet minister in the Callaghan government ten years later. The tour was suggested by and organised by Fitt as the local MP and Orme was accompanied by Paul Rose, the CDU chairman, and Maurice Miller, MP for Glasgow Kelvingrove. None were Catholic [in fact Rose and Miller were Jewish]. Their inclusion was probably the result of a deliberate decision.[34] A detailed and vivid account of the trio's experience is given by Rose in a book written some years later. He described the visit as 'The Highlight of the Campaign for Democracy'.[35] The objectives included an investigation of discrimination and electoral law and practice. But it was also hoped to inform a wide spectrum of citizens in the province of the activities at Westminster of Labour MPs interested in Northern Ireland affairs.[36] Rose recalled:

> Although only the opposition groups would meet us it was a remarkable tour. In some areas we were met by bands and led to the rostrum set up in the middle of the town like conquering heroes. Even the pubs closed. In Strabane virtually the whole town turned out at 11 at night, and television cameras were thrust upon us at one in the morning.[37]

The MPs met the Secretary of the Belfast Trades Council, Betty Sinclair, to discuss economic problems and they also saw representatives of the NILP and the nationalists 'commonly termed green Tories'. The gathering at Londonderry was most significant:

> it was the embryo from which the SDLP was born. The irony of Derry was that by concentrating Catholics in high rise flats in Bogside, the Unionist majority on the council could be preserved. It also provided a bastion for violence when ultimately the explosion came.[38]

In their subsequent report[39] the MPs came to a number of conclusions: there could be little doubt that discrimination in housing existed on a wide scale. Discrimination on political and religious grounds was substantiated by figures previously provided by the NILP and confirmed by all those with whom this was discussed. This applied in relation to Government appointments in the legal profession, in local government and in sections of industry. In the legal profession there were only 11 Catholics holding judicial offices out of a total of 142. In many public bodies Catholic, Labour and Trade Union representatives were excluded. In Londonderry there was 'irrefutable evidence of gerrymandering in order to perpetuate minority control'. The electoral franchise which excluded 250 000 voters from local government elections[40] was a UK anomaly. Unemployment was greater in Catholic areas. Neglect of the area west of the Bann was patently evident.

The MPs also commented on Unionist reaction to their visit which they described as 'hostile and provocative'. They were described as 'anti-Ulster' and 'interfering and unwelcome.' The Unionists refused to meet the members of the group. There was, however:

> a ready response at all the meetings to the simple statement of principle that the MPs demanded the same rights and privileges for Northern Ireland as in their own constituencies as an integral part of the UK. A policy which respects the right of Irishmen ultimately to decide their constitutional status for themselves but recognises Westminster's overriding obligation to ensure democratic government in the province is one which would commend itself to large sections of people, both Protestant and Catholic in Northern Ireland.[41]

The three MPs ended their report with the recommendation that the Government should set up a Royal Commission to investigate the operation of the Government of Ireland and Ireland Acts.[42]

Not all those concerned with the need for reform, however, welcomed the visit. Jack Hassard, a Dungannon NILP councillor who had a good local record on civil rights issues, complained that the MPs had only talked to 'Green Tories'.[43] The *Belfast Telegraph*, in a front-page editorial, commented that the MPs 'blew in and blew out' but was not otherwise hostile. It would be unwise, said the paper, for its opponents to write off the visit too soon:

> Considering that Northern Ireland prides itself on being an integral part of the UK and that these same Labour MPs will soon be asked to approve a further £50 million increase in Stormont's borrowing powers, the visitors have every right to interest themselves in our affairs.[44]

This was a shrewd observation by the author of the editorial [probably the Editor, Jack Sayers]. The so-called subsidy provided by the mainland British taxpayer to Ulster was increasingly taken up by Labour MPs as an argument for intervention. To their moral case they could now add the practical one that a considerable sum of money was being spent on shoring up an undemocratic administration. [The actual amount of this largesse is generally given at between £100 million and £130 million a year during the late 1960s, certainly more than a billion pounds in today's money].[45] Wilson himself [and ironically O'Neill too, against Unionist hardliners] was to make increasing reference to it as tension in the province grew.

The report of the MPs' investigative visit was submitted to the

Home Secretary, Roy Jenkins, who, the *Belfast Telegraph* lobby correspondent, Roy Lilley, believed, probably raised its findings with
O'Neill when Jenkins saw the Ulster PM on 10 May.[46] The CDU
report came on top of the secret intelligence that the Cabinet had
received the previous year about the IRA plan to mark the 50th
anniversary of the Easter Rising with a campaign of violence.[47]
However, according to Paul Rose, who of course knew nothing about
the intelligence, the CDU report was ignored by the government with,
in his view, appalling consequences.

> The very setting up of a Commission would have shown that we
> were aware of the problem. Instead the Government allowed the
> traditional, highly provocative Apprentice Boys' March to trigger
> off such opposition that there was a danger of the Ulster police
> running riot in Bogside. In that context no one could blame the
> Government for the initial decision to send in troops. And all
> because they ignored our report.[48]

However, for Rose and others to expect Jenkins to intervene at this
stage was unrealistic. The government was burdened by many more
pressing problems and, as Bloomfield was quoted earlier as saying,
conditions on the surface in the province in 1967 seemed 'unremarkable'. The hypothetical risk of serious civil unrest in Ulster was not
going to find its way onto the Cabinet agenda. Rose, in effect admitted this years later:

> over Northern Ireland he (Jenkins) had this historical perspective
> that Northern Ireland could be the political graveyard and knowing
> that he listened with great sympathy and he agreed to meet us
> (CDU) regularly but there wasn't any great change.... Jenkins is a
> non-interventionist because he has got other matters which he
> regards as far more important, a large number of important law
> reforms, and I think he was the best Home Secretary of the century.
> He wasn't going to get himself involved in a topic that might bring
> about his downfall when he had more important things, in his view,
> to worry about.[49]

This certainly seems a fair summary of Jenkins at that time.[50] As a
protest group the CDU were dwarfed by the more traditional factions
inside the Labour Party. For the Left, the Vietnam War, the collapse
of Labour's programme for expanding the economy, Rhodesia and
South African apartheid were the issues that mattered. A handful of
the CDU MPs, despite their assiduity, were unlikely on their own to

influence either Jenkins or Wilson. Moreover, they could not look to the press to publicise their cause as the newspapers, in the main, were continuing to pretend that Ulster did not exist. Brian Wenham, a former Director of Programmes, BBC TV, 'put his finger on the problem of the overly narrow, self perpetuating newspaper agenda' when he wrote that big issues, including 'the emerging crisis in Northern Ireland in the 1960s' had

> been openly evaded or effectively by-passed, sidelined from politics to the realms of economics or sociology, only to force themselves back eventually on to the harsh world of politics to general shock and surprise.[51]

However, the CDU were soon to be on their own no longer. Within a few days of the CDU initiative a second and potentially much more influential investigation into discrimination in Northern Ireland had been launched. This was the inquiry set up by the Society of Labour Lawyers [SLL]. The Society, which still exists, was not, and is not, a left wing or fringe pressure group but a highly respected body, the membership of which has included over the years prominent members of Labour governments including Lord Chancellors, Attorneys General and a Leader of the House of Lords. Therefore any report made by the Society could not be simply dismissed as propaganda by a left-wing pressure group. This perhaps is one of the reasons why the announcement of the investigation caused such disquiet among the Ulster Unionist establishment.

The papers of the Society of Labour Lawyers, deposited at the London School of Economics, are incomplete in the sense that they contain neither an interim nor a final report by the committee of investigation. It is possible that no final report exists because the committee's activities were overtaken by inquiries such as the Cameron Commission set up as a result of the tragic events of 1969. That at least is the opinion of several members of the Society (see below). The first reference to the Ulster investigation occurred in the Annual Report for 1966–67. This gave no explanation of why the Society decided at this point to set up the inquiry though it is likely that the violent events of the summer of 1966 were responsible. Instead it is merely reported that a sub-committee had been established during the year.[52] However, the minutes of the executive committee which met on 19 April, 1967 include a report of the first meeting of 'The Northern Ireland Sub-Committee' stating that the committee's procedure had been settled and noting that:

its appointment and operation has caused much interest in Ireland. Its terms of reference are 'To inquire into, and report on the working of the Government of Ireland Act 1920 and other legal and constitutional provisions affecting the administration of Northern Ireland with particular reference to allegations of religious discrimination, to receive evidence and to make any proposals which in the light of its inquiry it deems desirable.'[53]

The inquiry team included brilliant young lawyers who went on to hold some of the highest posts in Labour governments: Sam Silkin, Peter Archer and Ivor Richard. Silkin, chairman of the team and Labour MP for Camberwell, Dulwich, served as Attorney General 1974–79. Archer, now Lord Archer of Sandwell, was Labour MP for Rowley Regis and Tipton, and rose to Solicitor General in the 1974–79 administration. Richard, Labour MP for Baron's Court, was appointed Ambassador to the United Nations 1974–79. After Labour returned to power in 1997 he served for 15 months as Leader of the House of Lords. The two other members were Lord Gifford and Ulster-born Cedric Thornberry, secretary to the inquiry, who became a senior United Nations official based in Geneva. The *Belfast Telegraph* greeted news of the inquiry with a major front page report headlined: 'Inquiry is opened. Labour lawyers prepare list.' It said:

> First steps have been taken by the committee of inquiry into Northern Ireland Affairs set up by the Society of Labour Lawyers to collect evidence and memoranda which may help in the investigation. The committee points out that it is independent of the party to which it is affiliated.[54]

The inquiry was announced within days of the CDU fact-finding mission and just before *The Times* published its own survey of tensions in the province. There was clearly alarm in the O'Neill camp that the gradualist agenda of the so-called liberal Unionists would be undermined by such scrutiny. As the *Belfast Telegraph*'s London Editor, Percy Diamond, put it,

> [there were increased] fears in Unionist circles that the province is about to undergo one of the most dangerous phases of criticism that it has had to endure for a long time. There is apprehension that the building up of attacks linked with the activities of the committee of inquiry of the Society of Labour Lawyers and the Ulster debate which can be expected before long in the House of Commons will increase the climate of hostility making difficult the

task of those anxious to see the liberalisation of Northern Ireland proceed in a steady and fruitful manner.[55]

One man who was intimately concerned with the SLL inquiry was Brian Garrett, now a well-established Belfast solicitor and then a young lawyer prominent in the Northern Ireland Labour Party. Garrett recalled that young, left-wing lawyers in Britain and in Northern Ireland were becoming frustrated by the Labour Government's failure to respond to the work of the CDU and MPs such as Paul Rose and Gerry Fitt. He thought that this was the real reason the inquiry was set up:

> The argument that there was some sinister plot or propagandists' ploy with the SLL was not true. These were reformist people who wanted to move the thing along. I am referring to the SLL. The CDU had been in the background for some years. People wanted to move faster. The team we got was a mixture of establishment lawyers and the ones that had got a particular cause.[56]

Garrett believed that no final report ever appeared. That is also the view of Lord Archer.[57] [Lord Richard regretted that after such a length of time his recollection of the inquiry was distinctly hazy].[58] Lord Archer recalled that the inquiry was initiated by Gerry Fitt and other Labour MPs campaigning for the Catholics in Northern Ireland.

> At that time the parties accepted a bipartisan policy towards Northern Ireland. Our inquiry looked at the structures of the electoral system there and found that it was not a democratically elected Parliament. It spoke only for an artificial unit.[59]

His previous knowledge of Ulster had been based on 'private interests' at Queen's University, Belfast. He had not looked at the wider picture:

> None of us on the inquiry team was a Roman Catholic. Callaghan [who became Home Secretary and responsible for Northern Ireland at the end of the year, before the interim report came out] would not have regarded the Society of Labour Lawyers as troublemakers and would have taken us seriously.

None of the team, he said, were well informed about Northern Ireland. None of his friends in the province were Roman Catholic: 'It came as a revelation to all of us how bad things were, gerrymandering, Roman Catholics not being appointed to public office, etc.'[60]

Lord Archer cannot remember exactly what happened after the interim report but the Labour lawyers 'would have pressed the Labour Government to do something'. The government's policy was to leave it to the Ulster premier who was the nearest Ulster had to a reformer: 'But he could not deliver and Wilson and Co. should have realised that earlier.'[61]

Archer had not expected instant action by the government in dealing with Roman Catholic grievances. The SLL, he pointed out, carried out many reports which might not be acted on for years sometimes. However, he considered that there had been 'an element of blindness' by the Labour government.

The irony was that when something began to be done for the Roman Catholics, the violence started – the Unionist backlash. There were injustices crying out to be remedied.... I had the strong feeling that, though I was totally against violent protest, that the violence was understandable.[62]

The third of the investigations that spring was carried out by *The Times*. The paper, along with the rest of Fleet Street, had shown little interest in Northern Ireland. In this it was simply reflecting the fact that Britain had forgotten about Ulster, as Harold Evans, himself a future Editor, once remarked.[63] However, the paper had a new Editor, William Rees-Mogg. Rees-Mogg, a Roman Catholic, had been Deputy Editor of the *Sunday Times* the previous year when that paper had carried the article already referred to exposing discrimination against Catholics and demanding action from Westminster. *The Times* retained in the 1960s some of its legendary authority though its relations with the Wilson government were becoming sour. In 1966 the paper had lauded the Labour Prime Minister,[64] but Wilson soon felt that he was getting unfair treatment, particularly from *Times* Political Editor and veteran lobby correspondent, David Wood. It was said that Wilson advised Lord Thomson of Fleet, the paper's new owner, to sack Wood.[65]

The Times survey written by 'The News Team', was headlined 'Ulster's Second-Class Citizens'. Above, smaller type declared: 'Electoral System Weighted Against Catholics'.

The survey began with a full report on 'grave allegations of religious discrimination in the planning of Northern Ireland's prestige city of Craigavon now being built 20 miles south west of Belfast'. They were made by Professor Geoffrey Copcutt, former head of the city design team. He revealed that during the planning of the city he was told by a source close to the Stormont Cabinet that: 'the Ulster Government would not countenance any scheme that would upset the voting balance between Protestants and Roman Catholics in the area'. The Professor told *The Times*, 'the situation of the Roman Catholics in Northern Ireland was very similar to that of the Negro in the United States'. After he had resigned from the design team in protest he claimed that the Stormont government launched a concerted campaign to discredit him. He alleged that senior officials of the Northern Ireland government had told the United Nations that he was unfit for an appointment with them. *The Times* explained that the controversy over Craigavon came to light during the News Team's investigation into widespread allegations of religious discrimination in the province:

> The investigation found overwhelming evidence that the electoral system in some local elections was deliberately weighted against the Roman Catholic minority by a discriminatory system of more than 20 years standing.[66]

They found that segregation amounting to discrimination was widely prevalent in the allocation of council houses by local authorities. They also discovered 'that Catholics are discriminated against either deliberately or (more often) by the prevailing system in many senior government appointments and in many private firms'. The allegations were then put to the Ulster Prime Minister 'in considerable detail'. Captain O'Neill 'replied with charmingly varied versions of the proposition, "Reform takes a long time."' (The report said that no detailed evidence was given of counter allegations of discrimination by Catholics against Protestants in Ulster's 'scattered Roman Catholic strongholds'.) *The Times* survey then turned its attention to Londonderry:

> Religious discrimination is a burning political issue in Ulster where emotions run high and savage tactics including violence are not unknown. It is particularly controversial in Londonderry.... Because of its history Londonderry is far more emotionally important to the ruling Protestant majority than Belfast.[67]

Throughout the province there was evidence of boundary changes to maintain Unionist control of local councils, 'In Londonderry the Nationalists are greatly in the majority in population, yet greatly in the minority in the city corporation.' The Unionist reply was that in 1936 when the wards were decided the rateable value in their wards was relatively much higher than in the single Catholic ward thus justifying more seats for the Protestants. The survey found that religious segregation in council houses was a fact denied by neither party nor by O'Neill 'a remarkably frank politician. The usual explanation was that the two communities "cannot stand living near one another"'. O'Neill told *The Times*: 'The foundations I have inherited here are foundations of cleavage, hatred and intolerance.' There was also active discrimination in private employment. A foreman of a large Belfast factory told *The Times* reporters that he and his fellow foreman turned away Catholic labour. 'Even where applicants are not asked their religion, the name of the school they attended usually gives it away.'[68]

The Times survey caused fury among Unionists. Captain O'Neill went on the record immediately to denounce its main findings: 'This facile article is bound to disappoint all those who have expected of *The Times* some degree of detachment and critical sense.'[69] O'Neill went on to attack Professor Copcutt claiming that no one of any judgement would attach much weight to his charges. He dismissed the rest of the evidence in the survey as 'a mere repetition of the stock-in-trade of the so-called Campaign for Social Justice in Northern Ireland'. O'Neill was in Leeds at the time of his remarks, promoting the province during the city's 'Ulster Week'. According to *The Times* there were fears in Northern Ireland that the article would have a harmful effect on efforts to promote the province's trade and industry with Yorkshire. Meanwhile *The Times* reported that the Home Secretary, Roy Jenkins, had promised to meet the CDU MPs who had visited Ulster earlier in the month to discuss their report on discrimination in the province.[70] *The Times* pointed out that the CDU report reached conclusions similar to those arrived at by their News Team. The paper then reported the CDU findings at some length and also a tribute to the paper from Gerry Fitt. At the CDU annual meeting at Westminster Fitt said:

> The most significant happening of all the work that has gone on in the past to make people realise the discrimination in Northern Ireland was the article in *The Times* on Monday ... most people are offering a heartfelt prayer for what this paper has done.[71]

If the Stormont government at first thought it could shrug off *The Times* article with a few words in Leeds from O'Neill, by now it was having second thoughts. Three days later a lengthy article by O'Neill himself appeared on the paper's main opinion page. It is clear from the tone of O'Neill's remarks that Stormont was now seriously alarmed that the mainland's sudden concern for Catholic rights [as demonstrated by the establishment of three separate investigations] might lead to that previously unimaginable development, intervention by Westminster. In his article, O'Neill tried to discredit *The Times* reporters. Their survey 'lacked real balance and objectivity' and, he added:

> I know that there is a modern passion for 'depth' studies of current problems but we are dealing here with issues far too complex to be adequately grasped in a study carried out within a few days by a two-man team.[72]

He conceded, however, that there was concern about Northern Ireland in the Parliamentary Labour Party and elsewhere but 'Irish problems are deep-seated and not amenable to facile external solutions however well-intentioned.' Since becoming Prime Minister he had with some success begun to break down 'the old barriers'. But the violent events of 1966 had made many people realise that harmony could not be achieved overnight. *The Times* had commented as though he had said something rather whimsical when he told their News Team that reform took a long time.

> Perhaps this illustrates the difference between the idealism of the journalist who can propound his theories and leave for pastures new and the realism of the politician who has to cope with them on the spot.[73]

O'Neill listed reforms which he said were in progress, including an end to university representation at Stormont and of plural voting, and he ended with a demand that Westminster should keep out of Ulster:

> there really is no acceptable or truly democratic alternative to letting us find the solution for our own problems. Stormont is after all a democratically elected Parliament and no solution which is imposed upon the majority of the population could fail to provoke greater evils than it would solve.

This was 'certainly not the moment for an ill-judged intervention in our affairs' which might produce results which no one could foresee.[74]

It is difficult to believe that O'Neill would have written in these terms had he not genuinely feared a change in policy by the Wilson government. After all, nine months had gone by since the Chequers lunch and there was a growing opinion among MPs and journalists that Catholic grievances were still not being addressed seriously. Wilson was now meeting O'Neill every few months but as his comments in the House of Commons that week indicated (see below) he was aware that the momentum he had earlier claimed was simply not there. Even the *Belfast Telegraph*, normally the most loyal of supporters of O'Neill's 'quiet revolution', thought that the time had come for some plain speaking. The article was written by Roy Lilley and headlined 'Ulster Under Fire'.[75] Lilley's analysis is significant for two reasons. Firstly, it rejected the comfortable idea of a cosy relationship behind the scenes between Whitehall and Stormont officials. Secondly, Lilley, with his intimate knowledge of the Parliamentary Labour Party based on his experience as a lobby correspondent, suggested that Wilson would not be able to head off backbench demands for direct intervention for long. O'Neill, wrote Lilley, has declared that in its three years in office Labour 'has behaved quite correctly in its dealings with Northern Ireland' and Ulster had continued to receive fair treatment from the government in London. But, he warned, O'Neill's

comments are made to the accompaniment of a rising clamour by a numerically formidable flank of Labour backbenchers, unimpressed by O'Neill's programme for political reform, for direct Wilsonian intervention in Northern Ireland's affairs.

In what was an ominous phrase for the Northern Ireland government, Lilley claimed that 'Stormont's relationship with the power in Whitehall is enveloped in an atmosphere of unease and uncertainty.' O'Neill himself had virtually admitted that, when he last met Wilson, the British Prime Minister had raised the contentious issue of the role and rights of Ulster MPs at Westminster. O'Neill, said Lilley, was left with the thought that the Ulster MPs should consider 'a self-denying ordinance when it came to voting on issues not directly relevant to Northern Ireland', and that, 'one or two of the self-appointed Unionists who assume the role of baiting the Government might prudently leave this function to the Tory benches'. Lilley also observed that 'some Stormont officials in contact with their Civil Service counterparts in Whitehall detect signs of a stiffer approach and a questioning attitude to Northern Ireland'. [This is an ironic in the light of John Oliver's view that civil servants from London and Belfast, his 'technocrats', might have worked together to bring about reform.] Finally Lilley forecast that Wilson may yet seek a mandate to restrict the activities of Ulster MPs. Nor is it to be assumed that he will withstand indefinitely the criticisms of his backbenchers that there is no positive evidence that political change in Northern Ireland is advancing at an acceptable pace....

However, he conceded that it was questionable whether Wilson 'would be eager to embark on a major amendment to the Northern Ireland constitution'.[76]

The same day that Lilley's article appeared Wilson for the first time revealed publicly his government's 'acute concern' about Northern Ireland. The occasion was Prime Minister's Questions in the House of Commons.[77] Wilson said that there had been 'widespread concern in more than one part of the House about certain events which have occurred in Northern Ireland'. He had embarked on a series of talks about this with O'Neill and had already had 'two very interesting discussions and a third will take place in due course'. The Prime Minister turned down the demand for a Royal Commission but, significantly, reacted strongly when the Ulster Unionist leader, Captain Lawrence Orr, attacked the CDU whom he implied would be held responsible for any unrest in Northern Ireland. Wilson told Orr that MPs would not like the tone of his remarks. Calling on the House to back O'Neill's policy, he added, ominously for those in the province fearing intervention: 'There is still acute concern about many questions affecting the functioning of democracy over there.' Wilson assured the Conservative Leader, Edward Heath, that there would be no change in the constitutional position of the province without the consent of the electorate there. However, he added that he was sure that Heath would agree that, despite the progress so far, 'there is still a long way to go'.

CONCLUSION

By early summer of 1967 something of an impasse had been reached. After nearly three years of a government committed to reform little had been achieved. Wilson had banked on O'Neill delivering and so far this had failed. Asked what had been Stormont's reaction to growing demands for intervention unless changes were made, Dr Oliver replied: 'It was putting off the evil day'. There were, he said, 'half a dozen things we should have done in 1967'. These included introducing one man, one vote in local elections, 'that was an obvious shortcoming and it was an easy weapon to take up'; ending religious discrimination in the allocation of council houses, ending gerrymandering in Londonderry and tackling Catholic grievances over the role of the B Specials.[78] In fact there was no movement on any of these fronts partly because of Stormont's policy of the primacy of Unionist unity but equally because Wilson and Jenkins, though aware of the growing dangers, were not yet prepared to employ the authority of Westminster granted under Section 75 of the Government of Ireland Act, 1920. It is also true that potentially the most important of the three investigations that spring, that of the Society of Labour Lawyers, had only just begun. Nevertheless, the reaction of Stormont to this sudden interest from the mainland, and the defensive posture of O'Neill himself, suggest that in Ulster at least there was real fear that the days of fully-devolved government were numbered; not the abolition of Stormont – Wilson had never publicly threatened that – but for example the imposition of an Ombudsman.

The unfolding of events over the next two years strongly suggest that John Oliver, Lord Archer and others were correct in believing that earlier implementation of the range of reforms being advocated, with or without the spur by central government, might have prevented the spiral into violence. It could be argued that these measures were palliatives, attractive to 'liberal Hampstead' but not sufficiently far-reaching to transform Ulster into a genuinely democratic, non-sectarian region of the United Kingdom. This was certainly the view of Joe Haines for whom such reforms were mere 'tinkering'. He claimed that they would not have persuaded Catholics that their future lay with the United Kingdom 'because Britain was still the old enemy'.[79] However, the evidence suggests something rather different. Research into the views of Catholics in the late 1960s (discussed in the next chapter) revealed that the British link might not have been an insuperable barrier to reconciliation. Callaghan too considered that the recrudescence of the IRA might have been avoided if the Unionists had 'been more far-sighted' and 'allowed O'Neill to bring forward the reforms that simple justice demanded'.[80] We will, of course, never know, but at least they might have tried!

4 The Phoney Peace,
May 1967–March 1968

Few issues in the past have shown a greater capacity to divert and
dissipate the reforming energy of left-wing British Governments
than deep embroilment in Irish affairs.

Home Secretary, Roy Jenkins, during a rare House of Commons
debate on Northern Ireland in October 1967[1]

The eruption of violence in Londonderry on 5 October 1968 effectively began 'The Troubles', which continued until the first IRA
cease-fire of September 1994. Yet during the previous 18 months,
despite the warnings, internal and external, outlined in the previous
chapter, the British government appeared less concerned with events
in the province than at any other time since Labour came to power,
pledged to reform, in October 1964.

The series of crises, political and economic, which afflicted the
Wilson administration at this time partly explains the indifference.
Devaluation and a wave of hostility to the government demoralised
ministers, not least the man who was to become responsible for
Northern Ireland in December 1967, James Callaghan.[2] Wilson
himself feared moves to oust him, from within his own Cabinet,
orchestrated by dark forces outside.[3] Yet, as suggested earlier, intervention from Westminster to speed up reform might have prevented
the violence that was to engulf the province within two years.

A remarkable opinion poll carried out by Professor Richard Rose
in the spring and summer of 1968 (though not published until 1971)
suggested that Catholics were almost evenly split on what Rose called
the 'British connection'. The key question that was put to Catholics
was: 'There has always been a lot of controversy about the constitutional position of Northern Ireland. On balance do you approve of it
or disapprove of it?' The result showed that 33 per cent totally
supported the constitution, 34 per cent totally disapproved and 32 per
cent said that they did not know. Professor Rose's analysis of these
results was very cautious. He wrote: 'The aggregate profile of opinion
in the country is profoundly ambiguous. One can say that as much as

54 per cent of the people support the constitution or than only 54 per cent support the constitution.'[4] However, in Paul Bew's view, the poll was evidence that O'Neill's policies aimed at reconciling the two communities 'need not necessarily have failed'.[5]

What follows is an examination of the period between May 1967 and March 1968, which saw the policy of non-intervention emphatically confirmed by the Home Secretary, Roy Jenkins, to the dismay of Labour backbenchers in the CDU, and Jenkins' replacement in November 1967, by Callaghan. Callaghan's personal attitude towards the problems of Northern Ireland is considered and the relevance of the deep unpopularity of the British Government, as shown by local elections and by-elections during these months, is taken into account. Finally, at the time when O'Neill was celebrating five years in office, Wilson's fatal miscalculation of the Ulster premier's capacity for reform is analysed. First, however, the ambiguous policy of *The Times*, during this period, is considered in some detail because the paper was taken very seriously by politicians and civil servants in London. One of those civil servants, in a senior post at the time, recalled:

> Although as always people said that it was a not what it used to be it was still looked on as the most authoritative of papers, it still attempted to be a journal of record and reading it was compulsory.[6]

At a time when most of the media was ignoring Northern Ireland, the paper, under its new Editor, William Rees-Mogg, began to take an interest in events in the province. However, domestic 'in-house' considerations prevented the paper pressing more vigorously, as he would have wished, for an end to discrimination against Catholics in the province.

Only ten days after *The Times* had revealed serious discrimination, a leading article 'The Trials of Ulster' warned the Wilson government on no account 'to wade in'.[7] It may seem difficult to reconcile this caution with the malpractice that the paper had itself only just uncovered. However, this apparent contradiction reflected a significant disagreement on Northern Ireland policy right at the top of *The Times*. The Editor, William Rees-Mogg, and his Chief Leader Writer, Owen Hickey (described by Rees-Mogg as 'the two main influences on *The Times*' policy on Northern Ireland', the other being himself) disagreed on the line the paper should take.[8] Nearly 30 years later, Rees-Mogg admitted that his paper's policy on Northern Ireland would have been more radical had he not felt the need to defer to the more conservative Hickey who, ironically, was also a Roman Catholic.[9]

The leading article 'The Trials of Ulster' which Rees-Mogg said would have been written by Hickey, began with a tribute to O'Neill's leadership but then turned its attention to Westminster where:

> there is an itch to interfere, intensified by the arrival of Gerry Fitt. It has not so far penetrated the procedural defence of the House. Nor has the Government caught it.[10]

The paper then warned against 'overt interference'. If things were getting worse or not getting better there might be a stronger case for intervention but 'as it is Westminster should think on this before wading in'. The article concluded with a brief history lesson for the politicians:

> Since 1922 MPs here have no experience of ordering a society in which much political opposition takes the form of opposition to the basis of the constitution; and before that date they had little success and no joy in trying to do so.[11]

Looking back to the policy at the start of his editorship (he had taken over in January, 1967) Rees-Mogg said:

> We had come to think that there was a serious issue arising in Northern Ireland, that the truth was that there was a lot of discrim-ination in jobs, housing and so on against the Catholics and that this complaint was legitimate and backed up by the facts.[12]

However, he also sympathised with O'Neill who he believed would 'try to move things in the right direction'. He wanted *The Times* to support O'Neill 'relative to his critics in the Unionist party and to the Paisley position'. He remembered the way the 'story' developed and 'I had the feeling we were getting it right ... that we were right in saying that there was very considerable unease among quite moderate Catholics that the situation was deteriorating.' He had thought at the time that the people most to blame were the hardline Unionists, not just Paisley but the Unionists in O'Neill's own party who were very reluctant to surrender their predominance. He added, 'I felt it was the job of *The Times* to report it, that it was also the job of *The Times* to give every opportunity to people to put another side to the case to the side we were taking.' This was why he had willingly given O'Neill space in *The Times* to respond to the News Team's investigation into discrimination in the province.[13]

Explaining why the leading article following the News Team's confirmation of serious discrimination had told Wilson not to interfere, Rees-Mogg said, 'We had undoubtedly a somewhat unusual split on the paper.' However, he had decided to let Hickey, for whom he had a great deal of respect, continue to develop the paper's line on Ireland. Rees-Mogg now admitted, 'It is also true to say that my own position, had I not been trying to work out a position for the paper, would have been somewhat different from him.'

He had been been uneasy about Hickey's position 'because he [Hickey] was nearer to the orthodox Ulster Unionist position ... although we could both be described as being politically Conservative we actually had a different way of looking at the world'. But he was sure that had he stopped Hickey writing the Irish leaders, Hickey would have resigned.

> That would have had a very bad effect on the morale of the place and left a feeling that this was bumptious Canadian Thomsonism intruding on the way the paper was being run.[14]

So it seems that purely domestic considerations at *The Times* had prevented the 'Thunderer' from giving a more robust lead on discrimination in the province.

However, if *The Times*, because of its support for the so-called 'reformers' in the Unionist leadership, drew back that summer from pursuing the discrimination the paper itself had discovered, the Society of Labour Lawyers, felt no such constraint. On the contrary they managed to produce something akin to panic among Unionist circles. On 19 May, the Ulster Letter from London in the *Belfast Telegraph* reported that both Sir Elwyn Jones, the Attorney General, and Sam Silkin, Chairman of the SLL Committee of Inquiry on Northern Ireland, would be visiting the province in June. No explanation was given for Sir Elwyn's visit.[15] In August the Unionists demonstrated their alarm with an attempt at counter attack. A front-page report in the *Belfast Telegraph* was headlined: 'Unionists Reply to Pressure for Ulster Inquiry. Letter to Lawyers. Probe Might Hinder Better Relations'. The paper's Political Correspondent reported that officers of the Ulster Unionist Council had approved the draft of a reply to a letter from the SLL which indicated that it was determined to press ahead with the inquiry. The Officers said that 'the inquiry may well hinder rather than assist moves to establish better community relations'. The report then quoted the SLL as saying that the inquiry would centre chiefly on allegations of religious discrimination in the province. Written evidence had already been submitted to the inquiry from opposition quarters including the Nationalist Party in Londonderry.[16] The following month in was decided that Sam Silkin should appear in a television documentary about the inquiry to be broadcast by BBC Northern Ireland. and shown in the province only. The Northern Ireland Labour Party's Brian Garrett, wrote to Silkin informing him about the programme and adding:

> We would like, however, to address to you in a short film interview (to be conducted by John Cole of the *Guardian*) a direct question as to why in your view the inquiry has in fact been established at this time.[17]

Garrett recalled that he was asked to 'look after' Silkin's appearance in Ulster but could not remember the date. 'Sam was very ponderous – a very brilliant mind but very ponderous delivery and it would have been very hard to see Sam as a burning revolutionary.' Silkin explained to viewers why the SLL had come to Northern Ireland 'and rather well I thought'. In fact Garrett himself was 'hesitant' about the investigation.

> There was a rhythm going on in Ulster that I was not sure of and I was a getting a little uneasy. My sixth sense told me that if you provoked the Unionist community you would get a reaction. Historically that had turned out to be correct.[18]

It seems from the SLL archive that Peter Archer also appeared in the programme[19] though he cannot recall doing so.[20]

Only a few weeks earlier the Unionists had received another unwelcome broadside from across the water this time from their *bête noire* Paul Rose. The CDU chairman had been invited by the *Belfast Telegraph* to set out the case for reform. The article, entitled 'The Cancer at the Heart of Ulster Life', warned of the possibility of intervention from Westminster. He wrote: 'People in Northern Ireland must realise that if they want to be treated like Loyalists they must stop flag waving and act like Loyalists in every day life.' Rose argued for better relations between Dublin, Belfast and London:

> Until that spirit prevails my colleagues and I have a duty to ensure that civil rights and liberties in Northern Ireland conform to the

pattern in the rest of the UK.... So far we have had a few promises from the Prime Minister which he has not yet redeemed. If Stormont won't do the job then the less desirable alternative remains at Westminster.[21]

During the next few days the paper published a number of letters from readers bitterly critical of Rose's remarks. It has to be said that for Unionists he was, Jewish and left-wing, the archetype 'outsider' who could not conceivably understand their problems.

O'Neill was due to see the Home Secretary on 13 September for one of their regular discussions. The previous day the *Irish Times* reported that the Nationalist leader, Eddie McAteer, had met Jenkins to protest about the influence of the Orange Order. Afterwards in a statement McAteer said that after a full year 'there is little outward evidence of the reforms for which we were hoping'. However, the paper reported the following day that McAteer had the impression that Jenkins was sympathetic to his views on reform and that these would be relayed to O'Neill.[22] This was wishful thinking by McAteer. Neither Jenkins nor Wilson had any real intention of stepping up the pressure on Stormont. Surprisingly the Labour Party, which might have acted as a spur, reflected this reticence as was to be seen at the October conference in Scarborough. On the eve of the conference, the main front page story in the *Irish Times* reported that resolutions from two constituency Labour Parties (Croydon, North East and Camberwell, Dulwich) urged the government to use existing legislation to prevent discrimination in Ulster.[23] The *Belfast Telegraph* political correspondent reported that there were three resolutions from constituency Labour Parties calling for a Royal Commission to be appointed on Northern Ireland but suspected that no time would be found for them.[24] However, a way was found to raise the issue, albeit not in the conference hall. The front-page report in the *Belfast Telegraph* revealed that demands on the Government to apply strong pressure on O'Neill to speed up political reform would be made at a meeting being organised by the National Council for Civil Liberties (NCCL). The sponsors of the meeting believed that O'Neill was most sensitive to public opinion in Britain and that Harold Wilson should adopt a tough line with him without further delay. At Scarborough it was being recalled that in the 1964 General Election campaign Wilson had written to Mrs Patricia McCluskey, leader of the Campaign for Social Justice, promising 'action by a Labour Government'. It became clear that resolutions on Northern Ireland were almost certain not to be given time for debate at the conference.[25]

The NCCL meeting at Scarborough went some way to making up for the failure of constituency Labour Parties to get Northern Ireland on the official agenda. It was attended by a number of Labour MPs including one junior minister, Reg Freeson [Parliamentary Secretary, Ministry of Power]. A full report appeared in the *Belfast Telegraph*, under the provocative headline 'Action on Ulster or Else' (from 'our Political Correspondent'). It reported an uncompromising speech from Paul Rose who warned:

> Unless action is taken in the lifetime of the present Labour Government to right injustice against the minority in Northern Ireland many people in the province will be tempted to turn to 'extra Parliamentary' methods.[26]

Rose then appealed to Wilson and Jenkins to tackle the problem as one of urgency. The government had not yet fulfilled promises given before the 1964 General Election (The Political Correspondent reported that later Rose explained that he did not mean violence but 'other forms of protest in the form of civil disobedience'). The report also said that Rose had agreed that Jenkins was applying pressure on O'Neill – a surprising concession in view of his earlier strictures against Jenkins and Wilson – but then added that this pressure had to be increased because there was no evidence that O'Neill intended to carry out effective reforms. This could only be changed by pressure from Westminster. The *Belfast Telegraph* itself was sufficiently alarmed by the NCCL meeting to devote an editorial to denouncing it the same day. It declared:

> The political content of the statements at the NCCL meeting at Scarborough is too obvious. Paul Rose's attitude to Northern Ireland, while it may be well-intentioned, permits him to see no virtue at all, and Gerry Fitt again goes beyond the bounds of reason when he alleges that the Government 'pressurises' industrialists to keep them away from Derry, Strabane and Newry.[27]

The editorial maintained that very serious questions were raised

> when a Labour MP at a gathering, supported by the Connelly Association,[28] tries to provoke an intervention by the British Government with veiled hints of 'extra Parliamentary' methods and campaigns of civil disobedience by the minority.

The editorial claimed that

the calmer approach to the problem is that Capt. O'Neill and his government, as accepted by Harold Wilson, have adopted a liberalising policy and that the question is now one of judging at what pace that it can be implemented having regard to the feelings not only of the Unionist Party but of those Catholics who are waiting, and with patience, to benefit from that.[29]

Fitt himself was less than pleased with Scarborough. In his Ulster Letter from London, the following week, Percy Diamond reported in the *Belfast Telegraph* that Fitt had hoped for much more enthusiastic backing 'from his Labour friends' than he received at the conference, 'where he feels, I am told, that he was let down'.[30] However, a rare chance to bring the argument back to Westminster occurred later in the month. Under reforms initiated by the Commons Leader, Richard Crossman, brief morning debates were now held. Fitt had just over an hour to discuss the economy of the Northern Ireland Region which, being the ultimate responsibility of central government was not in breach of the convention. According to Diamond, Fitt was disappointed that a morning sitting had been allocated for the debate, presumably because few MPs attended so early in the day.[31] Nevertheless as it was to be answered by the Home Secretary, Roy Jenkins, ministers could not fairly be accused of trying to avoid the attention of press and public. The debate, on the adjournment, took place on the morning of 25 October.[32] The hope among the CDU MPs must have been that Jenkins, who had already proved himself to be the most radical Home Secretary since the war on social matters, would promise a much tougher stand by the government on civil rights in Ulster. Yet again he dashed their hopes. In any case, though he cannot have known it at the time, promotion to 11 Downing Street, in the wake of devaluation, was about to absolve Jenkins of any further individual responsibility for Northern Ireland.

The debate was opened by Fitt and, for once, the CDU could not complain of gagging by the Chair. As the Deputy Speaker, Sydney Irving, commented at one point, Fitt had 'managed to discuss under this Motion almost every subject he has wished to discuss'. Fitt began by complaining that since the Commons had last debated the province over 14 months previously, every other region of the country had been debated many times over, yet the problems of Northern Ireland were of such importance that a good deal more time should have been given by the government. During the last debate he had sincerely hoped than when Northern Ireland was next discussed there would have been 'dramatic changes', but, 'it is with a sense of deep disappointment that I stand here today and tell the House that no changes have taken place in Northern Ireland since the subject was last debated'. An analysis in the *Guardian* had estimated that the British taxpayer's subsidy to Northern Ireland was £117 million a year and, he claimed, 'That money, given to the Northern Ireland Tories, is being spent in the areas where they will gain the most electoral support.' Stormont had deliberately, over the years, engaged in a policy of industrial isolation because of the electoral complexion of 'anti-Unionist' areas. He said that no matter what the political complexion of an area in mainland Britain might be it was admitted by MPs of all parties that the people in it were entitled to a home and a job but, 'That is not how the Northern Ireland Unionists see it.' He told Jenkins that before any further financial assistance was given, strings should be attached saying where the money was to be spent, and that should be where the need was greatest.

Fitt maintained that the policy of the Unionist government was to deny people in anti-Unionist areas homes and jobs to force them 'to emigrate to Great Britain thereby taking away a danger which would otherwise arise threatening the Unionist electoral representation'. He assured the Home Secretary that the Northern Irish had great respect for him. They appreciated the stand he had taken against discrimination in Britain. Jenkins had thought it important to introduce legislation to protect minorities in Britain but said Fitt,

If the Government consider it necessary to have protective legislation of this kind how much more necessary is it that this same protection is given to United Kingdom citizens in Northern Ireland? I press here and now for all the legislation that has been introduced to protect minorities in this country to be made applicable to Northern Ireland.

Fitt said that he was only too well aware of the many urgent problems that beset the government he was supporting and which could distract ministers from Northern Ireland. These included 'an acute economic problem', Rhodesia, Vietnam, and the Middle East. Therefore in his opinion Northern Ireland was 'very low on the agenda of this House'. Arguing for race relations legislation to cover religious discrimination in Ulster, Fitt referred to a *Belfast Telegraph* editorial attacking the failure to appoint Catholics to public posts in the province. He also called for a Parliamentary Commissioner for

Northern Ireland, an Ombudsman, 'who would be aware ... of the discrimination ... and would take steps, perhaps, to remedy the situation.' He wanted to impress on the Home Secretary the need for urgent action. In a recent public speech he had warned that if people 'found there was nothing to be gained constitutionally, who could blame them if they themselves tried to do something to rectify their own position'. He had been condemned for this by the Ulster Unionist MP for Belfast, North (Stratton Mills) but he believed that such action would be morally valid. Finally, speaking directly to the Home Secretary he said:

> many people in Northern Ireland are looking to the British Government to impress on the Northern Ireland Government the necessity of bringing about reforms ... to ensure that we are all treated as British subjects. That is all we ask ... I believe the British Government have it in their power to do this.

He accused the 'allegedly liberal' Ulster PM, O'Neill, of getting away with a massive confidence trick and stalling over reform in the hope that Labour would be defeated at the next election. If, however, reforms were not brought in 'before the lifetime of this Government expires', he predicted that 'there will be trouble. I hope that I am wrong because I do not want to see trouble in Northern Ireland'. [A year later Fitt was proved all too tragically correct when the Londonderry riots began 30 years of violence and unrest in the province.]

In his reply the Home Secretary admitted that 'no one can pretend that we have had a full and exhaustive debate ...'. He began by giving a brief account of Ulster's economic difficulties. He believed that if these were solved it would then be 'much easier to solve the special social and political problems of Northern Ireland', and he added:

> People employed in a vigorous modern economy with a technological base which demands high management and other skills are less likely to be obsessed by old quarrels.

The Northern Ireland administration had been criticised and he assured MPs that 'the general feeling of concern which underlies many, although not all, of those criticisms, is something which the Prime Minister and I share'. But he then made it clear that, despite this concern, the Labour government had no intention of intervening. They could not 'simply put aside the constitution of Northern Ireland or ignore the historical facts which underlie the present position and present policy.' He added:

Successive Governments here have refused to take steps which would inevitably cut away not only the authority of the Northern Ireland Government but also the constitution of the province.

There was room for argument about the pace of reform which was practicable or desirable. 'But we must at least be satisfied about the direction. Provided we can be so satisfied there is a great deal to be said for not trying to settle the affairs of Northern Ireland too directly from London.' He had studied and written about nineteenth and early twentieth century history and he added:

No one can undertake detailed studies of that period of British history ... without being left with the conviction that despite the many attributes of the English a peculiar talent for solving the problems of Ireland is not among them.... Few issues in the past have shown a greater capacity to divert and dissipate the reforming energy of left-wing British governments than deep embroilment in Irish affairs.

At the end of his speech the Labour MP for Hampstead, Ben Whitaker, intervened to ask him to extend the Race Relations Act to Northern Ireland. The Home Secretary told him to do so would be contrary to the Government of Ireland Act (1920).

Jenkins' reply only confirmed the opinion of the CDU MPs that any hope they had that the Home Secretary's reforming zeal would cross the Irish Sea could now be forgotten.[33] However, the *Belfast Telegraph* was alarmed by Jenkins' warning that the Cabinet was still not happy with the rate of progress. In an editorial headed 'Jenkins' Ear' the paper described the tone of Jenkins' speech as 'fair and balanced with the principle of non-interference as the underlying theme'. He had, rightly, made it clear that interference would reduce the authority of Stormont. But, it added, 'even so there was a note of warning sounded that the Labour Government is not yet ready to sit back and leave O'Neill to get on with it'. The Prime Minister, the editorial feared, was listening 'with more than half an ear' to his backbench MPs. 'Criticism of Northern Ireland emanating from these quarters is clearly still getting a hearing in the British Cabinet ...'.[34]

The paper returned the following day to the theme that there was after all something to worry about in Jenkins' words when it reported that the speech was being closely studied by Ulster Unionists. Jenkins had 'seemed to be giving the *quietus* to any suggestion of appointing any inquiry on the Northern Ireland administration or interfering with the Government of Ireland Act'. However, he had also 'stressed the unanimity of the Prime Minister and himself in the concern they felt for what lay beneath many of the criticisms'. The paper accepted that the Home Secretary's remarks implied that the ball 'was fairly and squarely in O'Neill's court in the quest for common economic and social standards – a goal towards which many wanted to see rapid progress'. This 'pleased the CDU supporters, however glumly they reacted to other portions of Roy Jenkins' carefully worded speech'.[35]

Two days after the Westminster debate the Liberal Leader, Jeremy Thorpe, arrived in Northern Ireland on a three-day visit to carry out his own investigation into discrimination in the province. He was scathing about progress made by the Labour government on achieving reforms. The *Belfast Telegraph* political correspondent reported the Liberal Leader's demand for a Royal Commission to investigate the working of the Northern Ireland constitution, the very move the Home Secretary had just ruled out at Westminster. Thorpe said: 'I am personally disappointed that the Labour Government has not done more' and he accused them of 'behaving like good Tories'.[36] Thorpe's intervention was of greater significance than might now seem likely in view of the damage done to his reputation as a result of the scandal that overtook him in the 1970s. However, it is worth noting that at the time he and his fellow Liberal MP, Eric Lubbock, had been giving powerful moral support at Westminster to the CDU.[37] David McKie, who was a political correspondent for the *Guardian* in the late 1960s, has praised Thorpe's prescience before the violence erupted. He recalled that he had been very struck at the time by Thorpe's awareness of the urgency of events in Northern Ireland compared with the inertia of the other party leaders.[38]

More than 25 years later, Thorpe [by this time seriously ill] recalled his determination that the urgency for reform would not be ignored by the British government. He had been well-informed about the province through contacts there that included Sheelagh Murnaghan, a Catholic barrister and Liberal MP at Stormont where she represented Queen's University, Belfast. As a result he had become convinced that 'there would be bloodshed if the Catholic minority remained second class citizens'. Asked if he had contacted Wilson privately to pass on his fears after his visit to the province, he replied, 'I have some recollection of going to see Wilson about it … but I got the impression that the Government thought that everything was all right.' He had wanted the government to give the Ulster Unionists an ultimatum: either they pushed on much faster with reform or

Westminster would take over the administration of the province. He did not accept Roy Jenkins' view that left-wing governments should avoid being sucked into Irish politics. 'As a historian Jenkins felt that he had a degree of superior judgement over his fellow politicians.' The fact was that the Labour government was 'terrified of the Ulster Unionists marching in bowler hats with umbrellas'.[39]

Unionist fears that there really was a sub-text to Jenkins' speech implying renewed pressure from London for reform were soon allayed because within a month of his remarks the government was thrown into one of the worst crises of Wilson's Premiership. The cause was the devaluation of the pound on 18 November 1967 which Wilson and Callaghan had fought so hard to resist. While this was to have a devastating effect on what was left of the administration's reputation in general and Wilson's in particular, another casualty was Northern Ireland. The next few months were dominated by Wilson's struggle for survival. The last thing on his mind was Ulster. By the spring of 1968, according to one of his biographers, Wilson was 'living dangerously'. His personal approval rating slumped and the government was devastated by a series of disastrous by-election results.

> Every government suffers a mid-term political recession but no government since the war had experienced as severe an episode of public rejection as that of 1968–9…. At the time, with no reason to expect a rapid recovery, there was talk of Armageddon. A disaster at the next election seemed inevitable.[40]

Devaluation had another consequence for Ulster. Less than a fortnight later Jenkins replaced Callaghan at the Treasury with the former Chancellor now taking over the Home Office. There was little in Callaghan's past record to suggest that he would be more sympathetic to the redress of Catholic grievances, though his visit to the province in the mid-1950s, principally to investigate the region's economic problems, had also alerted him to discrimination against Catholics in the allocation of housing.[41] In any case it seemed that Callaghan had been so demoralised by his experience at the Treasury that his career as an effective politician was over.

In retrospect, however, it turned out that Callaghan's appointment was highly significant. He would be the first minister to intervene directly in Northern Ireland since the province was created half a century before. In personal terms his role in Ulster was to restore a political reputation that had been severely damaged by devaluation.

Callaghan's role in the 18 months before the decision to send troops to Northern Ireland was crucial. Had he been determined to compel Stormont to speed up reform, the province might not have been plunged into violence in August 1969.

However, Callaghan considered that Westminster's responsibilities for Northern Ireland were strictly limited. As he told the ICBH seminar:

> There was such a thing as Stormont. There was a parliament in Northern Ireland. It had a Prime Minister. It had a government and ever since 1921 it had been the policy of successive British governments to ensure that that government had as much self-government as was possible. It was laid down in the constitution. The 1920 constitution gave the Government of Northern Ireland powers that were distinctly separated and so it was an independent parliament.[42]

This view, particularly the 'independent' nature of Stormont, is not supported by Professor Griffith's analysis outlined in Chapter 1. And senior civil servants closely involved with Northern Ireland policy in the 1960s do not agree either.[43]

Callaghan himself has written at some length in explaining his initial reluctance to get involved with what he regarded as Ulster's domestic affairs. He believed that the chance for a peaceful settlement was lost between 1963 and 1966 when in the light of the failed IRA campaign of the late 1950s and early 1960s discrimination against Catholics could have been ended.[44] Lack of interest in Northern Ireland was immediately apparent to Callaghan the day he arrived at his new post. He asked his new private secretary to provide him with a despatch box containing briefs on the issues that would be concerning him most during his first months.

> When I opened the box it contained books and papers about the future of the prison service, the fire service, problems on race relations, a number of questions about the police, children in care and their future and the reform of the House of Lords – but not a word about Northern Ireland....[45]

However, ominously for the future of Ulster, Callaghan claims that he was not surprised by this because, 'the subject rarely if ever came before the Cabinet and its concerns had fallen into a settled routine at the Home Office itself'. Confirming this indifference, Callaghan wrote,

> Northern Ireland was crammed into what was called the general

department which was responsible for anything that did not fit into any of the major departments at the Home Office.

These included ceremonial functions, British Summer Time, London taxicabs, liquor licensing, the administration of Carlisle state-owned public houses, and the protection of animals and birds. Northern Ireland was in a division with the Channel Islands, the Isle of Man and the Charity Commission which came under the control of a staff of seven, of whom only one was a senior civil servant (in what was then called the Administrative class). Callaghan recalled:

> The day to day work and responsibility for Northern Ireland affairs was in the hands of my colleague and friend Lord Stonham ... Minister of State at the Home Office. Northern Ireland was one of the main passions in his life....[46]

Callaghan saw no reason to disturb this arrangement, particularly as he was immediately preoccupied with more pressing matters including race relations legislation, House of Lords reform and control of the immigration of Kenyan Asians. Then there were, he said,

> the day to day problems which force themselves on the attention of the Home Secretary and which arise at great speed ... these issues demand great care and take up a lot of time ... so with all this I had no occasion to seek more work or go out and look at the problems of Northern Ireland unless they forced themselves upon me.[47]

Callaghan thought that the public viewed Ulster as an area of heavy unemployment 'whose politics were a hidden mystery'. However, he admitted that the reality was very different. He remembered O'Neill's admission that 'the tinder for that fire in the form of grievances, real or imaginary had been piling up for years'.[48]

Callaghan's mood of indifference towards Northern Ireland did not last, according to his close friend Merlyn Rees. Of all the problems, it was Northern Ireland that revealed 'the political outlook and concern for people' that had brought Callaghan into the Labour Party and, Rees added, 'He showed a feeling for understanding the Irish question and for the people of that island. His job was to make the political changes that should have been made before.'[49]

The *Irish Times* was lukewarm in its welcome for Callaghan's appointment. An editorial agreed that no Labour Home Secretary could take the Ulster Unionists to his heart as their MPs at Westminster were 'consistently more Tory than the Tories'. However, it noted that when Callaghan, then in Opposition, had visited Ulster in the 1950s his concern was for the province's economic not its political problems.[50]

Within a few weeks of Callaghan taking over at the Home Office the civil rights movement lost a potential voice at the very heart of government, Lord Longford, Leader of the House of Lords. In January he resigned from the Cabinet over the question of the school-leaving age. Wilson's attitude to the peer had been at best ambivalent. In his record of that government he paid tribute to Longford's keenness in the field of social policy.[51] On the other hand, according to Cecil King, he had once remarked that Longford had a mental age of 12.[52] Longford had a lifelong commitment to the Irish cause. In the late 1940s he had told David Astor, the Editor of the *Observer*, that unless something was done about discrimination against Catholics in the North 'disaster would certainly follow'. In the late 1960s when the journalist Mary Holland submitted articles on the civil rights movement Astor recalled Longford's warning. 'Moved by a delayed feeling of guilt, he decided to publish the explosive articles, which for the first time brought the situation in Northern Ireland to the attention of mainland readers. "I would not have backed Mary Holland so confidently", admitted Astor, "if Frank hadn't implanted in my mind so many years before the idea that a terrible injustice was being done"'.[53] [Mary Holland's articles are considered in the chapter that follows.] In fact Longford was unable to exploit his membership of the Wilson Governments to help bring about reform in Ulster.

He has given two differing explanations for this failure. Writing six years after resigning he asked himself what he was doing or saying about the Northern Ireland question during his three-and-a-half years in the Cabinet.

> I might as well put on a white sheet and stay in it. I have of course my excuses one always has. There was certainly no special sympathy for the Ulster Unionist set up in Stormont to be found in the Labour Cabinet. Every now and then one of us would raise the question of whether any steps were being taken to end the grosser forms of gerrymandering and anti-Catholic discrimination. The facts about these were not of course anything like as familiar as they were to become much later. But I was by no means alone in being aware that much was wrong.[54]

To such enquiries, Wilson would reply that he was pressing the Ulster premier, but O'Neill was 'having great difficulty with his

(O'Neill's) colleagues'. That was true and, wrote Longford, 'I could understand but not condone my own action.'[55] However, interviewed in 1995, he backtracked. Now the emphasis was no longer on *'mea culpa'* but on a view of himself as a man without status or influence in the Labour Cabinet. Why should Wilson have taken any notice of what he said? He had been more arrogant than he was now when he had written (in 1974) that he could not condone his own inaction. He explained: 'A Cabinet minister without a department is a pretty impotent figure. The weakness of my position is my excuse. I had not been in the Wilson circle but Gaitskell's. Wilson wanted to get rid of me. Crossman said I was farcical. O'Neill was impotent. It didn't seem a big issue when I was sitting there.'[56] The fact that he was probably the only Catholic in the Cabinet did not give him the right to a hearing. On the contrary 'the fact that I was a Catholic, a bloody Papist, made it less likely'. He did wish the government had done more but he recognised that to have attempted to impose reform on Stormont would have meant a 'major war with the Ulster Unionists', and, he said, 'I can't find it in my heart to blame them. To have a major war with the Ulster Unionists would have been unstatesmanlike for a struggling government.' Nevertheless, Longford should have at the very least been able to put the CDU's case in Cabinet but he had no recollection of any of them ever asking him to do so.[57]

A leading member of the CDU, Kevin McNamara, has explained why they failed to exploit Longford's membership of the Cabinet. There were three reasons. First,

we assumed that, given his interest in the subject, he would raise it anyway, without being prompted. Second, we were young, inexperienced and rather naive backbench MPs. Third, we were largely from the left of the Parliamentary Labour Party. Longford, an old Gaitskellite, was not likely to have much sympathy with us. He was also a very junior member of that Cabinet without much influence in it.[58]

The year 1968 was to end with the violence which heralded the beginning of 26 years of continuous turmoil in Ulster and a courageous attempt by O'Neill to survive the political onslaught launched by his right wing enemies in the Unionist party. The year began, however, in a deceptive calm with the Ulster premier preparing to celebrate his 'first five years in office'. An item in *The Times* Diary alluded to this on 19 January. It reported that O'Neill was 'to make a big speech in Belfast' that night to members of the Irish Association, the first time in 30 years that a Prime Minister from either North or South had addressed them. The Diary continued: 'It will also be a landmark for O'Neill, a chance for him to look back over his first five years as premier ...'. He was expected to deal with community relationships in Ulster and his policy of promoting friendship with the South.[59] The following day *The Times*, beneath the heading 'Northern Ireland Plea for Goodwill', reported that 'in a major speech' the Ulster premier had called 'for a new endeavour by organisations in Northern Ireland to cross denominational barriers and advance the cause of better community relations'. O'Neill said that he expected neither total surrender of one point of view to another nor a sweeping under the carpet of major differences on points of principle. But,

> What I see is rather an occupation of the broad area of middle ground by reasonable men and its steady widening in the course of time.

In most issues which confronted a modern government the terms Catholic and Protestant were not really relevant. They were particularly irrelevant in the local civic setting.[60]

In March the *Belfast Telegraph* reviewed those five years of O'Neill's stewardship to which they had given such strong support editorially. Their lobby correspondent, Roy Lilley, recalled how O'Neill 'with foresight had arranged a meeting with Harold Wilson privately a few months before the 1964 general election and became acquainted with Mr George Brown'. After Labour's victory, wrote Lilley, O'Neill explained, 'it is our job to get on with the government of the day in London. This will be our intention'. O'Neill, Lilley pointed out, had recently admitted that the economic treatment of Northern Ireland by Labour had been 'generous'.[61] The following day Lilley analysed O'Neill's relationship with Wilson:

> While the British Prime Minister continues to create a suspicion about his attitude to Northern Ireland by comments on the rights of Ulster Unionist MPs at Westminster with an implication that they should be trimmed, he has revealed no taste for making constitutional change a live issue.

However, Wilson had 'left no doubt that he looks for positive evidence of political and electoral reform'.[62] *The Times* marked O'Neill's fifth anniversary with a special article by John Chartres, headed 'Captain O'Neill counts his five years of bridges'. The article was accompanied by a photograph of a relatively happy looking

Ulster premier above the caption: 'Proud of small achievements'. The article, based on an interview with O'Neill, is remarkable for its tone of confidence and hope. There is nothing to suggest the profound pessimism that it is now known that O'Neill was really feeling. The evidence for this comes from the recollections of Kenneth Bloomfield mentioned in the previous chapter,[63] and a letter a few weeks earlier from Jack Sayers, late Editor of the *Belfast Telegraph*, talked of O'Neill's Irish Association speech having a plaintive tone and of his worries about the Ulster Premier's 'loneliness and insecurity'.[64] Chartres' article began by recording that O'Neill that day (25 March 19) would complete five years

> as a controversial political leader of the last turbulent corner of the British Isles. He has survived two open onslaughts on his position and many more covert ones. He looks back with pride on the various 'bridges' he has built between people, looks forward to building more, but is under no illusion about dangers still in store.

At 53, wrote Chartres, O'Neill was celebrating his fifth anniversary as Prime Minister 'at a time when the province is unusually quiescent on the politico-religious front, and there are even glimmers of hope about the economy and unemployment'. All the tests of O'Neill during this time, including open riots in Belfast, had proved what he had staked his reputation upon – 'that the vast majority in Northern Ireland disliked extremism and believed in an adult approach to cross-border and religious problems'. An opinion poll had shown that 90 per cent preferred O'Neill to Ian Paisley as Prime Minister and a majority (including two-thirds of the Unionists) approved of his moves to improve North–South relationships. 'All of this', said Chartres, 'is immensely encouraging to Capt. O'Neill, but he still sees "Paisleyism" as a force to be reckoned with'. Chartres asked O'Neill what events he was most proud of during his Premiership:

> Oddly, quite small matters, which he thought I as an Englishman would find hard to understand. High on his list he put the estab-lishment of a direct relationship between the Government and the trade union movement, previously bedevilled by the fact that the unions' joint representative body was a committee of the Irish Congress of Trade Unions.[65]

CONCLUSION

Such optimism about Northern Ireland would not be possible again for over a quarter of a century, not until the IRA cease fire of August 1994. Perhaps that spring it was still possible to hope that the province could yet avoid disaster. Richard Rose's survey, although it would not be made known for three years, had found a substantial Catholic constituency for accepting the British link. But it was a slim chance. Those urging the British government to force Stormont to implement reforms before it was too late were not heeded. On the contrary, by ruling out intervention by Westminster, Roy Jenkins had at a stroke surrendered the one means of bringing them forward. However, even if Wilson and his new Home Secretary, James Callaghan, had been prepared to act, the realities of domestic politics ruled out any immediate initiative. The Labour government was prostrate, its leader, Harold Wilson, paranoid about the threats to his position. Positive action, which would have to be carried out in the teeth of Unionist opposition, would need a determined, confident government that still had some authority left. [And a great deal of Whitehall and ministerial time and effort.] This administration in the spring of 1968 had little. In any case the new Home Secretary, Callaghan, as much as his predecessor, Roy Jenkins, strongly believed that any progress would have to come from O'Neill – though Callaghan's faith in the Ulster premier was to be badly shaken by the violence which broke out in Londonderry in October 1968.

5 The Road to Londonderry, April–October 1968

we cannot continue indefinitely with the present situation.
Something has to be done.
> Harold Wilson three months before the outbreak of violence in
> Londonderry[1] 11 July 1968.

Callaghan does not see how he can intervene because the Northern
Ireland Government is responsible for law and order.
> Report in *The Times* on the eve of the Londonderry violence after
> Labour MPs had appealed directly to the Home Secretary[2]

In the six months covered by this chapter the political atmosphere
swung from the optimism and complacency surrounding O'Neill's
fifth anniversary in office to the sudden, and dangerous, polarisation
of the two communities on the eve of the Londonderry riot. Many of
the ingredients for the 25 years of violence which followed can be
discerned during those months. Wilson himself claims to have sensed
the unreality of this period. He wrote later, 'Throughout that spring
and summer there was an uneasy quiet in the streets of Derry and
Belfast, and with it an uneasy reprieve for Capt. O'Neill.'[3]

For many, looking back – participants in the demonstrations, politicians and civil servants alike, the crucial new fact was the world-wide
student 'revolution' that began in May. Expressed differently, they
come to the same conclusion. Kenneth Bloomfield recalled, 'All
across the continent one saw the characteristic linked arms of the
young demonstrators and style of protest drawing heavily on the civil
rights movement experience of black America.'[4] At the ICBH seminar
Paul Bew and Paul Arthur, now professors at Ulster universities, then
student demonstrators, spoke of the influence of the student 'revolution' on the Northern Ireland Civil Rights movement.[5] Callaghan said
that the students' revolt which spread round the world had provided
the 'spark or a match' which enabled the students in the province 'to
feel that they could really conquer'.[6] John Oliver, from the perspec-
tive of the Northern Ireland Civil Service, said, 'Another element …
was the 1968 atmosphere across the world … this was heady stuff and

it added to and exacerbated the feelings.'[7] Yet this 'heady stuff' was not reflected by the more prosaic Campaign for Democracy in Ulster who by June were talking bitterly, and prematurely, of their failure to achieve any progress under a Labour government.[8] Meanwhile the failure of the official Whitehall machine to register the change of mood was more understandable. As Michael Cunningham pointed out many years later, in the two years since the August 1966 meeting, when Wilson appreciated that violent opposition to O'Neill's policies might necessitate the use of troops, 'neither at official nor at ministerial level had Westminster increased its monitoring of Northern Ireland'.[9] Cunningham's conclusion is now supported by the new material released by the PRO in 1997, revealing that the Chiefs of Staff decided in 1966, at the time of the IRA threat of violence to mark the 50th anniversary of the Easter Rising, that intelligence gathering in the province should be left to the RUC.[10] As will be noted in the next chapter Merlyn Rees, who was Northern Ireland Secretary in the 1970s, has confirmed that MI5 were not operating in the province before August 1969 when the troops went in.[11]

That summer of discontent provides the backdrop to the rest of this chapter which analyses in detail the events leading to the fateful 5 October, the day of the disturbances in Londonderry and the immediate aftermath bringing in for the first time evidence from the diaries of Richard Crossman. As the next chapter will show, Crossman became increasingly alarmed by the failure of the Cabinet and the Inner Cabinet (he was a senior member of both) to tackle a crisis which he came to see as even more serious than any other faced by the beleaguered Wilson administration. The impact of the interim report of the Society of Labour Lawyers into discrimination in Northern Ireland is also examined. Finally, the influence of a new player on the Ulster scene, the London-based media, is considered. For too long, newspapers (with the honourable exception of *The Times*), periodicals and broadcasting were culpably silent. Now, with the eruption of violence they began to sit up and take notice.

One of the puzzling aspects of the events leading up to Londonderry is the role of Lord Stonham, Minister of State at the Home Office with responsibility for Ulster.[12] During early June he paid a three-day visit to the province at the end of which he gave a remarkably optimistic verdict on community relations which soon proved to be fallacious.

According to the *Belfast Telegraph*, whose report was headed: 'No Pressure on Stormont over Bias' – Lord Stonham, the Minister, denied that O'Neill was being pressurised by Westminster over discrimination. Lord Stonham said: 'That would be wholly wrong but we can certainly give friendly advice'. The British government had no intention of interfering in Northern Ireland's domestic matters. Such interference would be as resented by Opposition leader Edward McAteer as by Capt. O'Neill. Certainly, said Lord Stonham, the Westminster government desired fairly rapid change to remove what appeared to be legitimate grievances, but he had found community relations in the province were much better than he had been led to believe. 'The curse of Cromwell is a thing of the past …'. Referring to a meeting with McAteer he said that he believed that Stormont now had 'the effective opposition which was so essential to any democracy'. He felt that O'Neill was trying to pursue a very courageous course.[13]

On any reading this is a surprising statement. First, Stonham clearly felt none of the unease that his Prime Minister, Harold Wilson, had felt that summer. Second, who or what had misled him into believing that tensions between the communities were worse than he had found them? The finger clearly points at the CDU who along with *The Times*, Liberal leader Jeremy Thorpe and others had warned of the risk of communal violence. What evidence did he find during his brief stay in Ulster, no doubt 'protected' by his Stormont hosts as Alice Bacon had been before him, to come to this erroneous conclusion? Finally, his assertion that the Nationalists were providing effective opposition was being belied daily by the gathering strength of the civil rights movement.

It seems to have been an ill-judged statement by any standard. However, when Stonham's apparent indifference to the rising tension in the province for which he was responsible was recalled at the ICBH seminar nearly a quarter of a century later it was the cause of a sharp disagreement between Callaghan and a former member of the CDU, Labour MP Kevin McNamara. The incident occurred after McNamara had referred to the way in which Alice Bacon, Stonham's predecessor, had been 'cosseted' by Stormont.[14] When Stonham became junior minister at the Home Office, said McNamara, 'we went and tried to make representations to him and these things went on continuously'. Callaghan turned to McNamara angrily saying: 'About what, Kevin? Because I won't have a word said against Victor Stonham, who was a deeply concerned man about the position of Northern Ireland.' And he added:

when the records come to be published I am sure they will show the pressure that as a middle-ranking minister he put on when he succeeded Alice. So what representations were made that he treated badly?

McNamara:

I never said we were treated badly. I said we made representations to him and nothing happened. We made representations over discrimination in housing; we made representations over the electoral law; we made representations over the continued existence of the Special Powers Act and a whole host of things ... and a lot of things which were there which were not taken on board.

Callaghan:

They were taken on board. It is ridiculous to say they weren't taken on board. Of course they were taken on board and pressure was put on O'Neill to take them up.

McNamara:

All I can say is that we as backbenchers were not aware of this.

McNamara then went on to explain to the seminar his various attempts at Westminster to raise discrimination against Catholics [some of which have been covered in earlier chapters]. However, Callaghan, while paying tribute to McNamara's efforts, was determined to defend Stonham's posthumous reputation: 'Victor cared intensely' and was always putting pressure on Capt. O'Neill. However, what happened when O'Neill could not 'get it through his party?' asked Callaghan. Did you then say 'we're getting rid of Stormont and taking over ourselves?'[15]

Callaghan's spirited defence of Stonham, commendable though it was, failed entirely to explain why, if Stonham was so 'deeply concerned' about Northern Ireland, he so misread events in the summer of 1968? It is hardly surprising that there was indifference at the Home Office to the growing tensions in the province.

A week after Stonham's optimistic assessment the central committee of the CDU met at the House of Commons to discuss progress since its foundation three-and-half-years before. The confidential memorandum submitted by the secretary, Paddy Byrne, bordered on despair. Byrne, 'who was the real driving force of the CDU',[16] makes clear throughout the statement the sense of betrayal by Labour ministers felt by the CDU. The few members who gathered at that meeting could not know that events would soon move so rapidly that Catholic grievances, far from being ignored by ministers, would be high on their agenda. Equally, they could not have known that the days of the convention that had gagged them so successfully at Westminster were numbered.

In his memorandum Byrne acknowledged some small successes. For example, referring to the very few occasions when MPs were allowed to mention the province, he praised 'the splendid performance by our MPs during debates on Northern Ireland', the publicity from which had had an unnerving effect on the Northern Ireland government. Byrne also referred to the 'wonderful reception' given to the delegation of MPs to Northern Ireland in 1967 and to the campaign to send telegrams to Harold Wilson protesting about discrimination in Londonderry in which 100 organisations had taken part.[17] However, this was insignificant when compared with Byrne's list of failures. Although the central committee met monthly, its 'efforts appear to be in vain'. A meeting of the Labour Party and Trade Unions was a flop and only three resolutions on Northern Ireland had made it to the Labour conference agenda. Letters from the CDU to Labour home secretaries 'were treated with contempt'.[18] [Despite Callaghan's claim at the London seminar that Catholic grievances were 'taken on board' this appears to have been the case. McNamara for example, later confirmed that the letters from the CDU had indeed been treated 'with contempt' by Callaghan and Jenkins.][19] A public meeting in Kilburn in April was attended by only 20 despite the fact that 7000 Irish attended mass there every Sunday. Only three constituency Labour parties had affiliated to the CDU. Byrne's conclusion was devastating:

> In short no mass movement has developed and there is no indication that one will. In the present situation in the Labour movement the people most likely to aid our cause, the British left, are far too concerned to save socialism from extinction than to bother about Northern Ireland about which the mass of the British people know little and care less.

Byrne saw only one hope:

> A new start might be made by a meeting in the House of Commons in the autumn similar to the inaugural meeting, having the single objective of ending the convention. If only this were achieved the CDU would not have lived in vain.[20]

Later that month there appeared to be confirmation for the CDU's gloom in remarks made by the *Belfast Telegraph*'s London Letter. The writer, presumably Diamond, referring to the forthcoming Northern Ireland annual debate at Westminster on those subjects which were not devolved to Stormont, echoed Byrne's assessment. 'Labour back-benchers are finding themselves far too pre-occupied with other problems to pay more than scant attention to Northern Ireland affairs.'[21] On 11 July, however, came the first signs that the CDU had been premature in preparing its obituary. During questions to the Prime Minister in the Commons,[22] the left-wing Labour MP, Ben Whitaker, asked why members of the Orange Order were able to vote on the Race Relations Bill, which applied to England and Wales only, when MPs at Westminster were 'not allowed to do anything about religious discrimination in Ulster?' Wilson called it 'a very good question which I have asked myself', and added:

> I recall that when this government had a majority of three in this House we could have been voted down by the Northern Ireland Members voting on Rachmanism in London when English Members and United Kingdom members had no opportunity of voting on Rachmanism in Northern Ireland.

He said no doubt the question would 'be discussed in the fullness of time.'

Commenting nearly three decades later Whitaker said that he had not been asked to put the question to Wilson. [The practice of 'planted' questions to the Prime Minister was a feature of parliamentary life then as now.] It had been spontaneous. However, despite Wilson's hint that the issue would be tackled it never was. In Whitaker's view Wilson had been deterred from direct action over Ulster by advice that the army was divided on Northern Ireland as it had been over Rhodesia. However, said Whitaker, 'if he (Wilson) had had a free hand, if it had been left to him, he might have done something. He had so many Irish in Huyton and I cannot think of anyone in the PLP who was sympathetic to the Unionists'.[23] Evidence for Whitaker's claim that Wilson feared disloyalty from the army is hard to find. Sir Frank Cooper, who was Deputy Under Secretary at the Ministry of Defence at the time, believed this very unlikely. 'It was much more that the army had said: "We cannot fight both Protestants and Catholics. Don't push the army in to a difficult situation." Wilson was always very cautious of involving the army.'[24]

Jeremy Thorpe now pressed the case for by-passing the convention that Westminster could not deal with Ulster's domestic affairs. He told Wilson that as far as human rights were concerned the House had the right to demand that the same standards would obtain in every part of the UK, and he asked, 'since we technically have those powers under the 1920 Act can we now take the proper Parliamentary powers to exercise them?'

Wilson's response was, at first, the familiar tribute to O'Neill. But his tone changed after Gerry Fitt had raised discrimination against Ulster's Catholics. The Prime Minister said:

> The Prime Minister of Northern Ireland and his colleagues know we cannot continue indefinitely with the present situation. Something has to be done. I certainly do not believe that this matter can be left to depend on some of the pressure and prejudices to which Captain O'Neill is subjected.... We in this House have duties in this matter both nationally and internationally.

'We cannot continue indefinitely with the present situation' can hardly be reconciled with Stonham's emollient tone only a few weeks previously and certainly rang alarm bells in Ulster. On 23 July headlines on the front page of the *Belfast Telegraph* declared: 'Explain PM's Stricture'. The paper reported that O'Neill was to be asked at Stormont to explain Wilson's statement.[25] The following day the main story on the front page reported that at Stormont the Unionist MP Capt. John Brooke, son of the former premier, had taken the lead in criticising Wilson. It was 'gross interference in our internal affairs', an attack on the people of the province.[26]

This was nothing to compare with the furore which broke out when the Society of Labour Lawyers published its interim report on discrimination in the province the following month.[27] Even the *Belfast Telegraph* temporarily abandoned its normally fair approach. The findings of the report, which clearly should have led the paper, were consigned to page six and banner headlines on the front page declared: 'Unionists Slam Labour Lawyers' Report'. The story below said, 'Unionist Party chiefs today slammed the interim report of the committee set up by the Society of Labour Lawyers into Northern Ireland Affairs describing it as a propaganda operation'.[28] The item, however, did concede that 'the report by the lawyers is a cautious one'. In their page six coverage, which was not extensive, the paper reported that the Labour lawyers had found anomalies in the Ulster electoral areas. There was criticism of the voting system in use for Stormont and local government elections and of the disparity in the size of the electoral areas. The lawyers, however, it was reported, had come to no conclusion yet on these matters.

Considering the build up of community tension in Ulster that summer, the Labour Lawyers' report could hardly be regarded as provocative despite Unionist claims to the contrary. But what was happening on the ground was indeed becoming serious. A detailed examination of the civil rights movement in the period leading up to the 25 years of violence which began at Londonderry in October 1968 is beyond the scope of this study. However, it would be difficult to evaluate the response of ministers without briefly recording the events in Ulster during the critical weeks before Londonderry. What indeed *was* their position at that point? Wilson, to judge by his recent comments in the Commons, seemed to be preparing for greater governmental involvement in Northern Ireland. Yet Callaghan's resolution not to intervene remained as strong as ever, despite the fact that he was the Cabinet Minister ultimately responsible for peace in the province.[29] This is not just a matter of treating letters from the CDU 'with contempt' in Byrne's words. At the end of August after the first civil rights march in the province, *The Times*, beneath the headline 'Civil Rights Demand', reported that more than 60 Labour backbenchers had signed a Commons motion deploring police action against a civil rights procession at Dungannon, Co. Tyrone. The motion, tabled by Gerry Fitt, demanded 'that citizens of Northern Ireland should be allowed the same rights of peaceful demonstration as those in other parts of the United Kingdom'.[30]

Significantly, the MPs went on to recall the words used by Wilson in the Commons on the subject of civil rights, 'we cannot continue indefinitely with the present situation'. The motion also asked the government to use powers under Section 75 of the Government of Ireland Act, 1920, 'to achieve equality in civil rights for the citizens of Northern Ireland'.[31]

Any immediate government reaction, however, was unlikely. It had only been possible to table the motion because Parliament had been recalled from its summer recess to discuss the Soviet invasion of Czechoslovakia. As so often happened [a recurrent theme of this story] crises elsewhere overshadowed events in Northern Ireland. The Labour Party conference in Blackpool offered Labour MPs a last chance to appeal to ministers to act before it was too late. The *Belfast Telegraph* reported on page one, under the headline 'Call for probe into Bias in Ulster', that resolutions condemning discrimination in Northern Ireland had been tabled by two London constituency

Labour parties.[32] But the CDU failed to interest the conference as its secretary Paddy Bryne recalled five years later:

> For the sake of history I would like to add a word ... to this story about the first battle of Derry. I was attending the Labour Party conference at Blackpool.... I saw Northern Ireland had not been included on the agenda.... I did meet the Standing Orders Committee, chaired by Reg Underhill of Transport House [Labour Party HQ]. Our pleadings were in vain.[33]

The unfortunate truth was that the Labour Party simply did not consider Ulster to be a vital issue. It has been suggested that one reason for this failure to take up discrimination was anti-Catholic bias in some local parties, particularly in Scotland. For example at a meeting of the Parliamentary Labour Party only a few weeks after Londonderry, George Lawson, MP for Motherwell and a former deputy government chief whip, warned of dangers of trying to impose changes in Northern Ireland. He said, 'It would do great harm if it were thought that the Labour Party was on one side or the other.'[34] [However, no evidence has been found to suggest that anti-Catholicism was behind the Labour Party's lack of commitment to reform in Ulster or for that matter the ultra-cautious approach of the Wilson Cabinet.]

On the Friday of the conference week, the eve of the Londonderry march, Labour MPs made a direct appeal to the Home Secretary to intervene. According to *The Times* Callaghan saw Labour MPs and members of the Northern Ireland Labour Party at Blackpool. Referring to Stormont's decision to ban the march, they told Callaghan that a ban on a civil rights demonstration amounted to a denial of normal democratic rights. However, wrote George Clark, the paper's political correspondent, 'Callaghan does not see how he can intervene because the Northern Ireland Government is responsible for law and order.' In view of the difficulty of raising the subject of civil rights at Westminster five Labour MPs, including the CDU chairman, Paul Rose, had 'decided to go to Londonderry to see what happens and to join the demonstration if it proves possible to hold one'.[35] Stan Orme, one of the MPs who saw Callaghan at the conference, said afterwards: 'When we get back to Westminster we shall demand the right to raise this matter in spite of the Commons convention that home affairs in Ulster should not be debated.'[36]

The build-up to the Londonderry violence, recalled the historian and former civil rights campaigner, Paul Arthur, began in June when

Austin Currie, a young Nationalist Stormont MP, illegally occupied a council house in County Tyrone. The house had been allocated to a 19-year-old unmarried Protestant girl, and Currie exploited the publicity to highlight the 'miserable conditions of many of his Catholic constituents'. In August the first of a series of civil rights marches took place in County Tyrone. 'Publicity was again valuable and whetted the appetite for further marches.'[37] The next site chosen was Londonderry on 5 October. The hardline Home Affairs Minister, William Craig, banned part of the route of the march. [The march would not be permitted within the walled city or in the Waterside ward.] Arthur explained:

> He reasoned that it would encroach on traditional Protestant territory.... And he claimed that the march would clash with a traditional Orange demonstration which had been arranged for that day. In fact the latter had been arranged hastily as a device to be used against NICRA [Northern Ireland Civil Rights Association] plans. The march still went ahead over the original route.

The RUC threw up a cordon and a riot ensued. Over 70 civilians and 11 policemen were injured as rioting spread over into the Catholic west side of the city and continued through the night.[38] The scenes transmitted on TV 'focussed world attention on the Northern Ireland situation'.[39] Gerry Fitt, in 1992, claimed responsibility for the massive TV coverage. He had gone round all the TV companies,

> all the television journalists ... who I had got to know over the years, particularly at Westminster and I told them, look I said 'if you're not doing anything send one of your camera crews ...' I said 'send an English camera crew over to Derry for the fifth of October' because I didn't trust BBC Television or UTV [Ulster Television], it can always be edited out, Northern Ireland being Northern Ireland....[40]

The Irish historian, Roy Foster, partly blames the police for the trouble. The violence that began at the march was 'notably on the part of the police – Royal Ulster Constabulary as well as B-Specials'.[41]

The event made a major impression on the British Prime Minister. Wilson wrote later that the violence signalled the beginning of a period of mounting unrest. 'Gerry Fitt, a Westminster MP was taken to hospital with a head wound and many more suffered injury. Three of our backbenchers were there and sent a written report to Jim Callaghan as well as seeing him.'[42] Callaghan too had been shocked.

In 1992 he described how he felt when he heard about the violence at Londonderry and the attack on Fitt:

> I felt indignant of course. I felt the way in which the police had behaved ... could not have taken place and would not have taken place in London in similar circumstances.... I felt that the police had over-reacted on that particular occasion. I can't say now at this lapse of time ... what my whole feelings were, but I don't believe in any civil rights marcher being hit over the head by anybody at any time, full stop.[43]

Significantly the event also marked a major change in the Home Secretary's assessment of O'Neill:

> I don't think I utterly lost faith in O'Neill's ability ... in his belief, in his desire. I began to lose faith in his capacity, his ability, to carry out what I thought he really wanted to do.[44]

There is evidence that O'Neill knew immediately that Londonderry had been a disaster for his policy. It comes from his close aide Kenneth Bloomfield. who recalled that 'the scenes that day secured press and television coverage all over the world', and added:

> O'Neill was from the outset extremely pessimistic about the longer-term consequences. With the events of 1966 still vividly in his mind, he felt that the genie of sectarian animosity would now well and truly escape from the bottle.

The Ulster premier knew, says Bloomfield, 'that from London and elsewhere pressure upon him to achieve more speedy reform would multiply and he did not look forward to fighting the cause of reform through a divided Cabinet ...'.[45] Brian Faulkner, at that time Minister for Commerce in the Stormont administration, wrote later that much of the damage done to Stormont was the fault of that television coverage, 'selective screening' showing marchers being beaten up by the police which 'had a very adverse effect on public opinion in Britain and left the incident judged in advance of anything the Northern Ireland Government might say or do'.[46] This attempt to put the blame on the messenger would not have impressed one of the most acute observers of Ulster's descent into tragedy, Jack Sayers, the liberal-minded editor of the *Belfast Telegraph*, who died the following year. Writing a month later, not in his newspaper but in *The Round Table*, he suggested that a shortage of world news that weekend ensured that Londonderry became a focus of international attention and there could be no denying the power of television to highlight not to say over-illumine, such local situations. However, the protest of the civil rights movement against 'outrageous' discrimination in Derry was 'authentic enough'.[47]

Perhaps the most significant outcome of Londonderry was that for the first time since the UVF violence of 1966 Northern Ireland was taken seriously by the British press. In the next few weeks many editorials and articles appeared in the broadsheets and periodicals. *The Times*, which unlike most of its rivals had shown some interest in Ulster, led the way. The following Monday, the paper had the full story on its front page. The headlines across three columns said: 'Appeal to Harold Wilson as Violence Flares Again in Derry. Street Battle Brings Injury Total to 96' and the coverage included a picture of the injured Gerry Fitt.[48] The next day a major leading article warned Stormont of the risk that political intervention by Westminster might become inescapable. The leader, under the heading, 'Right to be Cautious', began by saying that Wilson was 'not yet abandoning his so far successful endeavours to keep the internal affairs of Northern Ireland out of Westminster politics'. Wilson had found support for his policy in the procedural rules at Westminster. However, 'An energetic band of Labour MPs galvanised by the arrival among them of the Republican Labour member for Belfast West, Mr Gerard Fitt, have been trying for years to give the civil grievances of Ulster citizens a run at Westminster.' For this they invoked powers under the Government of Ireland Act. But, said *The Times*, that was 'not the open door it sounds'. For, it reported, most matters out of which the grievances arose were not the responsibility of ministers at Westminster. Wilson's policy had been to allow that the alleged grievances had

> been causing anxiety without definitely committing himself to belief in their reality and to confirm that they form part of the subject matter of his regular talks with … O'Neill without disclosing the substance of those talks.[49]

However, the paper continued, his critics believed that he was 'just stonewalling'. This was 'the reluctance of a politician who has more than enough on his plate'. But, said the paper, there was 'a more creditable explanation of the Prime Minister's reluctance to disturb the conventional relationship between the two Governments'. The extent of Catholic grievance was disputable, its presence was not. It was intensified by the existence in Northern Ireland of a political opposition which challenged 'the basis of the constitution and of extreme factions whose politics are the gun'. Providing Stormont gave an unequivocal lead in the direction of tolerance and impartial government, 'there is much to be said for letting the inhabitants of the province work out their own salvation'.[50] *The Times* acknowledged that the rate of progress of O'Neill's reforms had disappointed many but the difficulties he faced could 'be gauged by the insecurity of his own position, plotted against by the ultras within his party and publicly assailed by the clerical demagogue, Mr Ian Paisley.' And it asked whether the Londonderry violence should cause Wilson to switch to 'a policy of open intervention?' The protest movement had

> now found able leadership and broader support. It has learnt the value for a neglected cause of provocative mass action in the streets and the Minister for Home Affairs fell into the trap. But the underlying situation is as it was before.

The Times warned:

> If the Northern Ireland authorities cannot lace their firmness with reform, it may deteriorate to the point at which political intervention from this side is inescapable. Just now the responsibility and the next move are with Belfast and so is the best hope of retrieval.[51]

The Observer had sent their correspondent, Mary Holland to Londonderry for the march[52] and her despatch was published in the paper the following day under the headline 'John Bull's White Ghettos'. Above the heading smaller type declared:

> Mary Holland on the cause of Londonderry's rioting: Houses in Northern Ireland are a crucial political weapon, and people don't get houses if they don't vote the right way.

The despair in Ulster was greater, wrote Holland, because a few years previously 'it did seem things might change'. In 1963 the new Prime Minister, O'Neill, 'spoke of justice and seemed determined to purge the old hates from the body politic'. A teacher told her: 'O'Neill made liberal speeches but he has singularly failed to come across with the liberal goods.' Now, cynical mistrust had replaced hope. O'Neill, the teacher went on,

> spins a tolerant line which goes down well in London. He's stalling with Wilson. If he can prevaricate until the next election, the Tories will get back and then nothing will ever be done. Heath needs the Unionists at Westminster.

However, in Holland's view the Labour government's inaction was also responsible for this mistrust. Ulster reformers had been convinced that a Labour government would act but whenever Fitt or Labour MPs tried to raise reform the Government had followed the Conservatives in invoking the convention of not interfering in the affairs of the province. But, she claimed:

> The convention does not bear close scrutiny. The Government of Ireland Act expressly reserves the supreme authority for Northern Ireland affairs to Parliament at Westminster.

And she added:

> Westminster has interfered. The Prices and Incomes Act 1966 was extended to Ulster against the wishes of Stormont – unlike the Ombudsman whose powers do not extend to Northern Ireland.

The political weeklies too decided that it was time to cover Northern Ireland. The *New Statesman* at that time had a circulation of nearly 100 000, a remarkable figure for a heavyweight weekly,[53] and broadly supported the Labour government but by no means uncritically. Its Editor, Paul Johnson,[54] a Roman Catholic, at that time was regarded as an advocate of left-wing policies although he later moved right across the political spectrum, and became an avowed Thatcherite. The first edition of his paper after Londonderry carried a front page article headlined 'Ulster will be Wrong' [a play on Randolph Churchill's slogan, 'Ulster will fight and Ulster will be right'] making a powerful case for a major switch of Government policy towards intervention. This could take two forms.

> There is a financial argument, resting on the £110m. which Northern Ireland receives annually from Whitehall. But in practice this only gives power in its own realm of financial administration – defeating for example the politically loaded and socially brutal proposal that increases in family allowances should not be paid after the third child.

The second was the Government of Ireland Act.

> To put the argument at its lowest, a Labour Government expecting a close-fought election need not be saddled with 11 Conservative seats whose allegiance bears no relation to national policy. To go

one stage higher a British government need not submit its most particular legislation to those unconcerned with it, having no rights in their backyard in return.[55]

But, most important, Northern Ireland had 'waited long enough for political democracy'. It was nearly five years since O'Neill's regime, 'allegedly appealing to reasonable men in the middle ground was established' and, declared the article: 'The disenfranchised in Ulster look to this country for the benefits promised to all by their unique status. If Ulster thinks they can wait indefinitely, Ulster will be wrong.'[56]

From a more centrist position politically, the *Economist* suggested that the right policy was to continue to support O'Neill rather than threaten intervention. A long leading article concluded that the violence on the Saturday though 'thoroughly nasty' was not tragic. Nobody was killed. 'The real sorrow is that this well-televised fracas should have broken out now. After long years of the higher lunacy, faint glimmers of reason and progress had begun to come to Londonderry.... Much of the credit for this beginning (however timid) lies with ... O'Neill.' However, extremism was catching and

Ulster desperately needs a leader who can hold as many people as possible to middle-of-the-road opinions.... Since two-thirds of its inhabitants are Protestants the leader must be of that religion. By far the best middle-of-the-road Protestant politician on the horizon is Captain O'Neill.[57]

But, warned the *Economist*, if the convention that Westminster kept out of the province's affairs was openly broken by Wilson, O'Neill could hardly stay in office. His successor, suggested the paper, would not be more liberal, 'far from it'. Instead of overt intervention there was another method of making Westminster's influence felt:

It should be made covertly plain to hard-line Unionists ... that British public opinion will not stand for intransigence or gross incompetence, in Ulster: that if there is a switch towards less democratic tendencies in policy ... then the necessary millions for motorways and other desirable luxuries will not go on flowing across from one Treasury to the other.[58]

Though the *New Statesman* and the *Economist* differed on the question of intervening directly in Ulster both seriously considered using the British taxpayers' subsidy as a means of persuasion. This was more significant than either could have known because only the previous month – before the Londonderry violence – the Cabinet had attempted to discuss the subsidy with less than satisfactory results as is made clear in the following extract from the diaries of Richard Crossman. Crossman, a senior member of the Cabinet and long-time left-wing confidant of Harold Wilson, was to become increasingly worried by the government's failure to grapple with civil unrest in Ulster. [Part of the following is from the unpublished version of the Diaries, see references.] Crossman recorded that at a meeting of the 'Steering Committee' on Strategic Economic Policy (SEP) on 12 September while discussing subsidies for Shorts of Belfast, Wilson had asked,

> Why should we pay vast sums to a firm in Belfast? What good do we get out of the twelve Ulster MPs? What social results do we achieve by pouring into Belfast money which we deny to Millom or the North-East coast?… At this point I said, 'I am an ignoramus; may I be told what is the exact financial arrangement?' Nobody could say. Neither Jack Diamond [Chief Secretary to the Treasury] nor the Chancellor [Roy Jenkins] knew the formula according to which the Northern Ireland Government gets its money. In all these years it has never been revealed to the politicians and I am longing to see whether we shall get to the bottom of this very large, expensive secret.[59]

The secret, Crossman added in the unpublished manuscript, was

> of the huge subsidies and subventions Northern Ireland gets from us under a political settlement made by our predecessors, carried out by a Labour Government for four years, which is therefore subsidising an area of high Tory reaction at the cost of those in England.

It was, he said, 'a fantastically conventional [*sic*] politics in defiance of their political interests'.[60] After the Londonderry violence, as is recorded in the following chapter, Wilson was to raise the question of using the subsidy to exert pressure on Stormont and O'Neill expressed his fears that this was in the mind of the Labour government. [The Treasury subsidy was necessary because of the lower tax yield in Northern Ireland. 'This amounted to £74 million in 1969–70.'[61] The province's 'budget was settled in discussions between the Finance Minister and Treasury officials in London and there was a Joint Exchequer Board to consider any disputed matters'.][62]

Though there is no evidence that Wilson really intended using the financial weapon against Stormont, politically the Unionists were heavily damaged by Londonderry. The violence had made a mockery of their argument that the province's internal affairs were a matter for Stormont alone and it was clear that the Parliamentary convention was at last dying. In Paul Rose's words:

> it was not until millions of television viewers saw Gerry Fitt, with his head streaming with blood, following a Royal Ulster Constabulary of Northern Ireland baton charge, that the convention was shattered.[63]

Evidence for this was provided as soon as Parliament reassembled after the summer recess. When Fred Peart, Leader of the House, told McNamara that the administration of the province could not be discussed, he retorted: 'That is a most disappointing answer particularly in view of the brutalities we witnessed on TV in Derry....' Fitt warned Peart that it was only by questions and answers in the Commons 'that we can relieve the frustration that has brought about such a tense situation in Northern Ireland'. The Liberal leader, Jeremy Thorpe, said that the government had not merely stood by the 1920 Government of Ireland Act 'but have interpreted certain conventions that have no juridical validity to suppress debate in this House'.[64] However, the following day, during questions to the Prime Minister[65] it became clear that times were changing when Wilson and the leader of the Ulster Unionists at Westminster were involved in a highly charged exchange. The Prime Minister had been increasingly critical of the Ulster Unionist MPs as his exchange with Ben Whitaker, had demonstrated,[66] but he had generally avoided open confrontation with them. Now he threw off all restraint and launched an unprecedented attack. The opportunity came when Paul Rose asked the Prime Minister to remove control of the RUC from the Northern Ireland Home Affairs minister and what matters he intended discussing in his forthcoming meeting with Captain O'Neill. Wilson told him that the talks would cover all the main factors arising out of disturbances in Londonderry. Rose then asked Wilson to make it clear to the Ulster premier that Westminster was prepared to legislate directly for Northern Ireland or to use financial subsidy to compel the restoration of civil rights to Northern Ireland. Wilson prefaced his reply with his customary tribute to O'Neill but added:

> I do not think anyone in this House is, however, satisfied with what

has been done and the feeling that he is being blackmailed by thugs putting pressure on him is something the House can not accept.

Obviously stung by this the Unionist leader, Captain Orr called Rose's remarks 'a slur upon what is probably the finest police force in the world' and accused him of 'mischief making'. The Prime Minister turned on Orr angrily and, in effect, branded the Ulster Unionist MPs liars:

> Up to now we have perhaps had to rely on the statement of himself and others on these matters. Since then we have had British television.

Orr, describing Wilson's remarks as a 'despicable imputation', used a procedural device to try to block any further discussion. The Speaker refused but a few minutes later brought these remarkable exchanges to an abrupt halt. They had only taken a few minutes, but it was clear that Paul Rose had been right. The convention was dead!

CONCLUSION

In the few weeks between Wilson's promise to MPs that 'something has to be done' and Callaghan's refusal to do anything on the eve of the violence in Londonderry on 5 October, Northern Ireland had in effect spun out of control. Not until the IRA cease fire 26 years later was the province to experience a sustained period of peace. In August 1966 Wilson and Roy Jenkins had offered O'Neill a period without interference from Westminster to bring about the reforms that he, O'Neill, claimed he wanted. As recorded in Chapter 2, Wilson offered O'Neill this period of consolidation though admitted in retrospect that 'more time, the most precious commodity in the explosive Northern Ireland situation was inevitably being lost.' Two years later, for all O'Neill's public protestations, Ulster was on the brink of disaster, Wilson knew this yet still his Home Secretary quoted the Government of Northern Ireland Act back at anyone who demanded action. In fairness to Callaghan, however, a number of Labour MPs and, of course, all the Conservatives, still believed that the Stormont system, despite its faults, was best for the province. An example of the prevalence of this attitude is an article written for *The Times* by the highly respected constitutional historian and Labour MP, John Mackintosh, only a couple of months before the

Londonderry violence. The article entitled 'Nationalist eyes on Ulster's system' was in fact about the threat nationalism in Wales and Scotland was posing at that time for the Labour Party. Mackintosh advised a look at devolution in Ulster. There was, he said, 'a great deal to be learnt from the experience of the Government of Ireland Act of 1920'. The Stormont system, he claimed, started 'as something no one wanted and has now become positively popular'.[67] Callaghan, however reluctantly, came to accept after Londonderry that the policy might have to be modified. As the following chapter will show, preparations began almost at once for the possibility that troops might have to be sent in to preserve law and order and even, previously unthinkable, direct rule. Yet right up until the end – the tragic events of August 1969, even after O'Neill, described by Crossman as that 'poor incoherent inarticulate landowner',[68] had gone, Wilson and Callaghan could not bring them-selves to believe that intervention was inevitable.

6 'History is against Us',[1] November 1968 –April 1969

> The only solution – direct rule from London – will of course never materialise ...
> O'Neill, December 1968, four months before his resignation[2]

This chapter describes the final collapse of O'Neillism and with it the last vestiges of the Labour government's Northern Ireland policy. After the Londonderry riot on 5 October 1968, the Unionist leadership, pressed by Wilson, promised at last to bring in reform and a remarkable television appeal by O'Neill seemed briefly to succeed with large sections of both communities.[3] It proved a false dawn and four months later he was gone. However, it is now known that at least six months before O'Neill's sudden departure, the British government had begun to think the unthinkable and plan for the possibility of intervention to prevent civil war in the province.[4] These crucial developments will be covered in the final chapter. The present chapter considers the last, and doomed, attempts by politicians and public officials on both sides of the Irish Sea to find a solution after Londonderry. As Roy Lilley, *Belfast Telegraph* political correspondent, put it: 'By 1969 Northern Ireland was a major issue on the political agenda in London.'[5]

The following account of the last days of O'Neill begins with demands by Wilson and Callaghan, in the aftermath of Londonderry, that Stormont introduce major reforms at once. The fear at the heart of government that, despite O'Neill's acquiescence, these measures would turn out to be inadequate is revealed 26 years later in a remarkable document written only recently by a retired civil servant who held a senior post in Whitehall at the time (see below). O'Neill's unsuccessful bid to confront his Unionist enemies, first by his television appeal then by an ill-fated general election, is considered. The reaction to these events in Westminster, including the possibility of withdrawing financial support from the province, is examined, partly with the aid of material, some of it unpublished, from the Crossman diaries. There is, finally, an account of the dramatic events of April 1969, which began with the bombing of installations in the province,[6] included the election and extraordinary maiden speech of the militant young civil rights campaigner, Bernadette Devlin, and ended with O'Neill's sudden resignation.

What specific advice Callaghan received from his senior officials immediately after the Londonderry violence will not be known until the papers become available in 2000 and possibly not even then if key documents are considered still too sensitive for publication. However, an invaluable insight into what was going on in the minds of the top policy-makers in Whitehall has been provided, nearly 30 years after Londonderry, by a senior civil servant, now retired, who has asked not to be named. To help the research for this project he agreed to write the kind of memorandum he would have drafted for the Home Secretary, James Callaghan, after the Londonderry riots if so requested by Callaghan. He marked it 'Totally Fictitious' to make it clear that it was not literally a Home Office memorandum of 1968 nor even based on a genuine paper. Nevertheless, he was thus able to give a valid account of the thinking, and the attitude of Whitehall, as the crisis deepened. He began by admitting that the recent violence gave cause for real concern:

> I know that rioting has become fashionable and is going on all round the world; but it seems to me that there is something special about these troubles and that we are at risk [*sic*] of the Irish question, which bedevilled politics here for so long raising its ugly head again.[7]

He then admitted that it was surprising that the constitutional arrangements for Ulster had lasted so long:

> It has always seemed slightly comical to have the full array of Governor, Parliament, Prime Minister and Cabinet for a province of $1^1/_2$ million, and although there have been some very talented Ulstermen, it is asking a lot to expect the Protestant element of such a small total to produce enough people of quality.[8]

The tradition had grown up that Whitehall did not interfere (apart from helping with the public expenditure). But despite the tiny staff at the Home Office involved with Northern Ireland, 'we can claim to

have some knowledge of what goes on and in particular of the stir-
rings of dissent and dissatisfaction'. They knew that some of the
Roman Catholics – although not all – would welcome unification with
the South and that Catholics were discriminated against in employment, by the local authorities, in housing, and that the police were in
effect closed to Catholics. They also knew that there was no Labour
Party in Northern Ireland, as Callaghan kept reminding him, that the
civil servants, able though some of them were, could hardly help
thinking like the politicians they had served for half a century, and
that some of the politicians are simply not 'reasonable men' on both
sides. And he continued: 'There are questions about the suffrage, civil
rights and the special powers legislation. But I need not go on.'

Turning to what action was needed, this informant made the significant admission that the government at Westminster had done very
little for years but this inaction was not going to be possible any longer
– 'there are too many indications, apart from Londonderry, to suggest
that the uneasy calm is likely to erupt'. Callaghan himself, he thought,
ought to go to Ulster and make 'something of a splash to mark the
fact that the days of benign and distant tolerance are coming to an
end'. It was inevitable that Stormont would have to be pressed to take
action over discrimination in housing and unemployment, to investigate the special powers legislation and open up the RUC. But,
becoming increasingly pessimistic, he added:

> I do not think this will be enough; and we must recognise that we
> cannot tell where we shall get to. We are dealing on the one hand
> with unscrupulous men of violence and on the other with obstinate
> men who are quite prepared to retaliate and are well aware that
> obstinacy has paid dividends in the past.[9]

He was unable to offer a solution which had eluded generations of
politicians. He thought there should be some form of coalition
government in Ulster to include the minority 'but I am baffled to
know how to achieve it'. It had to be made clear to Stormont that
Westminster could no longer leave it all to them and that 'we must
press them to take action which they will find distasteful. If, as I
suspect, this turns out not to be a solution the prospect becomes
pretty gloomy'.

This informant went on to say that the possibility of sending police
officers over 'from some of the big English forces', had been considered but that would only be a short-term measure. He then warned of
the dangers of sending in troops: 'Once in it will not be easy to get

them out.' Then there were 'the other horrors' to be considered. These included the role of Northern Ireland MPs at Westminster. This was, he said, a constitutional issue likely to arouse the PM's keen interest. All this, he feared, was going on with the eyes of the world, especially those of the USA and the Irish Republic, on Britain. 'If only Northern Ireland were made up of a couple of ordinary shire counties', he wrote, 'with major policy settled in London! But history is against us. It is simply not like any other part of the UK'.[10]

It is easy to see here where hindsight comes into the retired civil servant's 'memorandum' [the suggestion that Callaghan might make a 'splash' in Ulster, for example, was indeed what happened] nevertheless, this, in his own words, 'pretty gloomy' analysis provides a valuable benchmark for judging the actions of ministers over the next six turbulent months. If this was the kind of advice he was indeed giving, and there can be little doubt that it was, the gamble Wilson and Callaghan had taken on O'Neill restoring order and tranquillity to the province was very great.

Wilson himself has given a detailed account of the changes in government thinking brought about by Londonderry and of the fact that the House of Commons as a whole was beginning to take events in Northern Ireland seriously. He wrote that in the Queen's Speech debate that autumn, 'Northern Ireland, for the first time in many years became a focal subject for discussion.' On 4 November O'Neill, Faulkner and Craig met him and the Home Secretary. Wilson recalled:

> During the discussions, I made clear our determination about the urgent reforms which were required in the local government franchise, in housing allocations, and in the appointment of a Parliamentary Commissioner with powers comparable to those of own Ombudsman, to review allegations of maladministration in the Stormont Government.[11]

He and Callaghan expressed concern about the operation of the Special Powers Act for which, he told the Ulster ministers, Britain, as the sovereign power, had to accept international responsibility. He pointed out that Labour MPs from all sections of the party were 'united in their determination to establish human rights in Northern Ireland'.[12] Wilson had said much of this before but what was entirely new was that he threatened the Stormont ministers with punitive action. He said that only 'speedy reform could avert irresistible pressures for intervention by Westminster under the Government of

Ireland Act 1920', though he added, 'none of us wanted that'. He also stressed that at a time when his government had been forced to take unpopular measures to restrain public spending, 'there was a strong feeling among Labour MPs about the large and growing provision of UK finance for Northern Ireland'. And

> while this was contributed under the Consolidated Fund and not voted annually on the Estimates, its provision in the last analysis, depended on the goodwill of the Westminster Parliamentary majority.[13]

Wilson also attempted to shore up O'Neill's precarious position in Ulster: 'As a personal warning and expecting the message to be carried back', he wrote,

> I made it clear that if Captain O'Neill were overthrown for no other reason than opposition to his reform measures, and if he were replaced by a more extremist leadership, a new situation could arise in which Westminster's inhibitions about taking some of the measures pressed upon us would disappear.[14]

Wilson has been accused of sometimes adopting a Walter Mitty stance when recalling confrontations such as the above.[15] However, comments by O'Neill in his autobiography, suggest that Wilson has not exaggerated his menacing tone. Before meeting Wilson, says O'Neill, he Faulkner and Craig went through the notes he had brought with him. 'By their joint decision we went naked into the Cabinet Room. In the end, of course, they were forced to agree a package of reforms.'[16] Callaghan too has confirmed Wilson's resolute attitude. The Prime Minister, said Callaghan, told the Ulster ministers that pressure was growing at Westminster:

> If the Ulster Cabinet could not introduce the necessary reforms ... we might have to apply sanctions such as reconsidering the financial arrangements between the two countries, or even changing their constitutional relationship. Wilson pointed out that whereas the 12 Ulster MPs at Westminster could vote against the Government and even defeat it, we could not even debate Northern Ireland at Westminster. He did not spell it out at the time but what he had in mind was cutting off Northern Ireland's representation at Westminster.[17]

Wilson's new, and apparently uncompromising, stance continued the next day (5 November) when he reported on the meeting to the

House of Commons. He recalled, 'for good measure I repeated my private warning of the previous day'. In answer to the Opposition Leader, Edward Heath, who had called for support for those in Northern Ireland who favoured a moderate policy, he replied 'I very much agree.' But, he added that the Government could not get into the position where O'Neill's vulnerability to pressure from the extremists 'could be used as an occasion for blackmail and could be used as an occasion where we failed to press for reforms which are necessary'. If O'Neill, or his measures, were overthrown the government would 'consider a fundamental reappraisal of our relations with Northern Ireland'.[18]

The change in tone was certainly not missed in Ulster. In his memoirs Faulkner, who accused Wilson of 'waving the big stick', claimed that at the meeting with the British Prime Minister, it was clear that the Government wanted reforms to conciliate the Catholics and he added:

> Harold Wilson made some remarks in the Commons the next day which were not very helpful to easing tension in Northern Ireland. He adopted a vaguely threatening posture and talked of a 're-appraisal' if things did not improve.[19]

Just what Wilson had meant also caused convulsions at the *Belfast Telegraph*. Its Editor, Jack Sayers, changed his assessment twice in 48 hours. On the eve of the Downing Street meeting Sayers had written a private letter in which he speculated that this was the last chance for O'Neill and warned that 'if Wilson goes even a little too far it could be the beginning of the end'.[20] On 5 November the day after the talks, Roy Lilley, writing in the *Belfast Telegraph*, suggested that O'Neill would tell his Cabinet that although Wilson was not contemplating any direct intervention he was looking to Stormont 'to act on its commitment to reform without delay'. The paper also reported that in the Commons Labour MP Frank Judd had spoken of 'the widespread feeling in Great Britain that there is much in Northern Ireland that is an affront to democracy ...' The rest of the sentence was lost in the shouting.[21] According to Percy Diamond, the London Editor of the *Belfast Telegraph,* confirmation by Wilson of the Attlee pledge on Northern Ireland's constitutional status 'greatly gratified O'Neill'. The assurance was entirely unprompted, wrote Diamond. In his leading article Sayers seemed convinced that his private fears about Wilson were unfounded. O'Neill, he wrote:

can be thankful that Wilson continues to show a politician's understanding of wind and weather and that the effect of the conference is to endorse reform while giving the government at Stormont a reasonable time span for action.[22]

However, the following day Lilley wrote that Wilson was prepared ultimately to consider the financial weapon to speed up reform. 'This well-founded view was gaining increasing ascendancy in Belfast and London today as MPs analysed his dramatic statement that in certain circumstances the Government would need to make "a very fundamental reappraisal of its relations with Northern Ireland".' Lilley reported that Stormont Ministers had been taken aback by the tone of some of Wilson's remarks. 'Without doubt Wilson is exerting extremely strong pressure on Stormont and the effect of his comments in the House of Commons is to raise the political temperature ever further.' He added that it was being emphasised in London [presumably by the Number 10 press office] that Wilson's statements were designed to be helpful to the Northern Ireland premier. However,

> another possibility not ruled out in political circles is that the fundamental reappraisal could in extreme circumstances lead to a direct assumption by Westminster of at least some of the powers now vested in Stormont.[23]

By now Sayers had decided that his anxiety about the direction Wilson was taking had been well-founded after all. In a front page leading article, headed 'A Time for Cool Heads', he wrote:

> Whatever his reason for speaking out so soon and so aggressively about Northern Ireland Mr Wilson has not after all lowered the temperature. It could be that he was over-reacting to perhaps complacent statements by the returning travellers but he has certainly put a new complexion on the diplomatic statement issued after Monday's meeting.[24]

Sayers admitted that it was anyone's guess what Wilson meant by his threat of 'a very fundamental reappraisal' of the relations with Northern Ireland. But 'this very straight if highly unusual talk from the Prime Minister of the UK' had been made before there was any excessive right wing reaction against threats to Unionist rights to choose their own leader. He added:

> At the very least it could mean that Mr Wilson could curb the voting power of Ulster MPs at Westminster, something that would

be popular with his own backbenchers, and at most could lead to a curtailment of Stormont's powers.[25]

The other possibility Sayers saw were financial sanctions but he warned, 'no one likes to have to act under duress and on this score Mr Wilson has miscalculated'.[26] We know from Gailey's biography of Sayers that the liberal-minded editor believed that Wilson's financial sanction threat had had the opposite effect of what the British Prime Minister intended and had weakened O'Neill. It had 'stirred up a furious debate within the Unionist party over Westminster "interference".'[27]

Not all those present at Number 10, however, thought that Wilson really meant it. According to Bloomfield, the hard-line minister William Craig, one of the trio at the Downing Street meeting, believed the talk of intervention to be bluff. 'If … the Northern Ireland government were to turn a resolute face towards all pressure, the established convention of non-intervention would hold.'[28] The normally perceptive members of the *Sunday Times* Insight Team concluded that Wilson's threats had not been genuine. In their account of the events that autumn they claimed that the Downing Street meeting 'was the first revelation of the characteristic Westminster policy on Ulster ever since: reversing Theodore Roosevelt's dictum to walk softly and carry a big stick, British politicians stamp around the topic of Ulster but carry no stick at all'. Despite Wilson's warning in the House of Commons of a very fundamental reappraisal if O'Neill were overthrown 'no steps were actually taken against that contingency. Ministers continued to cheer themselves with the thought that O'Neill would somehow survive'.[29] The conclusions of the Insight Team might have been a little different had they been aware that the Government was in fact beginning to plan for the possibility of a major intervention (see below).

The fruits of Wilson's pressure on the Unionists were revealed on 22 November. Wilson records that throughout most of the month violent clashes in Londonderry had continued, then 'the Northern Ireland Government after a meeting of the Unionist Parliamentary Party made an important and courageous announcement of its reform proposals'.[30] The so-called 'Five Point Programme' of reforms promised a points system for housing allocations, an Ombudsman, the ending of the company vote in council elections,[31] a review of the Special Powers Act and the setting up of a Londonderry Development Commission. Wilson wrote, 'recognising our international responsibility the Stormont Government agreed that as soon as they considered that it could be done "without undue hazard" those of the special powers that were in conflict with international obligations would be withdrawn from current use …'.[32]

The historian of Ulster, Jonathan Bardon, writing 20 years later, saw the Five Point Programme as a major advance in civil rights:

> In just forty-eight days since 5 October 1968 the Catholic minority had won more political concessions than it had over the previous forty-seven years. O'Neill observed later that 'the civil rights movement brought about reforms which would otherwise have taken years to wring from a reluctant Government'. This very fact galvanised many loyalists now convinced that a Wilson–O'Neill–Lynch [the Irish premier] conspiracy, was afoot to undermine their position.[33]

John Oliver saw the measures as essential but thought they should have been taken in 1967.[34]

Others were less sanguine at the time and later. Gailey, justifiably, argued that the programme 'could never have stilled the civil rights momentum and the vicious cycle of march and counter-march continued unabated'.[35] O'Neill himself clearly had grave doubts. On 5 December in a letter to his editor-friend, Sayers, who had been ill, O'Neill wrote, 'I do hope you will soon be completely fit again. I only wish we could find some remedy which would have an immediate effect upon the health of the body politic....'[36] In the view of the Insight Team, those reforms which were carried within a year made little difference. 'The only visible gain for the Catholics was the Derry Commission.'[37] Professor Bew considered that the Five Point Programme marked the moment when O'Neill 'was probably doomed'. For the Ulster Prime Minister the dilemma had been excruciating, wrote Bew:

> On the one had, placating the civil rights movement was likely to mean consolidation of the opposition to him. On the other, failing to do so would probably lead, in his eyes at least, to British intervention and a complete dissolution of local autonomy. O'Neill chose the road of minimal appeasement … emphasising that Wilson had made it 'absolutely clear that if we did not face up to our problems the Westminster Parliament might well decide to act over our heads'.[38]

Wilson himself was soon to learn that many in the Labour Party were dissatisfied with O'Neill's 'courageous' programme. In an article in the *Belfast Telegraph*, under the heading 'Mr Wilson and the Pace of Reform', Percy Diamond said that his soundings in Westminster suggested that the Cabinet would have liked to have seen even faster progress. The problem was universal suffrage 'which is certain to come to the forefront when further top level talks take place'.[39] Diamond said that it seemed to many Labour MPs that the points conceded by the Unionists 'were comparatively minor compared with the principle of one man one vote to which they attach an almost mystical significance'. The likelihood that the goal would be achieved after local government reform in Ulster in 1971 was, said Diamond, 'a cold appeal' to the Labour MPs. What they wanted was 'to see the major part of the Ulster grievances met during the lifetime of the present government'.[40]

More violence, this time in Armagh, brought Ulster back to the floor of the House of Commons within two weeks of O'Neill's programme. Gerry Fitt unsuccessfully applied to the Speaker for an emergency debate.[41] The *Belfast Telegraph's* front page lead story the following day, under the headline 'Westminster shows signs of concern', reported the contention by the Labour MP, Michael Foot, that Northern Ireland was directly a matter for Parliament to consider. This, claimed the paper, was 'widely regarded as an omen that government backbench pressure on this issue may soon be power-fully increased'.[42] O'Neill himself was well aware that a critical point had been reached in his relations with both Westminster and his own party. He decided that the only way out was a direct appeal on tele-vision over the heads of the politicians to all the people of Ulster. Bloomfield has explained that O'Neill had been stung into making what became known as the 'Crossroads speech' by Craig who, discon-tented with the direction of events, 'began to give public evidence of his divergence from the O'Neill line'.[43] As a result on 9 December O'Neill went on BBC TV to explain that 'Ulster stands on the cross-roads'. He spoke of the need for justice to all section of the community and of the inevitability of intervention by Westminster if Northern Ireland 'did not put its own house in order'. Bloomfield recalls:

It was a time of great excitement.... The short-term impact was phenomenal. Encouraged by the *Belfast Telegraph* (then, under Jack Sayers' principled editorship, firmly in the O'Neill camp), over 150,000 people during the next couple of weeks indicated their support for O'Neill's policies....[44]

The reaction of politicians and press on the mainland was one of virtually unanimous admiration for O'Neill. Denis Hamilton, the Editor-in-Chief of Times Newspapers Ltd., wrote to congratulate Sayers on O'Neill's performance and on the *Belfast Telegraph*, 'an outstanding paper'.[45] *The Times* itself put a report on O'Neill's TV appeal on its front page: 'O'Neill gives Ulster an Ultimatum. Either they must accept his liberal policies and "bridge building" or look for a new PM.' A leading article applauded his warning that the legislation which reserved supreme authority to Westminster was 'not a dead letter'. Progress on reform had been slow so O'Neill's 'plea to organisers of the agitation to desist is fully justified'.[46] In Whitehall and the corridors of Westminster, according the *Belfast Telegraph*, O'Neill's speech had been 'studied with special interest and appreciation'. The report, headlined 'London is Impressed by Sombre Words', and written by Diamond, said that Whitehall's reaction was generally favourable. A highly placed source had told him, 'O'Neill is working on the right lines'.[47] As Diamond was a member of the Parliamentary Lobby the 'highly placed source' was probably a minister, perhaps Wilson himself or Callaghan.

The CDU, which had been riding high since the events of 5 October, claimed some of the credit for O'Neill's speech. Speaking at a meeting of the group at Westminster the Chairman, Paul Rose said 'we have broken through'. However, he warned, 'we must not, by breaking the dike, cause such a flood that all reason is swept away.' Rose said that all those who had carried on the fight for civil rights in Northern Ireland must acknowledge that the TV speech was remarkably outspoken and courageous. 'He has staked his political future on meeting our movement part way. To snub him would be foolish and dangerous.'[48]

The encouraging reaction to the 'crossroads' speech wrote Bloomfield, gave O'Neill the confidence to sack Craig.[49] Harold Wilson recalled the move with satisfaction, 'not before time'.[50] Roy Lilley, who knew Craig well, explained many years later that Craig had been genuinely convinced that the civil rights movement was really a Republican conspiracy plot with the objective of achieving a united Ireland. 'He would probably say now that events have proved him right.' However, said Lilley, one might equally argue now that Craig's actions 'might have fuelled precisely what he was talking about and in a way he was partly responsible for its development'.[51] A significant point arises out of Craig's role at that time. As Home Affairs Minister he might have been expected to be taken seriously at the Home Office in London. The real nature of that relationship was revealed at the ICBH seminar in exchanges between witnesses. It began when Kevin McNamara said that Craig told him that as Minister for Home Affairs, he had received information from MI5 'that civil rights was riddled with IRA'.[52] If what Craig had told McNamara were true, it would clearly have coloured the attitude of the British government to the objectives of the civil rights movement and could arguably have been a reason for not pressing Stormont earlier (and harder).

However, at the seminar Callaghan went out of his way to stress that Craig, far from influencing London, was simply 'not believed'. Callaghan told McNamara:

> You really mustn't assume that what Craig said was therefore accepted. None of us believed in the Home Office that it (the civil rights movement) was riddled by the IRA.

The British government knew that there were 'IRA people on the fringe'. But, he added: 'The real point is that the IRA was incapable at that time.'[53] Callaghan went on:

> what Craig was saying was utterly dismissed by people like O'Neill and people like myself if I may say so. We knew.[54]

Callaghan was backed by Merlyn Rees, who served as both Northern Ireland Secretary and Home Secretary in the 1970s. Rees told the seminar that he doubted that Craig had received a briefing from MI5. The security service was not operating in Northern Ireland at the time. 'Where he had his briefing from was the Home Affairs Department at Stormont.'

McNamara: 'He (Craig) said specifically he got things from the British Government.'

Rees: 'I don't believe him.'

McNamara said that Craig refused to give him the MI5 information in writing, explaining, 'I cannot do it because I am bound by the Official Secrets Act.'[55]

These exchanges suggest that O'Neill's decision to sack Craig helped to convince the British government that a solution to Ulster's troubles was still possible without intervention. As Callaghan said, the IRA were incapable of the degree of subversion claimed by O'Neill's enemies in the Unionist Party and O'Neill himself was riding high. The Unionist Parliamentary Party gave him a substantial vote of confidence and on 29 December an Irish newspaper, the *Sunday*

Independent, announced that its readers had chosen him 'Man of the Year'.[56] Yet, as Bloomfield pointed out, within four months of 'this high point' O'Neill was to decide that he must offer his resignation.[57] Much earlier than that, on Christmas Eve 1968, a mere two weeks after the 'Crossroads' speech, O'Neill had sent Bloomfield another of his 'prophetic letters'. O'Neill wrote to his friend and colleague,

> My Dear K. What a year! I fear 1969 will be worse – or that portion of which we may survive. The one thing I cannot foresee in 1969 is Peace. As I look in the glass darkly I see demonstrations, counter demonstrations, meetings, rows and general misery. In such an atmosphere of hatred would one in fact wish to continue this job, I doubt it. The only solution, direct rule from London, will of course never materialise and so we shall drift from crisis to crisis....[58]

Three decades later it still seems astonishing that O'Neill, in private at least, was advocating direct rule from London which not even the CDU were demanding at that point. Sayers shared some of O'Neill's gloom as his biographer makes clear. What worried the Editor was the decision to shelve local government reform for three years. For the moment the talk was all of triumph but, wrote his biographer, 'such optimism was to be short-lived'.[59]

Their pessimism was justified by a new factor which had entered the Ulster equation, the formation of the militant civil rights movement, People's Democracy (PD). It is beyond the scope of this account to analyse in detail the 'politics in the streets', to borrow the apt title of Bob Purdie's study of the origins of the civil rights movement.[60] However, the impact of PD was such that something must be said about its origins. PD was founded at Queen's University, Belfast, in October, 1968, four days after the Londonderry violence. After a student march to Belfast City Centre to demand an impartial inquiry into 'police brutality' at Londonderry and the repeal of the Special Powers and the Public Order Acts, a committee of ten was established. The committee called for one man one vote, a re-drawing of election boundaries and action to outlaw discrimination against Catholics. Its leaders included Bernadette Devlin and Michael Farrell.[61] Bloomfield has recorded:

> A cloud no bigger than a man's hand passed over the sunny skies of December 1968 when towards the end of the year, the so-called People's Democracy announced that it planned to undertake a four-day march from Belfast to Londonderry....[62]

For Sayers, too, the march and its aftermath was to prove a turning point.[63] The march began on New Year's Day 1969 with between 40 and 70 people taking part. It was criticised by loyalists for being provocative and was harassed by 'extreme elements' along the way. 'The most serious incident was at Burntollet Bridge, in Co. Londonderry, when the marchers were ambushed by some 200 loyalists. Stones and sticks were used in the assault and 12 students had to have hospital treatment.'[64] Afterwards the RUC was criticised by civil rights spokesmen who claimed that it had given 'the marchers little or no protection',[65] and the protests led to the establishment of what became known as the Cameron Commission, to look into the violence in the province since 5 October 1968.[66] The *Belfast Telegraph* took a sympathetic line to the marchers arguing in a leading article that civil rights had become a political demand with which Northern Ireland must reach a just settlement if it was to have a hope of peace and lasting stability. The paper also carried a news story reporting that Wilson was keeping himself fully briefed about the violence. 'Downing Street is receiving continuous reports from the Home Office as part of the normal relationship between the two governments.' The Northern Ireland Labour Party, said the *Belfast Telegraph*, had directed a constant flow of reports to the British Prime Minister about civil rights issues in recent months, and the recently formed Derry Central Labour Party was urging the British Government to consider the necessity of direct intervention.[67]

Since these events, however, doubts have grown about the role of the so-called 'Battle of Burntollet' in the civil rights campaign. It is now suggested that far from advancing the cause the march was a major error and may even have destroyed all hope of O'Neill's widely backed appeal succeeding. At the ICBH seminar Professor Bew admitted that he now had a 'great deal of reservation about the civil rights movement'. He said,

> I was at Burntollet. I think it was a mistake. I think O'Neill might just have pulled off some kind of accommodation with the Catholic middle class before Christmas. He wasn't able to after Burntollet. I say might just have – I actually suspect the system wasn't reformable.[68]

Another witness, Paul Arthur, who helped to organise the march, said he had begun to have reservations about it from the start. He said, 'Burntollet in retrospect may have been a mistake. But ... so many other things were mistakes ... but I believe that before Burntollet

O'Neill was gone.'[69] Interviewed three years after the seminar Professor Arthur said he could not recall saying that Burntollet might have been a mistake. He said:

> O'Neill was gone because of internal problems, ultras v the liberals (in his own party). Burntollet pushed it over the edge. Wilson continued to support O'Neill because the alternative was too much to contemplate.[70]

John Hume, he said, had been against the march: 'We went to see him and he told us not to go.' Burntollet, said Arthur, 'in hindsight, was a mistake', but it was not 'the cause' of the violence of August 1969 but 'it speeded things up'.[71]

O'Neill himself did not help matters by over-reacting to Burntollet. Bloomfield recalled that O'Neill

> feared that it would prejudice the uneasy armistice that had followed his 'Crossroads' speech and that fear led him to an immediate response that was felt by many Catholics to be a one-sided criticism of the marchers without adequate condemnation of those who had sought to prevent them from exercising their rights under the law.[72]

O'Neill's immediate action was fly to London to brief Callaghan on the growing violence and this sparked off a wave of rumours that he was going to ask for British troops to counter the increasing threat to law and order. British officials denied that any such request had been made.[73]

Another effect of Burntollet was to provoke renewed British press interest in Ulster. A front page editorial in the *New Statesman* forecast – accurately as it tragically turned out – that 'People are likely to be killed in Ulster if things get worse', and spelled out the circumstances in which intervention by Westminster would have to come. The paper said, 'The situation in Northern Ireland is deteriorating every day.' Stormont, which had failed to provide civil rights, now could not even guarantee civil order. It was extremely optimistic to assume that the Northern Irish could control themselves. Clearly referring to Burntollet, the editorial said,

> the forces of the state cannot guarantee the safety of a peaceful demonstration. Now they are not trusted by the Catholic poor to protect or even to leave unmolested their streets and houses.

The *New Statesman* conceded that O'Neill's programme was

genuine and its time table not unreasonably gradual but added, 'It is not Captain O'Neill's sincerity or virtue that is in question but his power.' If he could not 'deliver the goods' it would be necessary to take a stronger line. At present the idea of moving in British troops created incredulity and scorn. But 'how many will have to be killed before the idea of mobilising British soldiers seems less laughable?' O'Neill, said the paper, need not be left to handle his extremists alone. 'The British government could address a few words to them direct in a language which they understand. If they choose to break down civil order in Ulster, we shall restore it.'[74] The voice of the Editor, Paul Johnson, comes clearly through the unsigned editorial.

The Times provided space on its prestigious leader page for a major article advocating abolition of the Unionist monopoly of power in Ulster as the most effective way of ending the crisis. The author was Dr R.J. Lawrence, Senior Lecturer in Political Science at Queen's University, Belfast. He put a closely argued case for an end to single party rule as a way of binding the Roman Catholics into the UK. It was a solution that Heath was to try unsuccessfully five years later but which became the nucleus of the Good Friday agreement in 1998. The real trouble in Ulster, wrote Lawrence, was single-party government: 'A permanent minority cannot alter the rules in its own favour.'[75] The Unionist administration, even after the emergence of a reforming Captain O'Neill, failed to end the old abuses (such as discrimination in council house allocation) that drove poor Catholic families 'to despair'. The result was the civil rights campaign, pressure from British opinion and specially by Wilson and Labour MPs and O'Neill's reform package. Lawrence thought that the civil rights campaign might have opened the way for an end to single-party rule. It would need all opposition parties to accept that Ulster would remain part of the UK.

It was becoming by the day increasingly difficult, however, to imagine a solution based on co-operation between the two communities. More sectarian violence flared at Newry and the *Belfast Telegraph* followed the *New Statesman* in warning of a 'a shooting war'. A leading article [possibly not by Sayers who was ill] said: 'The British Government ... will not stand idly by if Northern Ireland shows it is unable to bring the trouble to an early end.'[76] A week later Wilson himself suggested that intervention by Westminster was now a real option. The *Irish Times*, under the headline 'Intervention in Northern Ireland if needed – Wilson', reported that in a television interview the British Prime Minister had said he would not shrink from intervening in Northern Ireland if that was needed to ensure order there. Wilson had been asked, on the BBC Television programme, *Panorama*, how near the province was to intervention by Westminster.[77]

Three days later the crisis deepened when Brian Faulkner, the Deputy Prime Minister, caused a 'major surprise' by resigning in protest against O'Neill's decision to set up the Cameron Commission. According to W.D. Flackes, the seasoned BBC Northern Ireland political correspondent, writing many years later, the move was obviously a climax to tensions between the two men.[78] Faulkner described the Commission as a 'major blunder', and he wrote: 'it was obvious that the Commission would report that one man one vote was the foremost demand of the protesters and would recommend that it be met'. The Northern Ireland Cabinet had already agreed that they would comply with the Commission. But at the same time O'Neill was proposing to say that there would be no change in the law until the review of local government had been completed in two years time. This, said Faulkner, 'was not only dishonest, it was a disastrous political tactic which could only damage trust between people and government'. In his view it would have been better to decide in favour of the reform, 'and put that view with honesty and determination to the people'.[79] O'Neill, in his memoirs, called Faulkner's resignation over the Commission 'a political manoeuvre'. He also recalled that in a television interview Faulkner, who now claimed to be in favour of reform – 'defending with enthusiasm' gerrymandering in Londonderry.[80] Roy Lilley has provided an independent assessment of the two men, both of whom he knew well at that time. Lilley said that 'a tragedy for Northern Ireland was that O'Neill became PM but Brian Faulkner thought he had title to the job as well as indeed, in all fairness, he had'. The problem was that Faulkner at that stage was still the 'dyed in the wool Unionist of the old school, the Orange Order'. He changed subsequently but too late. O'Neill had vision but he did not have Faulkner's political *nous*. Faulkner, claimed Lilley, could have delivered the Unionist party in a way that O'Neill could not. 'But the two of them never had any real understanding and Faulkner was always perceived as trying to undermine O'Neill.'[81]

The *Spectator* found an intriguing historical parallel between Brian Faulkner and Harold Wilson. In a leading article the paper compared Faulkner's challenge to O'Neill with Wilson's attempt to unseat Hugh Gaitskell, as Labour leader and added that now O'Neill had

disposed of those of his colleagues who were foremost in demanding defiance of Westminster, he should henceforth combine the
urgent pursuit of reforms with emphasis on his complete independence of action in so doing. Mr. Wilson ought from his own
experience to recognise that the end is well worth the means.[82]

Despite the turmoil among the Unionists so dramatically highlighted by Faulkner's resignation and his own warning of possible
intervention on *Panorama*, Wilson still had faith in O'Neill and this
won support from *The Times*. A leading article praised the British
Prime Minister for handling 'his less difficult end of the business
firmly and discreetly'. Wilson had warned that Westminster 'has the
means, financial as well as legislative, to promote redress'. In certain
circumstances, argued *The Times*, ditching O'Neill would bring nearer
'that intervention by London ...'.[83]
   It was at this point that O'Neill made what Wilson later called his
'disastrous dash for freedom' by calling a General Election.[84]
Bloomfield recalled that after Faulkner went 'the juggernaut of dissi-
dence accelerated'. A substantial number of Unionist MPs were
calling for O'Neill to go and 'it was difficult to see how he could
survive in the long term'. Yet there was huge evidence of popular
support following the 'Crossroads' speech. On 3 February O'Neill
took 'the phenomenal risk of appealing to the electorate'.[85] The news
of the election caused alarm in London. The *Belfast Telegraph's* Percy
Diamond wrote,

The warning lights have been flickering in Whitehall and
Westminster. However far fetched it may sound the possibility has
been made clear that in certain conditions it may be Britain's duty
to act directly in Northern Ireland affairs and one of those conditions, it is evident, is the blocking of the way to moderate and
steady reform as pursued by Captain O'Neill.[86]

As a lobby correspondent, Diamond was able to talk confidentially
to MPs and he said there was no doubt that the overwhelming hope
of all parties was that O'Neill's 'gamble' would result in an over-
whelming mandate for reform. But he added:

The greatest fear is that the outcome will be a regime more to the
right opening the prospect of a continuation of Ulster unrest which
will lower the standing of Northern Ireland in the UK and possibly
compel the British government to consider intervention....[87]

The *Spectator* clearly feared that the latter outcome was more likely. In a deeply pessimistic leading article on the front page, headed 'A Leap in the Dark', the paper said that O'Neill's calculation was presumably that even if the Unionist party lost a few seats it had a large margin of safety and he would 'find himself in the new Parliament leading a smaller but more coherent group, enjoying a smaller but workable overall majority'. However, the *Spectator* forecast that the most probable outcome was 'a return to the *status quo ante*', and warned that 'if this should happen it seems unlikely that Captain O'Neill could hold on to power for very much longer'.[88] Richard Crossman, however, did not share this gloom, as a long entry in his Diary for Sunday 9 February 1969 makes clear. Crossman wrote:

> Generally of course the big news all week has been the crisis in Ulster, the coming of a General Election (with) O'Neill the Progressive trying to test his strength of his hold over the Unionist Party, and his ability to defeat the old-fashioned Orangemen.

It was, said Crossman,

> getting very exciting this because O'Neill is the man we are relying on in Northern Ireland to do our job for us. To drag Northern Ireland Ulster [*sic*] out of its 18th Century Catholic–Protestant dispute.

O'Neill had called the election and Crossman had 'great hope he is going to bring it off. I have a great hope he will fragment the opposition, he will smash the old fashioned people and enable Ulster to go forward ...'. If, however, O'Neill was unsuccessful 'then we shall have to do something about it', responsibility would fall on the central government and 'Callaghan told me last week ... in the greatest secrecy, that he had to work out the plan for a take-over of Government in Northern Ireland if the government were in danger of collapsing. And that is one of the possibilities though I hope a remote one.'[89]

One outcome of the election campaign was that mainland citizens had a rare chance to see the Ulster crisis discussed on television when, on 17 February, the key protagonists were interviewed on the BBC programme, *Panorama*. Robin Day, a highly experienced and popular television interviewer, explained the election to viewers in terms that would normally be applied to a foreign country. Given how little coverage the province had in the British media he was justified in doing so. Ulster, he said, was facing an election which was like no other in the UK.... Normally an election in Ulster does not arouse immense interest anywhere even in Ulster. But this time it is different. The Prime Minister, Captain O'Neill, is fighting for his survival against a challenge from within the ruling Unionist party....

Day told viewers:

> So, unlike a normal democratic election, the object of this one is to decide not which party will govern, but how the governing party will be led.... Underlying it all, the historic feud between Protestant and Catholic and the recent clashes about minority rights.[90]

Those interviewed by Robin Day included the sacked Home Affairs Minister, William Craig, who claimed that Westminster non-intervention in Ulster was no longer merely a convention but virtually part of the constitution. He believed that Westminster no longer had, in practice, supreme power over Ulster. He told Day, 'you cannot give the people one day powers to exercise on their own behalf, and then because you disagree with their choice of policy take those powers away, that's a complete negation of democracy'. [The erroneous argument, that the convention had after 50 years constitutional authority, was discounted in Chapter 1.] O'Neill told Day that the issue before the electorate was the future of the province. 'Unless we can pursue and continue with moderate policies ... I cannot see any future for Ulster.... I am not clinging on to office at all.'[91]

The general election which Bardon called 'the most confused election in Northern Ireland's history',[92] took place on 24 February 1969. There were Unofficial Unionists who supported O'Neill against Official Unionists who opposed him. There were Independents who represented the broad civil rights platform and PD candidates who spoke for the more revolutionary wing.[93]

The result was equally complex. A number of the leading O'Neillites, both 'official' and 'unofficial' had won their seats. However, 11 candidates, who had stood on a specifically anti-O'Neill platform, had been returned, including some of the most important Protestant spokesmen such as William Craig.[94] O'Neill himself, who had been opposed by Ian Paisley and the PD's Michael Farrell, only just held on at Bannside.[95] The *Belfast Telegraph* feared that the inconclusive results might force Wilson to intervene and 'O'Neill's resignation as PM might be the first step to a period of turmoil facing Northern Ireland and could even end in intervention from Westminster.' [All of which happened within six months.] O'Neill's

gamble that there was a sufficiently vast middle of the road proportion of the electorate to rid him of his hardline enemies at Stormont
seemed to have failed. [96]

The London press was equally pessimistic about O'Neill. A prominent front-page report in *The Times* was headed 'Ulster poll result
may end O'Neill's reign as leader'. The paper's correspondent, John
Chartres, wrote, '... Captain O'Neill may have to offer his resignation', and Northern Ireland faced 'a long period of turmoil possibly
ending in intervention by Westminster'. Chartres also made the point
that a take-over by Westminster was 'quite simple under the 1920
Government of Ireland Act'.[97] Walter Terry, *Daily Mail* Political
Editor, and a personal friend of Harold Wilson, wrote:

> The Northern Ireland crisis now threatens to spread to London.
> With deep uncertainty in Ulster, Cabinet Ministers in London
> will have to consider whether and when intervention may be
> necessary.[98]

The following day David Wood, *The Times* political editor and
doyen of the Westminster lobby correspondents, gave his assessment
of the growing crisis in Ulster. Wood wrote:

> Westminster politicians pulled wry faces about the outcome of the
> Northern Ireland general election and then hurried on to say with
> hindsight that all political experience shows that coupon elections
> never mend party splits.

On both sides of the House of Commons, said Wood, there were
MPs who saw O'Neill's resignation as inevitable. Wilson, who had a
close personal relationship with O'Neill, had hoped that the election
would vindicate his policies. Wood predicted that Wilson would not
hesitate to strengthen his argument for steady progress with reform
with 'threats about economic aid to Northern Ireland'.[99] The
Spectator saw the significance of the election result in the success of
Paisley who 'must now be taken seriously'. Intervention, said the
right-wing weekly in a front page leading article, 'may turn out to be
inevitable if bloodshed and a collapse of public order are to be
averted ...'. but the one way of provoking a crisis was to act as if it
were inescapable. It would be 'inexcusable for Westminster to
threaten to reduce financial support (as both Mr Wilson and Captain
O'Neill have hinted that it might be) for that support is pledged in
recognition of the pressing economic and social problems of the
Province'.[100]

Writing in the *Belfast Telegraph*, the staunchly pro-Unionist T.E. Utley, warned that if O'Neill failed to produced strong government 'there is no perceptible alternative to intervention from Britain to maintain order and promote progress in Ulster'.[101] However, Percy Diamond believed that Wilson was still determined to avoid direct involvement in Ulster's affairs. In his *Belfast Telegraph* column he wrote, 'talk is being revived of a contingency planning on the part of the Home Office and the Ministry of Defence ...' But

> while Wilson, urged on by left wing supporters, will continue to throw his weight behind policies for the speedy levelling up of Ulster's democratic standards to those of the rest of the UK he is not in the least likely to take any precipitate risk of having a full scale Irish problem landing on his desk. [102]

At home, O'Neill was criticised by one of his most prestigious supporters, David Lindsay Keir, Vice-Chancellor of Queen's University, Belfast. In a letter to his friend, Jack Sayers, Lindsay Keir said that O'Neill's implication during the campaign that the financial subsidy might be cut off and that a breakdown of government might lead to direct rule was 'more likely to put Ulster's hackles up than make for submission'.[103]

Had the failure of the election to strengthen O'Neill really brought financial sanctions against Stormont nearer as David Wood, the *Spectator* and David Lindsay Keir believed? True, Wilson had made ominous noises in Cabinet about British taxpayers' money going to Ulster. In his memoirs Wilson's only reaction to the 'disastrous' election results was that Paisley's performance had dealt 'a shattering blow' to O'Neill's authority.[104] Crossman too was horrified by how close O'Neill came to defeat by Paisley, the 'leader of the reactionary Orangemen',[105] but in a lengthy entry for 25 February about the Ulster crisis, there is no mention of withholding money.[106] A warning that the subsidy could be at risk, however, came from Michael Shanks ten days after the election.[107] In a major article in *The Times* Michael Shanks wrote: 'It appears to be assumed in Northern Ireland that the British will continue to pay this £100 million subsidy without question. This seems a rash assumption.' Shanks was discussing prospects for the imminent budget which might take place against the background of world financial crisis. A no-change budget was probably right but the Chancellor might 'have to construct his strategy with an eye to the gnomes'. But recent events in Ulster could be significant.

Withdrawal of Britain's subsidies to Ulster now seems, as a result of Ulster's own actions, at least a possibility. If the situation in the province worsens, and if the economic pressures on the Chancellor increase, it could become more than that.[108]

'One would have thought that the maintenance of this subsidy, with all that it implies for Ulster's employment and standard of living was a consideration of major importance to the province. Yet it appeared to be assumed by all except O'Neill that 'the British taxpayer will continue to pay this subsidy without demanding any quid pro quo'. In Shanks' view 'no Ulster politician can any longer assume that Britain will inevitably go on footing the bill whatever happens'. However, O'Neill had 'at least shown he was aware of the situation, and he may well be literally worth £100 million a year to Northern Ireland'.[109]

But keeping O'Neill in place was fast becoming an academic question. Bloomfield had been with O'Neill as the returns from the election came in. The Prime Minister was 'morose and downcast', he wrote. 'We went through the motions of going on as before. The Unionist Parliamentary Party overwhelmingly confirmed O'Neill in the leadership....' However, 'O'Neill was right in his pessimistic judgement ... I could see in these final weeks that O'Neill felt he had been there too long for any good that he was doing.'[110] He hung on for another two months, 'courageously' laying his programme before Stormont, Harold Wilson recalled, 'and Bill by Bill his policies made progress. Despite this he was continually under attack. Riots continued'.[111]

'Two final blows then fell', wrote Bloomfield. The first was the bombing of water-supply lines and electricity installations in the province, thought at first to be the work of the IRA but later proved to be 'Protestant extremists trying to apply the coup de grace' to O'Neill. [112] Bloomfield thought it ironic that in the end 'the chance of peace was destroyed, not by Catholics, but by Protestants'.[113] O'Neill then 'suffered the final, stunning blow' of the resignation of his Minister of Agriculture, James Chichester-Clark, who was opposed to the timing (not the principle) of the abolition of the property vote at local government elections. 'O'Neill had had enough' and resigned.[114]

If Protestant bombers were about to achieve their objective they had also brought about the involvement for the first time of British troops. In response to a request from the Northern Ireland government, the Ministry of Defence announced that British troops would be used to guard key public installations. An Irish journalist in

London wrote, 'the Ministry of Defence told me categorically tonight: "There is no question of the use of troops to control crowds or demonstrations".'[115] The *Times* correspondent, John Chartres, in a prescient article saw the decision to use the army as highly significant. Under the heading 'Troops pointer to Ulster peril. Fears being realised' he wrote that Ulster had

> moved closer to the most-feared situation of all, a combination of violence and bloodshed on the streets, deliberate attacks on installations ... and continued internal strife within the Stormont government.[116]

Constitutional experts in London and Belfast had claimed after the general election that this was the only combination that could lead to intervention. The use of troops at this time, men already stationed in Ulster, was not strictly intervention as they had been requested by O'Neill. However, 'their visible presence guarding such installations as power stations and reservoirs may have its own dangers'.

While the case for intervention did not yet arise, Chartres warned: 'the British Government clearly could not stand idly by indefinitely if there were many repetitions of this weekend's events and particularly if lives were lost ...'. Chartres believed that an immediate danger was Protestant reaction to the victory of PD's Bernadette Devlin in the Mid-Ulster by-election. The triumph of the militant young Republican had apparently 'inflamed extreme Protestants both with anger and fear'.[117] The Liberal leader, Jeremy Thorpe, at a civil rights meeting in Birmingham, claimed that Devlin's victory told the Ulster Unionists that the days of their complacency could never return and he urged Wilson: 'While you are still in office do something constructive with it. Win at least one victory over reaction by insisting that Stormont does its duty to all the peoples of Northern Ireland.'[118]

The *Belfast Telegraph* was confident that despite the deepening crisis Wilson would still reject Labour backbenchers' demands for action under Section 75 of the Government of Ireland Act 1920. This was the judgement of Percy Diamond who in a front-page report revealed that the Cabinet had been holding urgent talks 'as indications grew that the Northern Ireland situation would erupt fiercely into the Parliamentary arena'. Diamond said that after the weekend violence

> Northern Ireland is again under the spotlight at Westminster. Harold Wilson, who dashed back to Downing Street last night after

Stormont asked the Home Office for troops, was again in consultation with senior colleagues ... but many Labour MPs will argue
that, in debating Northern Ireland, they should not be restricted
merely to the use of troops but should be able to discuss the reasons
behind the disturbances.[119]

The *Belfast Telegraph* also quoted a Press Association report which
said that 'contingency plans to use troops to maintain law and order
had been in operation for a long time. A lot of thought was given to
the possibility that the situation might deteriorate to the extent that
UK government assistance might be needed and final touches to the
plans for making troops available, if necessary, were given before the
election in Ulster ...'.[120] [Evidence that planning had begun even
earlier is provided in the chapter that follows.]

The following day Bernadette Devlin arrived at the House of
Commons to make her maiden speech after her triumph in the Mid-
Ulster by-election. One correspondent wrote much later, 'She
became the youngest woman ever to be elected to Westminster and
the youngest MP for nearly 200 years. She took her seat on her 22nd
birthday. It was, she said, "the arrival of a peasant in the halls of the
great". Her sponsors were Gerry Fitt MP and Labour's Paul Rose.
Ignoring tradition she made her maiden speech an hour after taking
her seat.'[121] Because her speech made such a major impact both in
Britain and in Northern Ireland it is worth considering it – and the
reactions to it – at some length.[122] Devlin had the opportunity to make
her maiden speech so early because Paul Rose had successfully
applied to the Speaker for a three-hour emergency debate on the
violence in Londonderry the previous weekend and the stationing of
troops at installations in Northern Ireland after the bombings.
Opening the debate[123] Rose, referring to the earlier violence in
Londonderry, on 5 October, commented: 'It was not until heads were
broken in Londonderry that attention of the British Press, public and
Parliament was focussed on Northern Ireland.'

Shortly afterwards Bernadette Devlin rose, explaining that she was
flouting the tradition of being uncontroversial because 'the situation
of my people merits the flouting of such traditions'. She agreed with
the Unionist MP, Robin Chichester-Clark, who had spoken earlier
that 'there never was born an Englishman who understands the Irish
people'. After discussing the renewed violence in Londonderry, she
told MPs:

The situation with which we are faced in Northern Ireland is one in which I feel we can no longer say to the people 'Don't worry about it. Westminster is looking after you.' Westminster cannot condone the existence of this situation. It has on its benches Members of that party who by deliberate policy keep down the ordinary people.

She herself was sitting on the Labour side of the House but she warned, 'I am likely to make myself unpopular on these benches.' And referring to the Ulster Unionist MPs she added, 'Any Socialist Government worth its guts would have got rid of them long ago.' George Brown, the former Deputy Prime Minister, she had heard, with horror, had suggested an O'Neill–Lynch United Party as a solution.[124] This brought home to her that British MPs 'do not understand what is going on. Of all the possible solutions ... the least popular would be an agreement between the two arch-Tories of Ireland'. The question before MPs she said:

in view of the ... lack of understanding which this House has shown to these people in Ulster which it claims to represent, is how in the shortest space it can make up for 50 years of neglect, apathy and lack of understanding.

If British troops went in, 'I should not like to be either the mother or sister of an unfortunate soldier stationed there'. Ulstermen shared one point in common, 'they are not very fond of Englishmen who tell them what to do'. Possibly the most extreme solution was the abolition of Stormont and rule from Westminster. 'Then we would have the ironical situation in which the people who once shouted "Home Rule is Rome Rule" were screaming their heads off for home rule, so dare anyone take Stormont away?' Another solution was for the government to threaten economic sanctions if 'true reforms were not carried out'. But the Unionist government, she said, could not carry out reforms. If they did 'what will the party which is based on and survives on discrimination do?' The government could impose sanctions but 'the Unionist Party will not yield ... one cannot impose economic sanctions on the dead'. Devlin sat down to an ovation and the Tory MP Norman St. John-Stevas remarked: 'Since the time of F.E. Smith I do not suppose that the House of Commons has listened to such an electrifying maiden speech.' Callaghan, who was winding up the debate for the Government, was unstinting in his praise too. She had faced an ordeal and 'emerged with very great brilliance', though he could not accept her negative conclusions.

Writing later Wilson recalled:

It was a remarkable debut, fluent, ordered, confident and not in the slightest degree self conscious. But as I commented to Jim Callaghan ... it was utterly negative.... In particular, she rejected, to the dismay of some of her friends on the Labour benches, the Westminster solution – legislation under Section 75 of the 1920 Act. Equally she rejected any idea of British troops taking over responsibility for law and order.[125]

Crossman's more immediate reaction was similar if harsher:

I am glad I didn't miss the occasion. I ... watched this black, dark, tiny thing standing up in the third row back. The crowded House was spellbound by a tremendous performance. She was ruthless. Everything was barred – the English were hopeless, the Unionists were hopeless, the Orange regime and the O'Neill concessions were hopeless, the Southern Irish government and the English government were hopeless. Everything would lead to disaster and everybody was to blame.... She spent her time building the barricades for a class war. The left-wing Labour backbenchers cheered, all the Members falling over themselves to congratulate her as actors congratulate one another. I suppose that in a few days' time they will realise the significance of what she said.[126]

Paul Rose, who had introduced her, realised the significance of what she said with increasing bitterness:

Her maiden speech was brilliant and then we looked at it and we thought this is totally negative and that business about the Englishman has not yet been born who can understand Ireland was a very chauvinistic remark. She came out with some pretty nasty stuff.

Rose said she regarded her Labour supporters as 'white liberals', and by the time of the 1970 general election 'she was the only MP, with whom I was not on speaking terms. I was on speaking terms with Paisley but not with her. She was totally impossible to work with'.[127]

In the short term, however, the CDU believed that Devlin's arrival at Westminster, like that of Fitt three years before, had done the cause nothing but good. This seemed to be confirmed by Percy Diamond in the *Belfast Telegraph*, who wrote that the debate was regarded by many as marking the end of the convention.[128] This was, of course, the CDU's main objective. Wilson recorded that the day after the debate the Unionists at Stormont voted to accept one man one vote for the next local government elections. However, Chichester-Clark resigned over the issue, and on 28 April Callaghan 'heard and immediately alerted me that Captain O'Neill was resigning'. His departure was marked by an eloquent and moving broadcast. He feared that 'a stormy summer lay ahead'.[129]

Just before O'Neill announced that he was quitting, George Brown, who admired the Ulster premier, decided that the sensation caused by Bernadette Devlin and her reference to him in her maiden speech gave him an opportunity to boost his own radical solution. Brown, who had resigned as Foreign Secretary in rather bizarre circumstances the previous year,[130] was still Deputy Leader of the Labour Party and, although he was later to be regarded with some contempt by his former colleagues, at that time the possibility that he might rejoin the government was raised whenever Wilson contemplated a Cabinet reshuffle.[131] Brown always claimed Irish origins: 'My father's side of the family is of Irish extraction. My grandfather came over from Cork, I believe at a very early age and settled in South-East London ...'.[132] He recalled that 'Irish politics figured large in my early childhood, for there were many Irish people where we lived. The stories of the troubles of Ireland made a very deep impression on me.'[133] On 24 April the *Evening Standard* carried a prominent article by Brown under the headline: 'My Answer to Bernadette'. Brown wrote that in her speech the young MP, 'having clobbered everybody else she then clobbered me'. But she had got it totally wrong, he said, and went on to propose a solution based on the economic integration of Ireland. When both the Republic and the UK joined the Common Market 'there would then be a United Ireland at least in economic terms. Clearly we should then be on the way to overcoming the real problem in Ireland which ... is the opportunities for jobs ...'. He claimed that when he was at the DEA (Department of Economic Affairs) he had tried to develop the economic possibilities of the province.[134] But in practice this was only possible by linking up with the Republic. Achieving this would lead to the 'real issue', Partition. If he were handling affairs he would bring together the Ulster premier and the Prime Minister of the Republic and 'we would then start to talk about how we reach a solution to the problems which are involved in the disappearance of the Border ...'.[135]

But the Deputy Labour Leader's ideas were light years away from those of his old Cabinet colleagues who, according to Crossman, were being dragged to disaster over Northern Ireland. [It should be noted that the material given in italics comes from Crossman's unpublished diaries.] There is a note of sheer despair in his diary entry on the eve of O'Neill's departure. Crossman wrote that the government was taking

> *great lunging leaps into crazy risks. We had leapt into Rhodesia and we had leapt into the European fiasco, we had leapt into that industrial relations bill, in my view we leapt into Anguilla ... and now I am desperately anxious that we are going to leap into another disaster in Northern Ireland. That is the other big story of the week.... Northern Ireland is of course far more important than Rhodesia, infinitely more important than Anguilla, here we are on the edge of civil war.*

O'Neill's government was 'tottering' while Bernadette Devlin was 'announcing a policy of absolutely suicidal class war and destruction'. British troops were committed to maintaining law and order and

> *we are being dragged closer and closer to the precipice of protecting the Orangemen in Ireland. Yet according to Jim Callaghan who has kept in careful touch with me on this here is the PM only concerned now to get over to Northern Ireland as soon as possible as he had to get to Nigeria three weeks ago or to get to Moscow....*

Wilson, wrote Crossman, had 'a passion for being on the spot, being in the news'. The Prime Minister wanted to be active internationally in the way he had stopped strikes at home. Just as he had waited for the chance to intervene in Rhodesia,[136] 'so he is now trying another such adventure and that is all the leadership he is giving us'. Crossman complained that he and Barbara Castle had been left off the Northern Ireland Cabinet Committee, which consisted of Wilson himself, the Foreign Secretary, the Home Secretary and the Minister of Defence. He goes on to say, 'Another sinister thing I have to mention is his Cabinet minutes.' He had noticed that the minutes about Anguilla had not been generally circulated and that though in that week's Cabinet Northern Ireland was discussed, 'that particular piece has not been circulated'. Crossman's private office explained that it would not be circulated without the Prime Minister's personal permission, 'This was news to me', wrote Crossman, adding: 'I had never heard it suggested before that members of the Cabinet should be denied access to minutes of their own meetings'.[137] This meant that Wilson did not want the Anguilla minutes circulated until he had made sure that they were 'tolerable for the historical record. So you will see why it is important that I describe in this diary what happens in Cabinet'.[138]

In that entry Crossman referred to the Northern Ireland Cabinet Committee. Unfortunately very little is yet known about this committee other than its membership. In the opinion of the *Sunday Times* Insight Team it was probably not set up until July. This is clearly incorrect because Crossman refers to it in an entry for April.[139]

CONCLUSION

It was tragic for Ulster's future that O'Neill's resignation, and with it the end of O'Neillism, should have coincided with serious turmoil in the Wilson government. Crossman is not always a reliable witness but on this occasion his alarm about the state of Cabinet government that Spring has been corroborated by leading British historians. Ben Pimlott wrote:

> Between April and June 1969 the main talking point in British politics was Wilson, and the leadership question. It was widely felt ... that the Prime Minister could not survive until the election.[140]

Much of the trouble was caused by warfare in the Labour Party over Barbara Castle's *In Place of Strife* programme for trade union reform, with Callaghan siding with the trade unions against the measure. 'Against a background of visible prime ministerial weakness the Government entered a phase of near anarchy. Wilson was attacked by almost everybody, and there were moments when he seemed to be kept in office only by the disunity of his detractors.'[141] Kenneth Morgan recalled that an Inner Cabinet was trying 'to reassert the Government's authority. But this was increasingly hard to achieve with a key minister like Callaghan in open revolt yet too important to sack ...'. There was 'a general feeling in the country that the government was in a state of perhaps terminal crisis'.[142]

The crisis also meant that the two ministers with most responsibility for Northern Ireland, Wilson and Callaghan, were at loggerheads, something which must have ruled out any initiative. Both men seemed to be governed, temporarily at least, by the primacy of their own personal prospects, political survival in the case of Wilson, ambition for the top job in the case of Callaghan,[143] and Ulster may have paid the price with 25 years of bloodshed. It has been argued that the essential nature of armed conflict is to destroy things and kill people:

> The highest duty on politicians in authority is, therefore, to ensure

that all steps that can be taken to avoid war, whether through early preventative action, quality diplomacy or high class intelligence, are taken.[144]

On this criteria the Wilson Cabinet failed to fulfil their 'highest duty'.

It is true that for the six months since the events of 5 October in Londonderry there had been faint hopes that Ulster would solve its own problems: O'Neill's Five Point Programme; the 'Crossroads' speech; the general election; but they had all come to nothing. The pessimism of the retired civil servant's 'totally fictitious' minute mentioned earlier had been borne out. In normal times a confident government would hardly have waited to see whether James Chichester-Clark, a weaker man than O'Neill whom he had replaced as Prime Minister, would take the necessary steps to stave off disaster. As is disclosed in the chapter that follows secret plans for an intervention were well under way in Whitehall. But as Crossman had shown these were not normal times and it was not a confident government.

A final word on O'Neill is appropriate here. A consistent theme of this account has been that Harold Wilson's policy of 'leaving it to O'Neill', was a risky business. Now it had collapsed. As recorded earlier, Paul Bew had regarded O'Neill's pro-Catholic reformism as 'non-existent'. In a recent reassessment of the Ulster premier, Professor Bew acknowledged that he was 'essentially a man of decent tolerant instincts'. Nevertheless Bew confirmed his original view that O'Neill saw little role for structural reform. He 'espoused a rhetoric of planning and modernisation by which nationalist grievances would be dissolved by shared participation in the benefits of economic growth'. Although he had inflicted a heavy defeat on the Northern Ireland Labour Party (in 1965) he was 'widely perceived to be a poor party manager. Normally secretive and aloof at times he was capable of indiscreet and hurtful sarcasm at the expense of prickly senior colleagues'. O'Neill's legacy, Bew concluded, was ambiguous ... 'He was a patrician figure out of touch with large sections of the population.'[145] Even a close friend like Sayers came to believe that O'Neill could not succeed. Sayers, in a private letter, wrote, 'I have never been able to satisfy my mind about the PM's liberalism – it's far more intellectual than emotional and even then much of it originates with Bloomfield.'[146] On another occasion Sayers described O'Neill as 'this somewhat lonely and sometimes arrogant and awkward man, stamped by Eton and the Irish Guards'.[147] Now that O'Neill had gone, Wilson had, in theory, three options: to turn the financial screw on Stormont [he had threatened this often enough]; to announce a deadline for intervention under Section 75 of the Government of Ireland Act; or to engage in masterly inactivity and wait and see what happened during the 'stormy summer' he himself had forecast.

7 To the Top of the Agenda, May–August 1969

> One saw a spectrum including troops in support of the civil power
> and including direct rule but not immediately
>
> Sir John Chilcot[1]

This chapter covers the brief period between O'Neill's resignation
and the British government's decision to intervene at last by sending
troops to contain the violence in the Bogside area of Londonderry.
The historian Geoffrey Bell has noted that Wilson later called
Londonderry 'the culmination of nearly fifty years of the unimagina-
tive inertia and repression of successive and unchallenged … Ulster
Unionist government'. The Labour government, said Wilson, 'had to
act at the eleventh hour after years of neglect'.[2] However, claimed
Bell, 'the Wilson administration of the Sixties was part of that inertia'.
Eleventh hour or not Wilson's own Cabinet 'had spent five years
watching the clock ticking and done nothing'.[3] Bell's analysis of
Wilson and his colleagues is largely accurate. However, he goes too
far in saying that nothing was done. As this chapter will reveal for the
first time, the government had begun, however reluctantly, to prepare
for intervention in Ulster during the winter of 1968–9: the '10th hour'
perhaps. The main evidence for this is provided by a senior civil
servant who retired in 1998. Callaghan, too, over the last 25 years has
thrown out some hints of contingency plans made by the government.
The question that arises then is not so much why was there no plan for
intervention? There was. The real question is why did the government
wait until the brink of civil war in the province before acting? And
why when at last the troops went in did the government shrink from
imposing direct rule from Westminster as so many have since argued
that it should have, not least O'Neill?[4]

The chapter also considers a damning report on civil rights in Ulster
compiled by the International Commission of Jurists and published
just two months before the eruption of sectarian violence. The
disagreement in Cabinet over whether the Apprentice Boys' March
on 12 August, 1969, should be banned and Wilson's own bizarre position, momentarily in favour of direct rule, are analysed. With the

entry of troops the chronological section ends. It seems the right place to stop: the Labour government's policy of non-intervention had failed and historians and journalists have provided a great deal of information about what happened next [not least the irony of the political rehabilitation of James Callaghan, whose handling of the Ulster question has often been contrasted with his difficulties as Chancellor of the Exchequer.] The Cameron report (Chapter 6, n.66) on the causes of the earlier violence, which was not published until a month after the troops went in, is also considered briefly. Though its terms of reference did not include the subject of this book's main argument, the Labour government's Northern Ireland policy, its conclusions are relevant because they seem to buttress the argument that the British government was guilty of inertia. This chapter will reveal, however, again for the first time, that the official who drew up the report now has misgivings about the conclusions, something which may go some way to exonerating the Labour government of the time.

The *Sunday Times* Insight Team, writing three years after the event, claimed that following O'Neill's resignation it was reasonable:

> to look for evidence that some major debate began at this point inside the British Government, perhaps the drawing up of contingency plans, to implement the threats now brandished at Stormont. None of this took place.[5]

This is simply not true. The year after the publication of the Insight book, Callaghan himself, without giving any details, wrote:

> On my initiative contingency plans had been drawn up in the winter of 1968 making provision for the government of Northern Ireland.[6]

In addition, the entry in Barbara Castle's diary for 16 September 1969 [a month after the troops went in] recorded that a meeting of the Cabinet was informed that a Northern Ireland Bill providing for take-over by London was ready in draft. Wilson, wrote Castle, interposed, saying: 'Those who accuse of us of not preparing for events might like to know we got it ready in March.'[7]

At the ICBH seminar in 1992, though his memory appeared to be a little shaky, Callaghan gave some indication of what had been going on that winter. The question of sending troops to Northern Ireland had been raised and, he said, 'It was in 1968 as a matter of fact.'

Discussions took place with O'Neill who was insisting that such troops would remain under Northern Ireland government command. Callaghan added, 'I am pretty sure in my recollection that the record will show that we were discussing this with O'Neill in 1968 … and [O'Neill] being very resistant to them going in under the conditions that we would allow.' Callaghan recalled that he would say to O'Neill,

> Look here, they can be used in aid of the civil power of course, but if a riot of the kind of proportions that you envisage took place in Durham it would be the British government that would take charge not the Durham County Council. And frankly on this basis I regarded them as much like the London County Council.

The province's population, he pointed out, was only million and a half: 'We weren't going to hand over to a government especially of that complexion.'[8]

Callaghan also talked more vaguely a few months later in an interview for the BBC television programme, *Timewatch*. He said: 'I think there were preparations [for military intervention] … there was some discussion with O'Neill.' Protesting that his recollection was 'so foggy' after 30 years, he said he recalled O'Neill, 'in posing this possibility that troops might be needed wanted them placed in his hands for him to control'. Callaghan said he had made it clear that it 'was for the British Government to handle British troops not for them to be placed under the hands of a Parliament which is in certain circumstances independent, namely Stormont'. Callaghan was asked about Crossman's claim [recorded in the previous chapter] that in early 1969 he (Callaghan) told him about secret contingency plans to deal with a possible collapse of the Northern Ireland government. Callaghan replied: 'Well, of course, you always have to take anything Dick says with a pinch of salt. But if he says I told him that, probably it's true.'[9]

However, until the present research was carried out, little further was known about these contingency plans initiated by Callaghan. The new light has been provided by Sir John Chilcot, who retired from his post as Permanent Secretary at the Northern Ireland Office in 1998. He was a young civil servant in the 1960s and was involved in drawing up the plans at the Home Office for intervention in Northern Ireland.[10]

Chilcot was responsible for most of the United Kingdom government's relations with the Northern Ireland government, other than matters of finance, etc. as one half of the workload of his post at the time. He said:

I remember there was relief over O'Neill's liberal policies and the North–South *rapprochement*. The civil rights protests came as a surprise, an unwelcome surprise to the Unionist government.[11]

At the end of 1968 he was given other responsibilities but within a few weeks he was asked to carry out a task for the Home Secretary.

Jim Callaghan wanted preparatory work done seeing the coming crisis. He wanted ... this work done in the event of a worsening situation. Was the potential for violence exceeding the power of the local authorities to cope with it?[12]

It was then that a contingency planning process was initiated. 'I wrote a book about it', said Chilcot, 'covering scale, the law, logistics and constitutional legislation. It included the constitutional position that arose when the civil power was "challenged."'[13] His next remark confirmed that the abolition of Stormont and the imposition of Direct Rule was being considered long before the intervention in August 1969. He said: 'One saw a spectrum including troops in support of the civil power and including direct rule but not immediately.' Previously the only evidence for such thinking was Callaghan's rather opaque reference to making provision for the Government of Northern Ireland in his 1973 memoirs (see above).

Chilcot stressed that no change in the province's constitutional position in relation to the Republic was part of the planning. He added,

Nor, of course, was any such change implied either in Sunningdale or subsequently. Successive British governments have been unswerving in upholding the constitutional guarantee in both its 1920 and 1973 [Sunningdale] formulations.[14]

The most significant revelation by Chilcot relates to the legislation that was being prepared in secret. This was not, it is clear, to do with direct rule. 'When the Government papers for the period are available in 1999–2000 successive draft bills will be revealed', he said. 'We wanted some political footing for the policies.' These draft bills were dealing with security only but, he added:

that is not to suppose that the British government of the time had no interests in any address to the civil rights and nationalist agenda. Wider policies towards Northern Ireland were, of course, proceeding independently of the exercise in which I was engaged.[15]

Chilcot also made it clear that the government had been worried about the effectiveness of the Army in dealing with disorder on the streets if it came to intervention. It was, he said, a question of whether the Army 'had the experience and training for dealing with civil unrest in domestic protest terms as against those in overseas and colonial situations'. He added:

> The Grosvenor Square Riot [1968] was the first taste we had had of such domestic protests. That event showed that the police service ... was going through a process of learning and experience in dealing with civil protest on a large scale and of a more violent kind than had hitherto been experienced in the post-war era.

Chilcot said that the Army would also 'have to undergo a process of learning and training in what was before 1969 an unfamiliar task'.[16]

The wide scope of Chilcot's plans makes nonsense of those who argue that the Wilson government did nothing 'as the clock ticked by'. Sir Oliver Wright, appointed UK Government Representative in Northern Ireland when the troops went in, recalled, 20 years later that he had been surprised how lacking the Home Office was in ideas 'for handling the current situation'. He explained, 'I had come from the Foreign Office where whenever there was a problem the department concerned had lots of recommendations that seemed to them to be the most promising action.' However, he had found a meeting at the Home Office 'a silent thing with all the officials waiting for the Secretary of State to speak'.[17] Yet had not Wright misjudged the Home Office? We now know that it was the equal to the Foreign Office when it came to plans, in Wright's words, 'to handle the current situation'. However, Chilcot's implication that Grosvenor Square was treated retrospectively as, in effect, a war game for dealing with civil unrest within the United Kingdom has been rebutted by another senior civil servant. Asked for his view, Sir Frank Cooper, who was Deputy Under Secretary at the Ministry of Defence at the time, said:

> I do not believe for a moment that Grosvenor Square rioting had more than at best a marginal effect in providing useful lessons in Ulster. At the time British police and Home Office links with Northern Ireland were very thin indeed. The Army ... were largely influenced by Colonial troubles ... Grosvenor Square did not lead to training for Ulster. The troops at first were conditioned by Colonial experience. Moreover, the Army hates being mixed up with rioting civilians....[18]

The admission by Chilcot that the spectrum of planning included direct rule 'but not immediately', is intriguing. As we shall see, Wilson himself was to consider direct rule, briefly, in the days immediately before the troops went in, only to reject it. A former Northern Ireland senior civil servant, Arthur Green, believed that the Cabinet was persuaded not only by Unionist politicians but by leading Catholics that Stormont was still 'reformable'.[19] There is more on this subject at the end of the chapter.

While the Home Office plans were being drawn up, the Cabinet itself still hesitated. Wilson was due to have talks with the new Ulster Premier, James Chichester-Clark, on 22 May when, it was presumed, he would be demanding no backsliding on reform. But according to Bell the government's Northern Ireland policy 'was now shrouded in secrecy, confined to discussion among the most senior members of the Cabinet'. Tony Benn [a member of that Cabinet], wrote Bell, once told a Labour conference fringe meeting that there were only two occasions when the Labour governments of the 60s and 70s ever discussed Northern Ireland in full Cabinet: when the troops went in and during the Ulster Workers' strike in 1974.[20]

However, as Bell pointed out, the Crossman *Diaries* mention several other discussions.[21] One of these was on 7 May 1969. Crossman wrote, 'the main subject is Northern Ireland again. Now the Cabinet was asking and insisting on its right to discuss it'. And, he added 'it became clearer and clearer today that the Cabinet wanted to know more about Harold's intentions in Northern Ireland. Barbara began to ask questions and the more we studied the paper giving the various so-called possibilities the more dubious we became. It was suggested that we were constitutionally bound to let our troops be used to defend law and order in Northern Ireland'.

Most of what follows is from the unpublished diaries of Richard Crossman; italics are used, here and in the rest of the chapter, as before, to indicate material that comes from the unpublished diaries.[22] When Crossman asked his colleagues, '*would it be a good thing with the possibility of civil war and suppressing the Catholics or not suppressing the Catholics if we know something about Northern Ireland*', he said, 'Callaghan replied, "I don't think we really need that. After all I am seeing Chichester-Clark every day". He resisted the whole idea saying it was absurd and that the Northern Ireland government would dislike our behaving in this way, though it would be all right if we were to ask them for ideas.' Crossman added that he was suggesting to his colleagues that the government needed political

intelligence as it had during the war: 'If we have to know about Russia
and every other country in the world, we should at least spend some
money finding out something about Northern Ireland.' Wilson
supported Callaghan, but

> Denis Healey came in on my side, saying 'Frankly, Northern
> Ireland has completely different conditions from Britain and we
> shall be as blind men leading the blind if we have to go in knowing
> nothing about the place.'[23]

Crossman also reported Callaghan, 'in the course of an hour of fighting, saying "I am working with a very small staff. I actually only have
two men on Northern Ireland".' After five years, Crossman wrote,

> in which I and others have believed that we must have a basis of
> sound intelligence and sound information on which to base our
> policy, this is the way we prepare for the possibility that we might
> have to take over direct rule of Northern Ireland.[24]

Crossman then recorded a remarkable conversation with Healey
about what was referred to as Wilson's 'crazy' attitude:

> As we went out of the room, Healey said to me, 'You have no idea
> what it was like before you came on to the Committee. The Prime
> Minister was always demanding active intervention early on, with
> this crazy desire to go there and take things over, that we should
> side with the Roman Catholics and Civil Rights movement against
> the government and the RUC, though we know nothing at all about
> it.'[25]

Crossman said that one of the questions he had asked during the
meeting was

> whether we had any reliable information about the work of the
> RUC. Did we have an objective view as to how far they were
> oppressive to the Catholics? Of course I gather they are oppressive
> but we haven't got any reliable picture of the degree of their
> oppression.

Crossman then returned to his obsession with Cabinet secrecy
mentioned in the previous chapter. '*I have noticed the Cabinet minutes
as usual, this bit of the Cabinet minutes are kept for Top Secret, and I
have yet to see what is in it and what commitment we have made.*'[26]
Wilson meanwhile did not share Crossman's despair. Unaccount-
ably he seemed to feel that Chichester-Clark might succeed where

O'Neill had failed. Three years later he observed that Faulkner 'became a tower of strength' to Chichester-Clark helping him to carry through the decision to bring in universal adult franchise at the next local government elections. Chichester-Clark himself, said Wilson, 'quickly became the Prime Minister who saw it through'. Wilson also noted that the Ulster premier had introduced an amnesty for political offenders 'designed to cool the continuing disturbances'.[27] In the House of Commons Wilson spoke optimistically about his forthcoming meeting with the new Ulster Premier. He had been asked by Paul Rose, Chairman of the CDU, to impress on Chichester-Clark the need for the immediate implementation of reform. Wilson told him that everyone in a position of authority in the province knew what he and Callaghan had said to O'Neill and his colleagues at Downing Street. He added: 'We are not in any sense varying what we said to them … they are fully aware of the need for urgency….' Replying to the Conservative Leader, Edward Heath, who had indicated that the Opposition fully supported the reforms, Wilson said that O'Neill had paid 'a heavy price' for recognising what needed to be done. 'It is now important that this programme should continue.'[28]

There was some support for Wilson's renewed confidence from Ulster itself. *The Times* reported an apparent lull in sectarian bitterness. The headline declared: 'New policies bring calm at last to Ulster'. Their correspondent, Tim Jones, wrote, 'After months of bitter weekend clashes, the proposed reforms announced last week by Major Chichester-Clark seem to have taken the steam out of militants on both sides.' For the first time since October, said Jones,

> an air of normality has returned to the Province. Civil Rights marchers seem content to sit back and wait for concessions and that the extreme Protestants have accepted the situation for the present was shown on Friday when Paisley's victory meeting attracted only 400 people.[29]

In the run up to the talks with the new Ulster leadership the question of the subsidy for the province came up yet again. Writing in the *Belfast Telegraph* Roy Lilley referred to Chichester-Clark's claim that he would have 'a good story' on reform to tell Wilson when he saw him the following week. Lilley suggested that Wilson would emphasise to Chichester-Clark that London's view of this 'good story' would depend upon whether it persuaded him and the Treasury into making, in the official phrase, another special contribution to 'the economic well being of Northern Ireland'.[30]

However, the CDU had more ominous concerns in mind when, on the eve of the talks, their president, Lord Brockway [the former Labour MP Fenner Brockway], and secretary, Paddy Byrne, wrote to *The Times*. They had clearly not been impressed by the apparent relaxation of tension in the province. Instead they warned of the danger of 'civil strife' if reforms were not implemented immediately. In their letter, headed 'Future of Ulster', they feared that 'one man one vote' was 'being withheld until the grouping of various councils into larger units, suitably gerrymandered ... is completed ...'. They urged Wilson to make it clear to Chichester-Clark

> that to continue to deny fundamental human rights to one third of the population is intolerable. Unless immediate and far reaching concessions are made the only alternative is civil strife leading presumably to the suspension of the constitution and direct rule from Westminster.[31]

Tragically, the first half of their prophecy was to come true within three months. The second, direct rule, took another three years.

The talks, held the following day, were to be the last before the decision was taken to intervene. According to *The Times*, Wilson spent 90 minutes with the Ulster leaders, who told him about 'the new approach in Ulster'.[32] The British Prime Minister seems to have been convinced. In a special statement at the end of Prime Minister's Questions on 22 May[33] he said that he had been assured that the new franchise for local government elections would be clearly seen to be fair and impartial. The Ulster leaders had also told him that in future the system for allocating local authority housing would be 'of demonstrable fairness'. The Northern Ireland ministers had appreciated the embarrassment caused to Britain internationally by the Special Powers Act but its removal would require a period of calm. Wilson told MPs that he

> was reasonably satisfied yesterday on hearing the plans of the new government that what Captain O'Neill fought for will now become a reality, and within the urgent time-scale which all of us regard as being necessary.

Some members of the CDU however did not share Wilson's confidence in Chichester-Clark. Kevin McNamara told him that suspicion had been aroused by the delay in holding local elections in Northern Ireland and in abolishing the 'invidious' Special Powers Act. The Liberal MP, Eric Lubbock, was also worried about the delayed elections and called for the immediate rescinding of the Special Powers Act. Wilson replied that O'Neill's government had been on the point of abolishing the Special Powers Act the very week in April when installations in the province were bombed. 'In the circumstances nobody could blame them for not proceeding further.'

Gerry Fitt cast doubt on the genuine reforming instincts of the new Stormont administration which, he claimed, included 'an intake of extreme right-wing people who may prevent the new Prime Minister … from implementing reforms'. Tempers rose when the Conservative leader, Edward Heath, referred to 'extremists' sitting behind Wilson which McNamara assumed meant the CDU MPs in the Parliamentary Labour Party and unsuccessfully called on the Speaker to rule the remark out of order. Wilson, however, sympathised with McNamara, and criticised the Conservative leader for his remarks. Labour MPs and many Tories, he said, 'are showing great patience about the need for reform, considering that responsibility lies so heavily on those who had responsibility in Northern Ireland for 50 years'. Finally Wilson revealed to MPs that following the fall of O'Neill he had feared that his successor would renege on the reforms. However, 'I am now fully satisfied that everything for which he is working will be carried through on a reasonable time scale.'

In the light of Crossman's diary entry showing that he, and more significantly Denis Healey, the Defence Secretary, were alarmed about the British government's lack of knowledge about what was really happening on the ground in Northern Ireland it is clear that Wilson had no basis for an optimism that verged on the complacent. This, ironically, was a view shared by the *Belfast Telegraph*. A scathing editorial pointed out that several commentators had noted that Wilson's statement 'showed the same kind of optimism that was used to describe similar meetings over the past four years or more'. The paper said that 'the momentum of change which Roy Jenkins had commended when Home Secretary proved not nearly fast enough and the tendency to pigeon-hole the Northern Ireland problem from one commotion to the next has still to be resisted …'. Wilson should be given much of the credit along with the civil rights movement for the acceptance of the one man one vote principle but, added the editorial, 'it must be hoped that his confidence in the Stormont Government's intentions to produce an impartial boundary view is not misplaced'.[34] Sayers had retired through ill health and it is not known who wrote this bleak leading article but it showed a greater grasp of realities than the British government. Sayers, though unwell, was still watching events and, in a letter to a friend, reported that David Lindsay Keir had said of the Unionist Party, 'The tide has come in but the rocks are still underneath.' Sayers thought that this was 'very descriptive of people who had been forced to accept so much of Terence's [O'Neill's] belief but still don't like it'.[35] The following day Alice Bacon echoed these fears. She warned the Northern Ireland Labour Party conference that the agreement between Wilson and Chichester-Clark might be impeded by extremists.[36]

The period of relative calm in the province, the last for 25 years, continued until the riots of 12 July. During that time a highly critical report on the British government's policy in Northern Ireland was published by the International Commission of Jurists (ICJ).[37] *The Times* reported the Commission's findings under the heading 'Britain is accused on Ulster'. The report said that from its headquarters in Geneva the Commission 'criticised the Northern Ireland Government for police brutality, religious discrimination and gerrymandering in politics'. The criticism was made in the Commission's quarterly review. Its secretary-general, Sean MacBride, described by *The Times* as a prominent Dublin lawyer and former Irish Foreign Minister, said that the study of Ulster had been made by about ten members of the commission's legal staff of all nationalities. It was based on official documents and published material. MacBride said that 'the study was carried out in the normal course of events. Other countries had been surveyed'.[38] MacBride also claimed that legislation and conditions in Northern Ireland had frequently been cited by the South African government 'to justify their own policies of discrimination'. He added that the South African Prime Minister had said that his Special Powers Act was modelled on, but less Draconian than, the special powers of the Northern Ireland government. *The Times* also reported fears of the commission that the B Specials, 'regarded as the militant arm of the Orange Order', might be used in future to put down civil rights demonstrations. Other targets for criticism included the Special Powers Act 1922, which allowed indefinite internment without charge or trial, and 'gerrymandering ... which deprives Roman Catholics of proper representation'.[39]

The reaction of the Northern Ireland government was carried in the same report. A spokesman said that the Special Powers Act had not been used since 1962, adding, 'Northern Ireland is the only part of the UK which faces intermittent armed attack.' The government 'had said repeatedly that when it is able to do so it will repeal the Act'. It was also pointed out that one man one vote would soon apply to all council elections.[40] That somewhat low key statement in *The Times* was followed by a much more robust response by Stormont ministers in the local paper that afternoon. No doubt their anger was fuelled by the fact that MacBride was among the most prominent pre-war IRA leaders and was reputedly chief-of-staff for a time.[41] Stormont's fury was the main news story on the *Belfast Telegraph's* front page. The headline said: 'Government to protest over scandal allegations. Stormont attacks outrageous report'.

The paper reported, 'The Stormont government announced today that it would lodge a formal protest with the International Commission of Jurists at the earliest opportunity ...'. The paper quoted Chichester-Clark saying that the Commission's allegations were 'inaccurate incomplete and tendentious' and a front-page editorial called it a 'rather shoddy piece of work'. However, it was reported inside the paper that the Commission had added Northern Ireland to the list of Spain, Portugal, Greece and Eastern Europe 'where the protection of human rights is inadequately assured'.[42]

The argument over the Commission's findings, however, was soon to become academic as the province began the slide into turmoil. It started on 12 July after the traditional Orange parades,[43] and three days of looting and burning shops in Londonderry followed. The British Cabinet now began to consider the question of banning future marches as a matter of urgency. The outcome of their deliberations is still controversial, which is inevitable given that 25 years of violence followed the final decision to allow the Apprentice Boys' March on 12 August. The Cabinet papers were not due to be released until 2000 [if then] and Crossman for once was silent in his diary. However, the *Sunday Times* Insight Team wrote that both Wilson and Healey favoured a ban but not Callaghan, and 'Callaghan was a figure no one could ignore'.[44]

Callaghan had been told that the RUC had not the resources to impose a ban and Home Office officials persuaded him that 'there was a fair chance of the parades passing off peacefully'. Insight claimed that Callaghan talked to Chichester-Clark and reported that the Ulster premier would be brought down by a ban. 'Reluctantly the Cabinet agreed to the marches'.[45] Wilson is scathing, in retrospect, about this decision. Clearly referring to Callaghan he wrote:

Consideration had been given to prohibiting the march, and I had originally favoured this course. But unwiser counsels had prevailed....[46]

In 1992 Callaghan was asked whether he was one of Wilson's 'unwiser counsels'. He replied:

> I don't recall but probably … I don't remember whether the Apprentice Boys' march was intended to march through areas that would have provoked Catholics … but if so … I certainly ought to have taken a different view.[47]

Even at the time Callaghan had clearly been aware of the great danger of allowing the march to go ahead. McNamara recalled a CDU delegation going to see the Home Secretary to urge him to ban the march. 'Callaghan said he spoke [*sic*] to Chichester-Clark who told him they could contain it.' However, said McNamara, precautions were taken, 'battalions were put on standby and soldiers in mufti at the gates watching what was going on'.[48] At the ICBH seminar McNamara had put a similar point to Callaghan. He said that the army were watching every aspect of the march 'so you obviously were concerned about it'. Callaghan agreed.[49] Paul Rose took a more critical view of Callaghan. He said, 'We could not believe that they could be so stupid as to allow that march. It was going to be a total provocation.' He compared it with Mosley's marches against the Jews through the East End of London before the war and added, 'To allow that was going to create enormous confrontation. To this day I don't understand how it was permitted.' Callaghan, said Rose, was either naive 'or was he influenced by a predilection for the Unionists?' He thought the Government preferred trouble to come from the minority rather than the majority. 'That was the pattern throughout', he said, 'greater fear of the Protestant backlash by doing the right thing than fear of violence from the minority by doing the wrong thing'. Callaghan, he believed, had 'allowed himself to be manipulated by the Unionists'.[50]

It is difficult to be convinced by Rose's view that as sophisticated (not to say wily) a politician as Callaghan could be manipulated by a man who was in Callaghan's own mind not much more than leader of a county council. In fact when Callaghan saw the CDU delegation his sturdy defence of his policy suggests not so much a man being manipulated as one who was confident of success in the long run. The *Belfast Telegraph's* London Editor, who had 'doorstepped' the meeting, reported on the case made by the Home Secretary to a highly sceptical audience. Callaghan, he wrote, drew attention to the extensive programme of reforms undertaken by Stormont and urged how desirable it was that the problems of Northern Ireland should be solved in Northern Ireland without any outside intervention. Replying to a suggestion that Home Office observers should be sent to Ulster, Callaghan expressed doubt that this could be possible without the consent of Stormont. In any event, he said, the Home Office gained a pretty good picture of the situation in the province from the press and other sources. The Home Secretary reminded the deputation that many of the reforms taking place in Ulster were achieved without any intervention at all. The MPs were clearly not convinced by Callaghan. One of them, Stan Orme, Labour MP for Salford, West [who was to become a member of Callaghan's Cabinet], told Diamond later that the CDU did not believe that Stormont was strong enough to deal with the current and potential situation. Another, Russell Kerr, Labour MP for Feltham and Heston, predicted a major political and social breakdown following the march and said that they felt that this was not a matter from which any British government could stand aside.[51] Kerr, a popular figure at Westminster, but [from the government's point of view] marginalised by his left-wing stance, turned out to be right.

An alternative argument in favour of banning the march has been provided by Roy Hattersley[52] who, as his number two at the Ministry of Defence briefly deputised for Healey during the Defence Secretary's illness. Hattersley said of the proposed march,

> We were against it ... for military reasons. We weren't against it for reasons of civil rights or the pressure of the minority population. We didn't believe we could manage it. We didn't believe we could control things if it got out of hand. We did not think there were enough troops there to deal with it.[53]

Jack Sayers too was fearful of what the marches could bring. Sayers, who as it turned out had only six weeks to live, explained, in a letter to a friend, how distressed he had been by the violence after the 12 July march.

> if I were still editor I would not know what to say. Both extremes are gaining strength and the more they do the more I fear for Northern Ireland's ability to survive.[54]

Sadly, Sayers had a massive heart attack on 30 August and died. On Sayers' retirement Lindsay Keir had spoken of Sayers' influence over events in Ulster and, on the first anniversary of his death in 1970, Terence O'Neill said that had Sayers been listened to, 'some of the terrible things that have happened might not have happened'.[55]

There was more rioting in Ulster on 2 August and Paul Rose publicly urged Callaghan to relieve Stormont of control of the RUC and take it over personally.[56] However, the Home Secretary was firm. After the Orange marches in July, he recalled later, 'the advice came to me from all sides: on no account get sucked into the Irish bog. We decided we would wait'.[57] In his view intervention along the lines recommended by Rose would simply make matter worse.[58] When, on 3 August Chichester-Clark requested help from the Army, the Cabinet agreed in principle to the use of troops, but Callaghan made it 'very clear' to Northern Ireland ministers that 'the last thing I would want would be to take over the government of Northern Ireland. We knew little enough at first hand of what was going on and had few reliable means of finding out'.[59] This was the result, presumably, of the decision of the Chiefs of Staff in 1966 not to recommend beefing up intelligence in the province at the time of the IRA threat of violence to mark the 50th anniversary of the Easter Rising.[60] It is in any case a remarkable admission from Callaghan in the light of his comment [as reported by the *Belfast Telegraph* London Editor] to the CDU that there was no need to send Home Office observers to Ulster because they had 'a pretty good picture of the situation in the province from the press and other sources'. Two days later *The Times*, which only a few months earlier had been hailing the apparent return to normality in the province, demanded a ban on the marches. An editorial declared:

> the causes of violence are so deeply implanted in Ulster society, hatred has come so near the surface again, and the prospect so uncertain, that it is necessary to contemplate the possibility of chronic violence beyond the capacity of the Ulster police to control.[61]

It was at this point that Wilson seems to have threatened direct rule if troops had to go in. John Bourne, the political correspondent of the *Financial Times* reported on 6 August that, 'British troops would be used to restore law and order in Ulster only if the Northern Ireland government first agreed to surrender its political authority to Westminster'.[62] The source for this, the *Sunday Times* Insight Team claimed, was 'Harold huffing and puffing about not being a rubber stamp for Stormont'.[63] Bourne was a highly respected and experienced lobby correspondent. He was one of small number of political journalists at Westminster who still retained Wilson's confidence and had probably spoken to him directly.[64] However, according to a civil servant, whatever Wilson had been saying he was bluffing about taking over control.[65] O'Neill certainly believed that direct rule should have been imposed once the troops went in,[66] and Paul Bew has asked why the Government did not take over immediately and 'cut the grass from underneath the Provisionals', instead of 'propping up the ramshackle apparatus of Protestant domination'.[67] Roy Lilley recalled that 'the big expectation at that time was that there would be dramatic political change.' But, he said,

> Wilson pulled back and again I think that was old thinking emerging again: no alternative to sending in the troops but we'll not get involved to a greater extent than was absolutely necessary. We'll still have the buffer state.[68]

Crossman suggested that the Cabinet went as far as threatening Stormont with direct rule in the days before the Apprentice Boys' March which *'everybody is dreading'*. Crossman wrote, *'We had it specially discussed in Cabinet and we had the Irish PM over here talking to Callaghan and talking about the place of British troops, Callaghan making it clear that the British troops should only be used in the last resort and if they are we can't hold ourselves responsible without becoming responsible for the country.'*

But, Crossman added, *'of course we are bluffing in all that'*. He thought that *'if a crisis did come the troops would go in and we wouldn't throw Chichester-Clark out and we would find ourselves supporting the Orangemen in Northern Ireland'*.[69]

When it was finally decided that Chichester-Clark's request for troops should be granted, direct rule does not seem to have been considered a serious option by the Cabinet. Callaghan was asked about this many years later. He said:

> Not only would it not have been politically possible at that time to have abandoned Stormont because public opinion wouldn't have been ready for it, but we would not have been in a position to handled the situation.

It was far better for Stormont to handle the problem providing they accepted civil rights and introduced the reforms that the British government wanted.[70]

The decision to send in the troops has been described by the man who actually gave the order, Roy Hattersley, deputising for Healey. Hattersley recalled that at first the request from Stormont had been turned down. He received a message from Wilson saying that 'we had been quite right not to rush into the momentous decision to send troops on to the streets of Northern Ireland. "Once we do that, they may be there for weeks".' However, with the eruption of communal violence after the Apprentice Boys' March, the request, now backed up by Bernardette Devlin in a personal telephone call to Hattersley arguing that 'Catholics would be slaughtered', could no longer be resisted. 'I went through the formalities of consultation', wrote Hattersley,

> sought and obtained James Callaghan's approval, and became after I had signed the Army Board Order 'the man who sent the army onto the streets of Northern Ireland'.

That was the accusation shouted at him by Republicans but 'they rarely added that I had responded to the urgent request of Bernardette Devlin ...'.[71]

The violence of the next few days resulted in Northern Ireland receiving attention from the press and television normally reserved for the mainland. Wilson had no doubt about the impact. For years the British people had thought that the violence that had occurred in the United States and France 'can't happen here'. But now, he wrote,

> the scenes of bloody violence reported by the press and still more dramatically shown on the television screens, brought home to the British people that law and order had totally broken down.

He recalled that he had said on television that 'this was not just on our door step ... it is in our house'.[72] An editorial in *The Times*, under the heading 'This Madness' said that the folly of allowing the Apprentice Boys' march was now tragically apparent.[73]

Crossman seemed to relish the way the crisis was dominating the news. Two days after the troops went in he wrote: '*And this week it has been Northern Ireland. Even the steel strike has been driven on to the bottom of the front pages, the French devaluation has almost been forgotten and the pound driven to low ebbs which followed the French devaluation.*' This '*has also ceased to be a great sensation because of Ireland*'.[74]

Crossman also recorded a conversation with the Home Secretary at Prunier's restaurant just before the troops went in. Callaghan told him that 'he was working out in the Ministry either a partial or a total take-over which would have to be presented to the Cabinet'. Crossman himself wondered whether a United Nations peace-keeping force might be the answer. He did not think the Cabinet could admit that the UN had the right to intervene in an internal affair but 'Barbara Castle might have this temptation and so might I. Otherwise I think we shall find that Cabinet will agree to a constitutional experiment fairly easily'.[75]

The political weeklies now had their first chance to comment on the dramatic turn of events. The Editor of the left-wing *New Statesman*, Paul Johnson, writing on the eve of the decision to send in troops, said the violence had been almost universally predicted. It proved that the Chichester-Clark regime was 'weak, divided, vacillating and incompetent'. Johnson feared that the 'drift to civil war has accelerated', and that the problem was beyond Stormont's control.[76]

From the right, however, the *Spectator* believed that Northern Ireland was very far from being out of control. Troops, it accepted, might be needed for longer than many people thought but that did not mean invoking Section 75 of the Government of Ireland Act, 1920 and abolishing Stormont. The Chichester-Clark government was going ahead with 'one man one vote' reform. There was 'no need whatsoever for any direct or overt political intervention …'.[77] The normally bland, middle-of-the-road *Economist*, was uncompromisingly bleak. The leading article, headed 'The Suicide Game', declared, 'Ulster is on the edge of civil war'. So far, said the paper, political intervention had been avoided but without a change of heart among Ulstermen 'direct rule from Westminster will be inevitable'. Wilson and Heath should spell this out to the people of Ulster. 'It may even be that such rule will have an increasing attraction for the law-abiding majority of Ulster', said the article, adding, 'What ought to have been plain was that the old ways were leading to the suicide of the state. What is plain now is that the very bases of the state can no longer avoid questioning.'[78]

This is the point where, logically, the analysis of Labour's policy of non-intervention in Ulster should end. The *Economist* was to be disappointed and direct rule would have to wait another three years, but the old days, when half a civil servant kept an eye on the province from the bowels of the Home Office were over. The new approach was symbolised by the despatching to Belfast of Oliver Wright, a senior diplomat, officially to represent the UK Government but, as Flackes put it, to act as watch-dog and monitor Stormont's reforms.[79] However, a postscript must be added to take account of the publication a month after the troops went in of the Cameron Commission's report on the earlier disturbances. As the Commission's secretary recently put it, 'We were simply overtaken by events'.[80]

The Commission's report is dealt with only briefly here because the focus has been primarily on the Labour government's policy which was not included in Cameron's terms of reference. The Commission had been set up, not by the British government, but by Stormont.

Its job was to trace the causes of the earlier violence. Its findings were highly critical of Stormont which it accused of being 'hide bound' and 'complacent'. The causes of the disorder included a rising sense of grievance among Roman Catholics particularly because of the unfair methods of allocating public housing. Other grievances included gerrymandering of local government boundaries in favour of the Unionists. The Commission also reported Catholic resentment against the 'B' specials and the Special Powers Act. The Commission found that the Civil Rights movement was not narrowly sectarian nor politically subversive. It was a movement which drew support from a wide measure of moderate opinion on many sides. Among the civil rights movement there were 'subversive elements' but

> while there is evidence that members of the IRA are active in the organisation there is no sign that they are in any sense dominant or in a position to control or direct policy of the Civil Rights Association.[81]

Cameron seemed to justify all those who had warned the British Government for nearly six years that Ulster was a bomb waiting to go off. However, Cameron has since been accused of being naive. The report, it is argued, was not aware that Republicans had been largely responsible for creating the Northern Ireland Civil Rights Association (NICRA) in the first place. Also the motives of IRA members in NICRA should have been questioned.[82] Patrick Riddell has asked why, if NICRA's sole intention was to secure civil rights for Catholics, did it accept men from an organisation pledged to the destruction of the state.[83] The most interesting revisionism is what appears to be a *mea culpa* from Arthur Green, the Commission's secretary, who in 1996 claimed that Lord Cameron 'turned a blind eye to the ambiguities of NICRA'. Green also said the report's conclusions about local government abuses were 'too slick', which, he accepted, was 'probably as much my responsibility as anyone'.[84]

CONCLUSION

In the three months since O'Neill's resignation Northern Ireland had been plunged into a state of near civil war. Despite Wilson's prediction of a stormy summer ahead, his government seemed to sleep-walk to disaster. Why he should have put such faith in Chichester-Clark's ability to deliver what Roy Foster has described as 'a minimal programme of reforms'[85] and restore order on the streets remains a mystery. Perhaps it was merely the wishful thinking for which the Labour premier was well known. It took the *Belfast Telegraph*, not left-wing journalists on the mainland, to question Wilson's faith in Unionist sincerity. The paper had been a mainstay of O'Neillism – sometimes even ahead of the Captain – but unlike the British government it was there on the ground and its forebodings were fully justified. There is also considerable doubt about Wilson's personal role. On the one hand he is praising Chichester-Clark,[86] on the other, as Crossman revealed, he has 'crazy' ideas of going out to Belfast himself to sort things out.[87]

In the end, when the decision in principle to send in the troops had been taken he vacillated over the crucial decision of whether to impose direct rule. Callaghan has said since that direct rule was never on, but Crossman suggested that it was at least considered and Wilson appears to have told one of his favourite lobby correspondents, John Bourne, that political control from London was inevitable if the troops went in. One other reason for the decision against direct rule has been suggested by Arthur Green, who claims that some leading Catholics let the British government know that they were against it. He has revealed that after the troops went in, a Catholic judge told him that the government should 'work through Stormont'.[88]

But if the charge of ambiguity can be levelled at ministers, that of failure to prepare contingency plans, so often made, cannot. This chapter has sought to show that by the end of 1968 Callaghan had in progress detailed planning including draft legislation. What was missing, if Healey has been reported correctly by Crossman, was any serious attempt to get information on the spot, hence the misreading of events immediately before the ill-fated Apprentice Boys' March. Merlyn Rees, who was Northern Ireland Secretary in the 1970s, has confirmed that MI5 were not operating in the province.[89] This meant that Intelligence was left to the Special Branch of the RUC. Rees was contemptuous of their ability. William Craig, Home Affairs Minister at Stormont, who had claimed that MI5 had revealed civil rights workers' links with the IRA, in fact had his briefing from the Home Affairs department of the Northern Ireland Civil Service The weakness of that department's intelligence work, said Rees in 1992, was shown up when internment was imposed in 1972: 'The information they came up with was so daft in retrospect'.[90]

Finally, what of the report of the Cameron Commission, which did not tell the Labour government anything it did not already know? The Catholic grievances outlined by Cameron had, after all, been reported to successive Labour Home Secretaries. The last of these assessments came from the International Commission of Jurists which arrived at the shaming verdict that the lot of the Catholics in Ulster was worse, in some respects, than that of the blacks in apartheid South Africa. Nevertheless, Cameron was at least confirmation that these reports were not alarmist. By the time its report was published in September 1969 Ulster had experienced the worst violence since the large-scale sectarian attacks on Catholic communities which accompanied the birth of the province in the earlier 1920s when 455 people were killed in Belfast alone.[91] Throughout the five years since Wilson promised to bring reform to Ulster the province was never considered a 'top agenda' issue. A succession of domestic and foreign crises had shoved it to the bottom. Now – at the twelfth hour – it was at last at the top.

8 Conclusions

Research for this book was approached with an open mind about the effectiveness or otherwise of the Labour governments' Northern Ireland policy prior to August 1969. This, broadly, was non-intervention in the governance of Ulster on the argument that, as Stormont was a devolved Parliament responsible for domestic affairs in the province, it should be left alone to get on with it. At the same time the Labour government had come to power in 1964 promising to address Catholic grievances and work to bring about reform. It would do this, not by direct intervention but by encouraging the apparently 'liberal' Prime Minister of Northern Ireland, Terence O'Neill, to press ahead speedily with the necessary changes.

In one sense the policy clearly failed. Though Unionist leaders reluctantly conceded some reforms, they came too late. And British troops had to be sent to the province to prevent civil war. But, given the terms of the Government of Ireland Act, 1920, and the Parliamentary convention that Westminster kept out of Ulster affairs, could the Labour government have acted any differently? And was it unreasonable to give O'Neill a chance? He seemed at first to be making headway. Wilson thought he had 'carried through a remarkable programme of easement'[1] so – give him enough time to finish the job. Finally, before accusing the Wilson government of reneging on its pledges to the Catholics, it would be unreasonable to ignore the appalling problems it faced at home and abroad compared with which Ulster's difficulties, although becoming more acute, were hardly a new headache.

These questions, it is hoped, have been considered objectively before any final conclusions have been reached. One argument, however, that has been outside the remit of this work is that put by Unionist apologists and some historians that discrimination against Catholics was grossly exaggerated, or that they were the architects of their own misfortune because, unlike citizens in mainland Britain, they did not accept the constitutional arrangements of the United Kingdom. Or again, that agitation that helped to bring down the administration was orchestrated not by genuine civil rights campaigners but by the IRA. However, the aim of the research has been to analyse the role of Cabinet, Whitehall and Westminster not Ulster's political and social arrangements.

In any case, the evidence that there was substance to Catholic grievances and that there were grave dangers in failing to address them seems to this writer to be overwhelming. Professor Richard Rose's findings that a large number of Catholics were prepared to accept, however reluctantly, the existing constitution suggests, as Callaghan himself agreed, that a real opportunity had been tragically missed. It is also worth noting that while the British press belatedly discovered 'John Bull's political slum', the local paper, the admirable *Belfast Telegraph,* was in no doubt that a third of the citizens of the province – unlike the rest of the United Kingdom – did not have equal rights. Another way of putting it would be to ask whether the Provisional IRA could have made such hay from 1970 on if the Catholic community [or at least large elements of it] had not felt victims of serious discrimination.

The argument that the Catholics had genuine grievances that it was in the interest of the rest of the United Kingdom to address was forcefully underlined when the papers for 1966 became available at the PRO. As has been shown, early on in the Wilson administration intelligence reports warned London of a potential explosion of IRA violence, which might be carried out by 3000 trained members to mark the 50th anniversary of the Easter Rising. Though in the end there was no serious violence, it seems extraordinary that, given the detail of intelligence passed at the highest level, ministers paid such little attention to Northern Ireland thereafter at least until the Londonderry riot of 1968.

All these points have been borne in mind before coming to the detailed conclusions that follow.

Dublin's neutrality during the Second World War influenced the Attlee government's Ulster policy, making it more accommodating to the Unionists than might have been expected from a 'socialist' administration which was supported by a number of backbenchers committed to decolonisation in general and a 'United Ireland' in particular. Wilson, and several key figures in his Cabinet, had been youthful members of Attlee's government and, in theory at least, could have imbibed this attitude – though Wilson's close aide, Joe Haines, stressed to the writer Wilson's lifetime sympathy for Ireland.

It was Labour in 1949, not the Conservatives, who gave Ulster cast iron guarantees that the Union was indissoluble. This may have led Soskice, and Callaghan (though not Jenkins) to treat Stormont with kid gloves. It is surely no coincidence that Callaghan, in discussions on Northern Ireland, always brings up de Valera's wartime role. The seeds of the CDU – whose campaign for reform was praised by Callaghan as deserving a footnote in history – were sown by the big rebellion in the Parliamentary Labour Party in 1949, led by Robert Mellish among others, against Attlee's Ireland Act, which gave the Protestants the guarantee. Labour's impulse for reform in Ulster, at least among some members of the Parliamentary Labour Party, was deep-seated. Michael Foot had written as early as 1953 of Ulster being 'the bomb on our doorstep'.[2] Even Partition was not totally off limits: both Gordon Walker and George Brown considered the matter of a 'United Ireland' in the 1950s.

By the General Election of 1964 Labour appeared to be genuinely committed to tackling Catholic grievances. The evidence for this is strong: personal letters from Wilson to civil rights leaders – which were published in Ulster – a private meeting with O'Neill when he made it clear to the Ulster Prime Minister that a Labour Government would expect implementation of reforms, and Wilson's light-hearted but still significant, references to the aspirations of the huge number of Irish Catholics in his constituency. Further evidence that for a brief period Wilson was serious about getting something done were the gestures to Dublin such as the return of Casement's remains and the St Patrick's Day Dinner proposal in March 1965 to bring the two Irish premiers together for settlement talks. But this commitment did not last and the conclusion must be that for whatever reasons – and these are suggested later – the impulse to sort out Ulster was weakening. Further confirmation of backtracking comes from the attitude of Wilson's first Home Secretary, Sir Frank Soskice, who publicly – and, in the light of what he must have known about, sickeningly – praised Stormont. Any hope the CDU had of using the House of Commons as a battering ram to force open real debate on Ulster was soon crushed by the Speaker's continual use of the convention and the refusal of ministers to be questioned on the subject. Professor Griffith has shown that the convention could have been waived if the government had so wished.

It is now clear that by the 1966 General Election Wilson, despite his big new majority, was unwilling to put real pressure on Stormont to get reform on the ground. Instead he appeared to be contemplating constitutional change – curbing the powers of the Ulster Unionists MPs at Westminster – which might at least have ended their self-appointed role of preventing the truth about Ulster ever reaching the Commons. But how serious was he about this? Research suggests that though he continued to express his contempt for the Ulstermen he backed off the idea of taking any action against them, possibly considering that it would not be worth the Parliamentary row and the backlash in Ulster, particularly given all his other problems. Perhaps he thought threats would be enough to make the Unionist MPs exercise self-restraint.

To what extent did the CDU fail? Up to the summer of 1968 they themselves believed that they had achieved nothing after nearly four years of Labour governments. Three successive Labour Home Secretaries had ignored them. However, in retrospect it is clear that the arrival at the House of Commons of Gerry Fitt in 1966, signalled the end of 50 years of pretence that Northern Ireland did not exist. Fitt's driving force in Parliament and the bloody events in Londonderry on 5 October 1968 played a key role in breaking the convention. From then on Stormont governments grudgingly conceded reform. But the changes came too late to avoid the disaster of 12 August 1969 when the explosion of violence in the province forced the British government to send in the troops. So the final judgement must be that the CDU never had the impact of other publicly led campaigns post World War Two such as the anti-apartheid and anti-poll tax protest movements.

They failed because of the determination of Wilson, Jenkins and Callaghan 'not to get sucked into the Irish bog'. [Callaghan's actual phrase.][3] The CDU simply had not the punch or credibility needed to turn this policy around. Though nominally supported by 100 MPs, including prominent politicians such as the veteran Manny Shinwell and a young David Owen, the work was carried out by about a dozen dedicated backbench Labour MPs, sometimes supported by Liberals including Jeremy Thorpe.[4]

It was also unfortunately true that the CDU and the civil rights workers in Ulster received little attention from the media, at least until Londonderry. They were simply not interested. Ulster was a far away place that did not sell newspapers or attract viewers. The policy throughout was 'let BBC Northern Ireland cover the news from the province'.[5] Mainland journalists, with the exception of *The Times* from 1967 and the radical writer, Mary Holland, usually ignored Ulster.

Could the Wilson Cabinet, had it so wished, have broken the convention and put through measures to tackle discrimination in Northern Ireland? Griffith and Calvert (Chapter 1) have made clear they could and there is some evidence to support this. The Prices and Incomes legislation, enacted in 1966, was imposed on the whole of the United Kingdom despite the contention that Westminster did not get involved in the province's domestic affairs. However, when it came to Race Relations legislation and the Bill to create a Parliamentary Commissioner for Administration (the 'Ombudsman'), special provision was made to exempt Northern Ireland. A close reading of Hansard for the years before Londonderry in October 1968 shows that the Speaker, no doubt with the tacit approval of Harold Wilson, applied the convention rigorously. It was not only the Speaker who was guardian of the 'Gag'. Ministers refused to answer questions which they said were the business of the devolved government in Belfast and the Table Office took their cue from the ministers and ruled such questions out of order.

The point remains, however, that the convention was not a statute. Statute cannot be changed except by statute and statute always overrides convention. Had the will been there, the Labour Government, re-elected in March 1966 with a majority of 97, could have used Section 5 or Section 75 of the Government of Ireland Act, 1920, and chose not to do so. A credible threat to do so might have been enough to spur Stormont into action sooner. The Home Secretary of the time, Roy Jenkins, explained why nothing was done in the House of Commons in October 1967. Given the hopes that had resided in the great 'liberal' reformer, Jenkins caused near despair among the ranks of the CDU at Westminster and civil rights campaigners in Ulster who, quite understandably, saw his refusal to act as a betrayal. In August 1966 Wilson and Jenkins, at a private lunch, had told O'Neill of the need to speed up reform. Only eight months earlier, as we now know, all three had received top level intelligence of IRA preparations to mark the 50th anniversary of the Easter Rising with a campaign of violence. Time was running out, as Wilson wrote afterwards. Fifteen months later more time had run out yet Jenkins still stuck to the old line.

Between the lunch with O'Neill and the Londonderry eruption of October 1968 the government, as has been shown, had been continuously warned that without reform serious sectarian violence was inevitable. Still the government did not act. Wilson, in the summer of 1968, told the Commons 'we cannot continue indefinitely with the present situation. Something has to be done'.[6] However, he did just that and even after the Londonderry violence it was still being left to Stormont to implement the necessary measures against the wishes of a large section of the Unionist Party.

After Londonderry, ignorance on the mainland about deteriorating communal relations in Ulster was no longer tenable. For the first time the press and television told Britain something of what was going on 'in their own back yard'. This did not mean that pressure on the British government to intervene was growing to any serious extent. The Labour Party, as mentioned earlier, did not want to get involved in a part of the United Kingdom where their writ did not run, and the Conservative leadership still backed their Unionist allies, though it is now known from the Party's archive that they soon began to have doubts about Stormont's long-term future.

Instead, Wilson and Callaghan seemed to be gambling on O'Neill's ability to outwit his own right-wing and implement reforms fast enough to prevent worse outbreaks of communal unrest. Just how great a gamble it was we now know from the remarkable (but 'fictitious') memorandum provided by that now retired civil servant of the time. He wrote of his fears that these immediate steps would 'turn out to be inadequate' and his striking phrase, 'History is against us,' could well have been the title of this book.

It is easy to see now, 30 years and more than 3000 lives later, that it was unlikely that these late reforms could have prevented the slide towards disaster in the province. O'Neill's attempt to go over the heads of bigots on both sides, first with his television appeal and then with his snap general election, though commendable, was doomed. The Crossman *Diaries* later revealed the Cabinet's disappointment and growing fears after O'Neill's departure: but it was not until Catholics and Protestants were at each other's throats in August 1969 that ministers acted at last.

The irony is that, as the research has discovered, in late 1968 the Wilson government had prepared detailed contingency plans for intervention including direct rule, though it was the last thing they wanted to do. The invaluable recollections of Sir John Chilcot make this clear. Callaghan had emphasised early on to O'Neill that if they went in, even 'only in the aid of the civil power', Westminster would retain control of the forces. About this time a Northern Ireland Cabinet Committee had been set up but, apart from the names of the ministers who made up its membership, virtually nothing is known of its deliberations. It is not clear when ministers seriously considered intervention. Crossman suggested that it was shortly after O'Neill's resignation. Whatever the truth, the minutes should be of great interest when the PRO makes them available.

My object here has not been to condemn the Wilson government for failing to replace Stormont with direct rule from Westminster before the Troubles returned. After all it was not until the civil rights movement had switched to a policy of direct confrontation with the Stormont regime (covered by world-wide television) that ministers began to accept that Ulster's problems were insuperable after all. In addition, it would be naive not to recognise how drastic a step it would have been at that time to abolish an elected Parliament with 50 years of life behind it and the solid support [however exaggerated by gerrymandering etc.] of the local majority before blood on the streets justified such extreme measures. In the 1960s, before the Troubles began, when even constitutional experts like John Mackintosh were praising Stormont, such a move seemed out of the question. Direct rule could only have been quite literally a last resort.

Instead, the argument has centred on the failures of British politicians from 1964 on to bring increasing pressure to bear on the Unionist administration to muck out their own stables. John Oliver, from his vantage point in the upper reaches of the Northern Ireland Civil Service, believed this could and should have been done. It is a credible argument. It is at least possible, surely, that an ultimatum that, without real progress on reform, financial sanctions would be imposed, or the powers of the Unionist MPs at Westminster limited, might have convinced Stormont at last that the Labour government meant business.

To what extent can this policy failure be blamed on the inadequacy of the four politicians on whom it depended – Wilson, Jenkins, Callaghan and O'Neill? Wilson vacillated from one idea to the next – curbs on Unionist MPs, financial sanctions – even going for direct rule, momentarily. The determined action needed possibly required a leader more in the mould of a Thatcher, a de Gaulle or perhaps even an Attlee. Thatcher showed the required steel to draw up the Hillsborough agreement in the teeth of Unionist and right-wing Conservative opposition [though there is good anecdotal evidence that she did not altogether understand the implications of the agreement]. De Gaulle got the French out of Algeria and Attlee the British out of India. The trouble was that Ireland was like no other part of Empire nor was it quite part of the home islands but a hybrid, posing unprecedented problems for 'Imperial' government.

Jenkins was only Home Secretary for a short period but, unlike Soskice and Callaghan, he did not take the trouble to visit Ulster [he said O'Neill did not want him], and his elegant inactivity must tarnish somewhat his cherished reputation as the great reformer of the 1960s. Wilson and Callaghan for much of the crucial time in 1969 were bogged down in internal strife in the Cabinet and the Labour Party over trade union reform. This vitriolic personal battle and Wilson's own fight for political survival hardly left time or energy for dealing decisively with Ulster even if either man had been prepared to do so.

As for the earlier period, it is only fair to take into account the over-whelming economic problems faced by the Government from day one in October 1964 and after the 'July cuts' of 1966 especially. The rolling economic crisis and Wilson's paranoidal fear of a Cabinet coup against him were hardly conducive to dealing with a little local difficulty like Northern Ireland.

The fourth man, O'Neill, is a tragic figure. For the Labour polit-icians who met him, he was 'little more than a souped-up county council leader'. Paul Bew, initially a bitter critic of the Ulster leader, convinced that he was not serious about structural reform, has soft-ened his analysis but still believes that O'Neill was out of touch with a large section of the population. A damning verdict on the man – as Crossman put it – entrusted by Wilson to bring Northern Ireland into the 20th century.

Counterfactual history is a precarious business. But it is surely worth arguing that the evidence presented here confirms that the final disaster could have been avoided and Britain and Ireland spared the loss of some 3500 lives and the expenditure of million of pounds of taxpayers' money if the Wilson administration had acted differ-ently. It is a big 'if'. If the government had not been distracted by economic problems at home and growing political unpopularity. If only ministers could have done a little more, and done it sooner, to convince the Unionists that they had no alternative but to give the Catholics their civil rights and to tackle other grievances at source.

Harold Wilson at the outset wanted to do something for Ireland. Despite the disturbances in Belfast during the 1964 election, it can be argued that he could have been forgiven for treating Ireland with benign neglect at least until late 1965 – early 1966 when he received intelligence warnings about the seriousness of potential trouble. As Harold Macmillan graphically put it in his diaries:

This Irish story is a very queer one ... hundreds of years of bitter quarrels … civil war amongst the natives following the complete surrender of the British – and now, peace – perfect peace.[7]

That Wilson did not, metaphorically speaking, take his cue from a by now old man, reflecting somewhat cynically on his time in office, is much to his credit. He knew Macmillan's 'peace' was a phoney peace and that Ireland would soon come to the boil again if nothing was done for the Catholics in the North. How sad, for both the British and the Irish, that his good intentions of 1964 should have come to nothing.

Notes

AUTHOR'S PREFACE

1. See particularly Bob Purdie, *Politics in the Street* (Belfast, 1990), which includes well-documented sections on the Campaign for Social Justice in Northern Ireland, NICRA and PD. On the NILP also see the following: an illuminating insider's view is C.E.B. Brett's *Long Shadows Cast before Midnight* (Edinburgh, 1978). Brett, who was described as one of the party's political ideologues, was chairman of the NILP's policy committee for 15 years. *The Northern Ireland Question in British Politics*, edited by Peter Catterall and Sean McDougall (London, 1996), includes a chapter on the NILP by Terry Cradden. For a more general overview see J. Whyte, *Interpreting Northern Ireland* (Oxford, 1991) and Tom Wilson, *Ulster: Conflict and Consent* (Oxford, 1989). Wilson acted as an adviser to the government of Northern Ireland while Whyte provides an apparently exhaustive bibliography.
2. Generally newspapers were consulted at the British Library (Newspaper Library, Colindale), periodicals at the University of London Library, Senate House.
3. Campaign for Social Justice in Northern Ireland pamphlet, *The Plain Truth*, 2nd edn, Dungannon, Northern Ireland, 1969.

INTRODUCTION

1. Public Record Office, Kew [Henceforth PRO]: PREM 4/53/2. Letter from Bevin to Churchill, 18 June 1940.
2. Bernard Donoughue and G.W. Jones, *Herbert Morrison*, London, 1973, p. 307.
3. Ibid. pp. 307–8.
4. Formerly Dr Christopher Addison MP.
5. PRO CAB 129/13 CP (46)381, 'Eire and Northern Ireland'. 16 October 1946.
6. PRO CAB 129/2, CP (45)152 'Relations with Eire'. 7 September 1945. It is reasonable to assume that de Valera's condolences on the death of Hitler (after the opening of the Belsen concentration camp) hardly endeared the Irish leader to Labour Ministers.
7. PRO CAB 129/13 CP (46)391, 18 October 1946. 'Eire and Northern Ireland'.
8. Kenneth Morgan, *Labour in Power*, Oxford, 1985, p. 56.
9. Paul Bew and Henry Patterson, *The British State and the Ulster Crisis*, London, 1985, p. 8.
10. David Harkness, *Northern Ireland since 1920*, Dublin, 1983, p. 106.
11. Ibid. p. 106–7.

12. Richard Crossman, *The Diaries of a Cabinet Minister*, vol. 3, London, 1977, p. 187.
13. F.S.L. Lyons, *Ireland Since the Famine*, London, 1985, pp. 568–9.
14. The Cabinet papers released in the late 1970s under the 30-year rule.
15. See particularly two of a number of Cabinet meetings where these matters were discussed: PRO CAB 128/13 CM 67(48)3 & 4, 28 October, 1948; PRO CAB 128/13, CM 74(48)6, 18 November 1948.
16. Ronald Hyam, *The Labour Government and the End of Empire, 1945–51*, London, 1992, p. lxix.
17. Ronan Fanning, *International Affairs*, vol. 58, 1982, No. 1. 'The Response of the London and Belfast Governments to the declaration of The Republic of Ireland, 1948–49'.
18. PRO CAB 128/13 CM 75 (48)2, 22 November 1948.
19. PRO CAB 128/13 CM 76 (48)2, 25 November 1948.
20. PRO CAB 128/13 CM 81 (48)2, 15 December 1948.
21. Fanning, *International Affairs*. op. cit.
22. PRO CAB 128/15 CM 1 (49)2, 12 January 1949.
23. PRO CAB 129/32 (1) CP (49)4. 7 January 1949.
24. PRO CAB 128/15 CM 1 (49)2, 12 January 1949.
25. Fanning, *International Affairs*. One effect of the refusal to join NATO may well have been to neutralise the usual American concern for Irish unity.
26. CAB 21/2263 Notes for weekly visits to the King, 1947–50.
27. PREM 8/1468 'The Royal Style Titles and the King's Signature'.
28. *House of Commons Debates*, 5th ser., vol. 464, cols 1856–62, 11 May 1949.
29. PRO CAB 128/15 34 (49)3, 12 May 1949.
30. This policy of non-intervention was based on a ruling given by the Commons Speaker, J.H. Whitley, in 1923 which is discussed fully in the following chapter.
31. *The Times*, 18 May 1949.
32. Ibid., 17 May 1949.
33. Ibid., 18 May 1949.
34. Ibid., 19 May 1949.
35. Bew, *British State*, pp. 9–10.
36. Ibid., p. 35.
37. Public Record Office, Northern Ireland. [Henceforth PRONI] COM 61/440 17 December 1940.
38. *Daily Herald*, 3 June 1953.
39. *House of Commons Debates*, 5th ser., vol. 517, col. 1018. 6 July 1953. Bevan's remarks were made during a brief debate on an Order to revoke all building controls in Northern Ireland.
40. Patrick Gordon Walker, *Political Diaries 1932–71* (ed.) Robert Pearce, London, 1991, pp. 212–14.

1 'LEAVE IT TO TERENCE': THE LABOUR GOVERNMENT,
OCTOBER 1964–MARCH 1966

1. Interview with Professor Griffith 19 December 1995. John Griffith, a
    friend of the author's brother, gave invaluable help in unravelling the
    intricacies of the convention.
2. Now housed at the National Museum of Labour History, Manchester.
3. In 1949 the NILP came out firmly for maintaining the link with Britain.
4. ICBH seminar, London, 14 January 1992.
5. *House of Commons Debates*, 5th ser., vol. 536, cols 778–85, 31 January
    1955.
6. James Callaghan, *Time and Chance*, London, 1987, pp. 271–2.
7. For five years the CSJ 'mounted a strong publicity campaign in Britain
    and abroad.... Its efforts were particularly effective in building up
    support for the civil rights movement within the British Labour Party'.
    W.D. Flackes, *Northern Ireland: a Political Directory 1968–79*, Dublin,
    1980, p. 35.
8. Brian Faulkner, *Memoirs of a Statesman*, London, 1978, p. 130; Bew,
    British State, p.11.
9. Interview with Haines, 12 September 1996. He had been appointed 10
    Downing Street Press Secretary in January 1969. The author has known
    him well for many years.
10. CSJNI pamphlet, *The Plain Truth*, 2nd edn, Dungannon, Northern
    Ireland, 1969.
11. *Irish News*, 3 October 1964.
12. Bob Purdie, *Politics in the Streets*, Belfast, 1990, p. 100.
13. NEC minutes, Home Policy Sub Committee, 2 December 1963,
    National Museum of Labour History, RD578.
14. Interview with Roy Lilley [later Editor of the *Belfast Telegraph*] 12 May
    1993.
15. Ibid.
16. *House of Commons Debates*, 5th ser., vol. 698. cols 1097–1152. 14 July
    1964.
17. *New Statesman*, 6 September 1975.
18. Jonathan Bardon, *A History of Ulster*, Belfast, 1992, p. 632.
19. Ibid.
20. *The Times*, 2 October 1964.
21. Ibid., 3 October 1964.
22. Bardon, *Ulster*, p. 632.
23. The Home Secretary, Sir Frank Soskice, told the Cabinet that the Irish
    Republic would have to give an undertaking that the remains would be
    reinterred in Republican territory and would not be subsequently
    removed. PRO CAB 128/39 CM1 (65)2, 14 January 1965. Wilson
    had previously told Soskice that he agreed with this condition.
    PREM 13/530, Casement, note from Wilson to Soskice, 5 January
    1965.
24. Harold Wilson, *The Labour Government: 1964–70*, London, 1971, p. 75.
25. *Irish Times*, 1 April 1966.
26. PRO CAB 129/123 C. (65)175, 'Negotiations for a Free Trade Area

Agreement with the Irish Republic', 8 December 1965.
27. *The Times*, 18 March 1965.
28. Ibid., 19 March 1965.
29. Ibid.
30. *The Times: Guide to the House of Commons, 1966*, London, 1966, p. 16. From an anonymous article in fact written by one of *The Times*'s lobby correspondents.
31. Interview with Oliver Wright, 8 September 1992.
32. Ibid.
33. PRO, PREM 13/980 'Relations between the United Kingdom and Ireland', Letter from the Northern Ireland Prime Minister, Terence O'Neill, to the Home Secretary, Sir Frank Soskice, 9 December 1965.
34. Ibid. Minute to the Prime Minister from Soskice, 10 December 1965. On it Wilson had scribbled in pen: 'I agree. Is Sec of State doing it or does he want me to do so – e.g. at lunch'.
35. Ibid. Letter from M.H.M. Reid, Private Secretary to the Prime Minister, to R.F.D. Shuffrey, Principal Private Secretary to the Home Secretary, 13 December 1965.
36. Ibid. Note for the Record written by P. Le Cheminant, Private Secretary to the Prime Minister, 4 March 1966.
37. PRO, DEFE 4/197, MOD Chiefs of Staff Committee, Confidential Annexe to COS 15th Meeting (66), 17 March 1966.
38. PRO, PREM 13/980, Minute to the Prime Minister from the Cabinet Secretary, Sir Burke Trend, 24 March 1966.
39. Ibid. Minute from Soskice to the Prime Minister, 4 April 1966.
40. PRO CAB 128/41 CM18 (66)2. 7 April 1966.
41. *House of Commons Debates*, 5th Ser., vol. 163, cols 1623–15, 3 May 1923.
42. Paul Bew, Peter Gibbon and Henry Patterson, *Northern Ireland 1921–1994*, London, 1995, p. 160.
43. Senior lecturer in Law at Queen's University, Belfast, in the 1960s.
44. H. Calvert, *Constitutional Law in Northern Ireland*, London & Belfast, 1968, p. 101.
45. Ibid.
46. Ibid. Section 5 precludes 'any penalty disadvantage or disability being imposed on account of religious beliefs'.
47. Ibid., p.103.
48. Interview with Professor Griffith, 19 December 1995.
49. Ibid.
50. The Government of Ireland Act states: 'Notwithstanding the establishment of the Parliaments of Southern and Northern Ireland ... or anything contained in this Act, the supreme authority of the Parliament of the United Kingdom shall remain unaffected and undiminished over all persons, matters and things in Ireland and every part thereof.'
51. Interview with Professor Griffith, 19 December 1995.
52. Ibid.
53. *House of Commons Debates*, 5th ser., vol. 803, cols 1365–66, 14 July 1970.
54. Ibid. vol. 707, cols 45–105, 22 February 1965.
55. Roy Foster, *Modern Ireland 1600–1972*, London, 1989, p. 583.

56. Mahon and Crawshaw represented seats with a high proportion of Irish voters.
57. Labour MP for Manchester, Blackley, 1964–79.
58. Paul Rose, The Northern Ireland Problem (2) Breaking the Convention, *Contemporary Review*, December 1971, vol. 219.
59. For example in 1971 he recalled going to the House of Commons to pay 'one of a long series of tributes' to O'Neill. Wilson, *Labour Government*, p. 671.
60. Ibid., p. 99.
61. Ibid.
62. For a full account of this meeting see Chapter 5.
63. *House of Commons Debates*, 5th ser., vol. 718, cols 22–114, 26 October 1965.
64. *Belfast Telegraph*, 29 April 1965.
65. Interview with Otton, 24 September 1996.
66. ICBH seminar.
67. This letter is quoted earlier in the chapter.
68. ICBH seminar.
69. Wilson, *Labour Government*, p. 177.
70. *House of Commons Debates*, 5th ser., vol. 720, col. 39, 9 November 1965.
71. Wilson, *Labour Government*, p. 178.
72. *House of Commons Debates*, 5th ser., vol. 711, cols 1560–62. 6 May 1965.
73. PREM 13/1077, Prime Minister's Personal Minute, Wilson to Bowden, 31 January 1966.
74. Waller was a personal friend of Wilson's.

2 THE 'CRUCIALLY DIFFICULT YEAR', APRIL–AUGUST 1966

1. Kenneth Bloomfield, *Stormont in Crisis*, Belfast, 1994, p. 86.
2. *Sunday Times*, 3 July 1966.
3. 'O'Neillism' was hardly a policy but more an imprecise phrase used to cover the Ulster premier's conviction that a more enlightened attitude to the minority community, coupled with economic growth (making everyone in the province, Catholic and Protestant alike, better off), would avoid the need for structural reform which, in any case, his party would never accept.
4. Bloomfield, *Crisis*, pp. 108–9.
5. Jonathan Bardon, *A History of Ulster*, Belfast, 1992, pp. 645–6.
6. W.D. Flackes, *Northern Ireland: a Political Directory*, Dublin, 1980, pp. 60–1.
7. Bob Purdie, *Politics in the Streets*, Belfast, 1990, p. 64.
8. *House of Commons Debates*, 5th ser., vol. 727, cols 437–46, 25 April 1966.
9. Ibid., cols 574–79, 26 April 1966.
10. See Chapter 5.
11. *House of Commons Debates*, 5th ser., vol. 727, col. 485, 25 April 1966.

12. In an interview for the BBC *Timewatch* programme made during 1992 but not included when the programme, 'The sparks that lit the bonfire', was broadcast on 27 January 1993.
13. *House of Commons Debates*, 5th ser., vol. 727, cols 574–79, 26 April 1966.
14. Interview with Lilley, 12 May 1993.
15. *Belfast Telegraph*, 26 May 1966.
16. PRO PREM 13/980. Note of a meeting between Minister (Army) and Lord Stonham, Parliamentary Secretary Home Office, 13 April 1966.
17. PREM 13/1077 Prime Minister's Personal Minute, Wilson to Bowden, 31 January 1966.
18. *House of Commons Debates*, 5th ser., vol. 729, cols 721–23, 26 May 1966. This was an early version of 'the West Lothian question' that bedevilled Labour during the Scottish devolution controversy in the late 1970s.
19. Ibid., vol. 736, cols 224–28, 15 November 1966.
20. *Belfast Telegraph*, 26 May 1966. For Wilson's Tory 'hacks' remark, mentioned by Diamond, see *House of Commons Debates*, 5th ser., vol. 711, cols 1560–62. 6 May 1965.
21. Interview with Paul Rose, 14 August 1992.
22. From transcript of BBC *Timewatch* interview, not broadcast.
23. *House of Commons Debates*, 5th ser., vol. 729, cols 923–951, 27 May 1966.
24. *Belfast Telegraph*, 17 May 1966.
25. ICBH seminar, London, 14 January 1992. For Clause 48 of the Finance Bill 1966 see Parliamentary Papers Session 18 April 1966–27 October 1967. vol. 3. Finance Bill Part V11 Miscellaneous. 48 MPs of Northern Ireland: Pension Fund and annuity premiums. pp. 54–5.
26. ICBH seminar.
27. Interview with McNamara 25 June 1992.
28. The Special Powers Act, passed in 1922, was designed primarily to repress the IRA and Republican groups. The Minister of Home Affairs was authorised 'to take all such steps and issue all such orders as may be necessary for preserving the peace and order'. It also provided that action might be deemed 'prejudicial to the preservation of the peace or maintenance of order'; even if not specified in the regulations. It made large blanket grants of authority, including the power to intern for years without trial or relief of *habeas corpus*. Richard Rose, *Governing without Consensus*, London, 1971, p. 128.
29. The above amendments are from the private papers of Kevin McNamara MP, Brynmor Jones Library, University of Hull.
30. Bloomfield, *Stormont*, p. 86.
31. Bardon, *Ulster*, p. 635.
32. Bloomfield, *Stormont*, p. 96.
33. Interview with Thorpe, 10 June 1993.
34. *Belfast Telegraph*, 28 June 1966. (Under headline of '100 MPs may sign motion on Ulster'.)
35. *House of Commons Debates*, 5th ser., vol. 730, cols 1585–87, 28 June 1966.

36. *The Times*, 29 June 1966.
37. Roy Foster, *Modern Ireland 1600–1972*, London, 1989, p. 585.
38. *Revue Française de Civilisation Britannique*, vol. V, No II, January 1989, p. 51. However, in his more recent contribution to the Dictionary of National Biography Professor Bew stresses that O'Neill was 'essentially a man of decent tolerant instincts'. [Dictionary of National Biography. Oxford, 1996, p. 337.] For a summary of his D.N.B. article see the conclusion to Chapter 6.
39. ICBH seminar.
40. Interview with Hattersley, 16 June 1992.
41. Ibid.
42. Bloomfield, *Stormont*, p. 75.
43. Ibid. p. 76.
44. Ibid.
45. Interview with Bloomfield, 1 December 1993.
46. Ibid.
47. The Orange Order, the largest Protestant organisation in Northern Ireland, with between 80 000 and 100 000 active members. From W.D. Flackes, *Northern Ireland A Political Directory 1968–79*, Dublin, p. 103.
48. Brian Faulkner, Prime Minister of Northern Ireland, 1971–2.
49. Interview with Bloomfield. The 'excesses' were some of the bizarre traditions of the Orange movement.
50. Ibid.
51. *Belfast Telegraph*, Ulster Letter from London 'A Breach of Convention', 1 July 1966.
52. Ibid.
53. For example, Kevin McNamara and Paul Rose in interviews with the writer, 25 June 1992 and 14 August 1992 respectively.
54. Interview with McNamara.
55. *Sunday Times*, 3 July 1966.
56. Ibid.
57. Ibid.
58. From the Foreword to *Ulster*, by the *Sunday Times* Insight Team, Harmondsworth, London, 1972, p. 8.
59. David Harkness, *Northern Ireland since 1920*, Dublin, 1983, p. 148.
60. *Irish Times*, 6 July 1966.
61. *Belfast Telegraph*, 13 July 1966.
62. Ibid., 'Ulster Letter from London', 8 July 1966.
63. Very brief interview with Jenkins, 3 October 1992.
64. Roy Jenkins, *A Life at the Centre*, London, 1991.
65. Bardon, *Ulster*, p. 646.
66. *Observer*, 6 October 1968, in an article headed, 'John Bull's White Ghettos'.
67. Letter from Bloomfield to the writer, 16 June 1994.
68. Harold Wilson, *The Labour Government 1964–1970*, London, 1971, p. 270.
69. Keith Jeffrey and Peter Hennessy, *States of Emergency*, London, 1983, p. 241.
70. Ben Pimlott, *Harold Wilson*, London, 1992, p. 405.

71. Kenneth Morgan, *The People's Peace*, Oxford, 1990, p. 254.
72. Pimlott, *Wilson*, p. 408.
73. Ibid., p. 428.
74. Morgan, *Peace*, p. 265–6.
75. Walter Bagehot, 'The Premiership', in Norman St. John-Stevas (ed.), *The Collected Works of Walter Bagehot*, vol. 6, London, 1974, p. 67.
76. Wilson, *Labour Government*, pp. 270–1.
77. Ibid.
78. Interview in 1994 with a former Whitehall Permanent Secretary.
79. Conor Cruise O'Brien, *States of Ireland*, London, 1972, p. 164.
80. Terence O'Neill, *The Autobiography of Terence O'Neill*, London, 1972, p. 83.
81. *Belfast Telegraph*, 6 August 1966.
82. ICBH seminar.
83. See for example Foley's speech earlier in the chapter.
84. ICBH seminar.
85. Interview with Paul Rose, 14 August 1992. The writer attempted to see Shirley Williams but she was not available for interview.
86. *House of Commons Debates*, 5th ser., vol. 733, cols 1276–1311, 8 August 1966.
87. The debate is given considerable space partly because at no other time during five years before the troops went in was the convention so strongly challenged on the floor of the Commons and also because the CDU MPs achieved, if nothing else, the clearest interpretation of the Government of Ireland Act 1920 yet given from the Deputy Speaker, Sir Eric Fletcher, and Alice Bacon on behalf of the Government.
88. *House of Commons Debates*, 5th ser., vol. 733, 8 August 1966.
89. Interview with Haines, 12 September 1996.
90. PRO PREM 13/980, Minute from Soskice to the Prime Minister, 4 April 1966.
91. Ibid.
92. 'Harold Wilson's failure to examine seriously O'Neill's policies may, ironically enough, be held in large part responsible for the eventual collapse of O'Neill's government. These policies could only have succeeded if there had been an early implementation of reforms in the area of local government and housing.' Paul Bew and Henry Patterson, *The British State and the Ulster Crisis*, London, 1985, p. 15.

3 PUTTING OFF THE EVIL DAY, SEPTEMBER 1966–MAY 1967

1. Interview with Dr John Oliver, 8 February 1995.
2. *House of Commons Debates*. 5th ser. vol. 745, cols 1821–23, 27 April 1967.
3. Oliver was chief adviser to the chairman of the Constitutional Convention, 1975–6. Born Belfast 1913, entered Northern Ireland Civil Service in 1936 and rose to be Permanent Secretary in the Development Ministry in 1970 and Housing Dept 1974. Retired 1976.
4. Interview with Oliver.

5. William Ewart Bell, Assistant Secretary, Commerce, Northern Ireland, 1963–70 (ended career as Head of Northern Ireland Civil Service, 1979).
6. Interview with Oliver.
7. Ibid.
8. Letter to the writer from retired senior civil servant, 31 May 1995. The DEA was abolished in 1969.
9. Ben Pimlott, *Harold Wilson*, London, 1993, p. 431.
10. In the years before the troops were sent to Ulster, in August 1969, the Conservatives had resisted any suggestion of intervention in Northern Ireland affairs by Westminster. However, after August 1969, their policy seems to have changed. During the 1970 General Election campaign Sir Alec Douglas-Home, speaking in Belfast, warned of the circumstances in which Stormont would have to be closed down. Professor John Ramsden, historian of the Conservative Party, has written that Sir Alec was 'foreshadowing' direct rule though few would have been aware of the fact. It was inconceivable that he had not cleared his remarks with Heath first. John Ramsden, *The Winds of Change*, London, 1996, p. 342.
11. *The Times*, leading article, 28 September 1966.
12. *Belfast Telegraph*, 28 October 1966.
13. Ibid. 29 October.
14. PRO PREM 13/1077, Prime Minister's Personal Minute, Wilson to Bowden, 31 January 1966.
15. Pimlott, *Wilson*, p. 428.
16. Private information.
17. *Catholic Herald*, 17 March 1967.
18. Interview with Waller, 15 March 1995. The same point about Wilson's deeply held commitment to Ireland was made by Joe Haines [see Chapter 1].
19. Ibid.
20. Ibid.
21. *The Times*, 20 December 1966.
22. Kenneth Bloomfield, *Stormont in Crisis*, Belfast, 1994, p. 97.
23. Ibid.
24. Terence O'Neill, *The Autobiography of Terence O'Neill*, London, 1972, p. 129.
25. Ibid., p. 61–2.
26. Ibid., p. 62.
27. Ibid.
28. Ibid., p. 76.
29. Ibid., p. 87. As mentioned in Chapter 1 the papers released by the PRO in January 1997 included a warning from O'Neill that IRA violence during the anniversary celebrations would be a serious setback to his efforts to cement a more friendly relationship with the Republic: PRO, PREM 13/980. 'Relations between the Unitred Kingdom and Ireland. Letter from the Northern Ireland Prime Minister, Terence O'Neill to the Home Secretary, Sir Frank Soskice, 9 December 1965'.
30. Ibid., p.137.

31. *Belfast Telegraph*, 4 January 1967.
32. Bloomfield, *Stormont* p. 101. Bloomfield also expressed the respect he felt for Sayers in his interview with the writer.
33. According to Cecil King, Harold Wilson once remarked that Longford had a mental age of 12: Cecil King, *The Cecil King Diary 1965–1970*, London, 1972, p. 19.
34. Paul Rose, *Backbencher's Dilemma*, London, 1981, p. 194.
35. Rose, *Dilemma*, p. 180.
36. Ibid., p. 194.
37. Ibid., p. 180.
38. Ibid., p. 181.
39. The report is reproduced by Rose in *Backbencher's Dilemma*, pp. 194–8.
40. Sub-tenants, lodgers, servants, and children over 21 living at home could not vote. 'About 250,000 adults were thus disenfranchised for local government elections. The great bulk of them were Catholics.' From the *Sunday Times* Insight Team, *Ulster*, 1972, p. 35.
41. Rose, *Dilemma*, pp. 197–8.
42. Ibid., p. 198.
43. Bob Purdie, *Politics in the Streets*, Belfast, 1990, p. 70.
44. *Belfast Telegraph*, 17 April 1967.
45. Richard Rose, *Governing without Consensus*, London, 1971, p. 119. Rose says that some 'estimates range as high as £140 million annually'.
46. *Belfast Telegraph*, 10 May 1967.
47. PRO CAB 128/41 CM 18 (66)2, 7 April 1966.
48. Paul Rose, *Dilemma*, pp. 181–2.
49. Interview with Paul Rose. 14 August 1992.
50. Jenkins was not prepared to give the writer a full interview. He spoke to him very briefly, and reluctantly, in a TV studio on 3 October 1992 after he, Jenkins, had appeared in a televised documentary.
51. Brian Wenham, 'Political Certainties and a Doubtful Truce', *Financial Times*, 27 August 1986. Cited by Peter Hennessy in 'The Quality of Political Journalism', *R.S.A. Journal*, vol. no. CXXXV, November, 1987.
52. The papers of the Society of Labour Lawyers, British Library of Political and Economic Science, London School of Economics, Temporary Box numbers 144–55.
53. Ibid., T.B. numbers 63–73. 19 April 1967.
54. *Belfast Telegraph*, 18 April 1967.
55. Ibid.
56. Interview with Garrett, 30 January 1995.
57. Interview with Lord Archer, 12 October 1994.
58. Letter from Lord Richard to the writer, 10 November 1994.
59. Interview with Lord Archer.
60. Ibid.
61. Ibid.
62. Ibid.
63. Harold Evans, in an introduction to *Ulster*, *Sunday Times* Insight Team, Harmondsworth, Middlesex, 1972, p. 8. The full quotation is given in Chapter 2.

64. The praise, mentioned in Chapter 1, was contained in *The Times Guide to the House of Commons 1966*, London, 1966, p. 16.
65. Pimlott, *Wilson*, p. 448.
66. *The Times*, 24 April 1967.
67. Ibid.
68. Ibid.
69. Ibid., 25 April 1967.
70. Ibid., 26 April 1967.
71. Ibid.
72. Ibid., 27 April 1967.
73. Ibid.
74. Ibid.
75. *Belfast Telegraph*, 27 April 1967.
76. Ibid.
77. *House of Commons Debates*. 5th ser. vol. 745, cols 1821–23, 27 April 1967.
78. Interview with Oliver.
79. Interview with Haines 12 September 1996.
80. James Callaghan, *Time and Chance*, London, 1987, p. 271.

4   THE PHONEY PEACE, MAY 1967–MARCH 1968

1. *House of Commons Debates*, 5th ser., vol. 751, col 1687, 25 October 1967.
2. Some years later his close colleague Merlyn Rees described how 'politically bruised' he (Callaghan) felt. 'Jim Callaghan and the Irish Problem', *Contemporary Review*, October 1973, vol. 223.
3. 'Peter Shore – a Wilsonite witness close to the throne – told Wedgwood Benn that the Prime Minister was still convinced about a deliberate plot to dispose of him …'. Ben Pimlott, Harold Wilson, London, 1993, p. 431.
4. Richard Rose, *Governing without Consensus*, London, 1971, pp. 188–9. Professor Rose suggested that the high level of 'don't knows' indicated confusion about the meaning of a complex four-syllable word.
5. Paul Bew and Henry Patterson, *The British State and the Ulster Crisis*, 1985, p. 15.
6. Letter to the writer, from the civil servant, now retired, who does not wish to be identified, 20 October 1996. He also said that the Editor, William Rees-Mogg 'was well respected, even if he was not looked on as one of the really great editors', and he added, 'it always had to be borne in mind that he [Rees-Mogg] was a Roman Catholic'.
7. *The Times*, 2 May 1967.
8. Interview with Rees-Mogg, 13 November 1995.
9. Ibid.
10. *The Times*, 2 May 1967.
11. Ibid.
12. Interview with Rees-Mogg.
13. Ibid.

14. Ibid. 'Canadian Thomsonism' is a reference to Roy Thomson, the Canadian newspaper proprietor, who had recently acquired *The Times*. In a letter to the writer, 22 January 1996, Hickey denied that he would have resigned if taken off Ireland 'provided that the reason was difference of opinion and not a general withdrawal of his [Rees-Mogg's] confidence'.
15. *Belfast Telegraph*, 19 May 1967.
16. Ibid., 1 August 1967.
17. Papers of Society of Labour Lawyers, LSE, temporary box numbers 63–73.
18. Interview with Garrett 30 January 1995.
19. SLL papers.
20. Interview with Lord Archer, 12 October 1994.
21. *Belfast Telegraph*, 3 August 1967.
22. *Irish Times*, 12 and 13 September 1967.
23. Ibid., 2 October 1967.
24. *Belfast Telegraph*, 2 October 1967.
25. Ibid., 3 October 1967.
26. Ibid., 4 October 1967.
27. Ibid.
28. '… a group which is generally thought to have close links with the Communist party of Great Britain; its title commemorates Ireland's best-known Marxist Socialist … James Connolly'. From Bob Purdie, *Politics in the Streets*, Belfast, 1990, p. 106.
29. *Belfast Telegraph*, 4 October 1967.
30. Ibid., 13 October 1967.
31. Ibid.
32. *House of Commons Debates*, 5th ser., vol. 751, cols 1662–88, 25 October, 1967.
33. Paul Rose and Kevin McNamara, in interviews with the writer.
34. *Belfast Telegraph*, 26 November 1967.
35. Ibid., 27 November 1967.
36. Ibid.
37. Some years later the Conservative Prime Minister, Edward Heath, offered him a post in a coalition Cabinet after the 'hung' general election of February 1974.
38. Letter to the writer from David McKie, 28 January 1993.
39. Interview with Thorpe, 10 June 1993.
40. Pimlott, *Wilson*, pp. 503–4.
41. Callaghan's own recollection of this visit is to be found in Chapter 1.
42. ICBH seminar, London, 14 January 1992.
43. For example Sir Kenneth Bloomfield, then Deputy Secretary to the Northern Ireland Cabinet, said that at the time he had written a 'position paper' on intervention explaining to the Unionists that they were wrong in claiming that the convention that Westminster did not interfere now had the force of law. [Interview with the writer, 1 December 1993.] Sir Frank Cooper, who was a senior official at the Ministry of Defence in the late 1960s and Permanent Secretary, Northern Ireland Office, 1973–6, described Callaghan's view as 'a rationalisation after

the event'. He said, 'Parliament is still sovereign so this is not an excuse that will stand up. It is this "let's not get involved" argument … There was gross failure in this country, and indeed in Northern Ireland itself, to appreciate that the thing was getting sourer and sourer and nastier and nastier'. (Interview with the writer, 11 January 1994.)

44. James Callaghan, *Time and Chance*, London, 1987, p. 270.
45. Callaghan, *House*, p. 1.
46. Ibid., p. 2.
47. Ibid., pp. 3–4.
48. Ibid., p. 4.
49. Merlyn Rees, reviewing James Callaghan's *A House Divided*, London, 1973, in *Contemporary Review*, vol. 223, October 1973.
50. *Irish Times*, 30 November 1967.
51. Wilson, *The Labour Government 1964–70*, London, 1971, p. 220.
52. Cecil King, *The Cecil King Diary 1965–1970*, London, 1972, p. 19.
53. Mary Craig, *Longford*, London, 1978, p. 189.
54. Lord Longford, *The Grain of Wheat*, London, 1974, p. 95.
55. Ibid.
56. Interview with Lord Longford, 10 October 1995.
57. Ibid.
58. Interview with McNamara, 26 October 1995.
59. *The Times*, 19 January 1968.
60. Ibid., 20 January 1968.
61. *Belfast Telegraph*, 12 March 1968.
62. Ibid., 13 March 1968.
63. Kenneth Bloomfield, *Stormont in Crisis*, Belfast, 1993, p. 97.
64. Andrew Gailey, *Crying in the Wilderness*, Belfast, 1995, p. 131.
65. *The Times*, 25 March 1968.

5   THE ROAD TO LONDONDERRY, APRIL–OCTOBER 1968

1. *House of Commons Debates*, 5th ser., vol. 768, cols 731–33, 11 July 1968.
2. *The Times*, 5 October 1968.
3. Harold Wilson, *The Labour Government 1964–70*, London, p. 671.
4. Kenneth Bloomfield, *Stormont in Crisis*, Belfast, 1994, p. 98.
5. ICBH seminar, London, 14 January 1992.
6. Ibid.
7. Interview with Oliver, 8 February 1995.
8. See account of CDU meeting at the House of Commons later in this chapter.
9. Michael Cunningham, *British Government Policy in Northern Ireland 1969–89*, Manchester, 1991, p. 17.
10. PRO DEFE 4/197 MOD Chiefs of Staff Committee, Confidential Annexe to COS 15th Meeting 66, 17 March 1996.
11. ICBH seminar.
12. Victor Stonham, formerly MP for Shoreditch and Finsbury 1954–8; created a life peer in 1958; Minister of State, Home Office, 1967–9; died, 1971.

13. *Belfast Telegraph*, 7 June 1968.
14. A full version of McNamara's remarks about Bacon can be found in Chapter 2.
15. ICBH seminar.
16. Bob Purdie, *Politics in the Streets*, Belfast, 1990, p. 109.
17. From the private papers of Kevin McNamara, Brynmar Jones Library, University of Hull.
18. Ibid.
19. Interview with McNamara, 25 June 1992.
20. From the private papers of McNamara.
21. *Belfast Telegraph*, 23 June 1968.
22. *House of Commons Debates*, 5th ser., vol. 768, cols 731–33.
23. Interview with Whitaker, 27 August 1996. [Whitaker, ironically, was a relative by marriage to Terence O'Neill.]
24. Interview with Sir Frank Cooper, 17 February 1997. Sir Frank went on to be Permanent Secretary to the Northern Ireland Office, 1973–6 and then Permanent Secretary to the Ministry of Defence, 1976–82.
25. *Belfast Telegraph*, 23 July 1968.
26. Ibid., 24 July 1968.
27. The report is not to be found among the papers of the Society of Labour Lawyers held at the BLEPS, LSE.
28. *Belfast Telegraph*, 22 August 1968.
29. See below comments of George Clark, *The Times*' political correspondent, 5 October 1968.
30. *The Times*, 28 August 1968.
31. Ibid.
32. *Belfast Telegraph*, 30 September 1968.
33. Paddy Byrne, typescript in the CDU archive, dated October 1973. NIPRO D3026/7.
34. *Belfast Telegraph*, 1 November 1968.
35. *The Times*, 5 October 1968. The other Labour MPs who went to Londonderry were: Russell Kerr, Feltham, his wife Anne Kerr, Rochester and Chatham, Dr David Kerr, Wandsworth Central [not related] and John Ryan, Uxbridge.
36. Ibid.
37. Paul Arthur, *Government and Politics of Northern Ireland*, Harlow, 1980, p. 103–4.
38. Ibid.
39. W.D. Flackes, *Northern Ireland. A Political Directory*, Dublin, 1980, p. 44.
40. BBC *Timewatch* transcript, provided by the BBC. The transcript was undated but the interview with Fitt was carried out during 1992 for the programme, 'The Spark that Lit the Bonfire', which was broadcast on BBC2 on 27 January 1993.
41. Roy Foster, *Modern Ireland 1600–1972*, London, 1989, p. 588.
42. Wilson, *Labour Government*, p. 671.
43. BBC *Timewatch* interview with Callaghan. Undated transcript provided by the BBC. As in the case of Fitt the interview was carried out during 1992.

44. Ibid.
45. Bloomfield, *Stormont*, pp. 98–9.
46. Brian Faulkner, *Memoirs of a Statesman*, London, 1978, pp. 48–9.
47. *The Round Table*, January 1969, No 233. The article is dated November, 1968.
48. *The Times*, 7 October 1968.
49. Ibid.
50. Ibid.
51. Ibid., 8 October 1968.
52. See reference to Holland in previous chapter.
53. 'The magazine's circulation peaked in the mid-sixties ...' from the *Guardian* 22 April, 1996.
54. Editor of the *New Statesman* from 1965 to 1970.
55. *New Statesman*, 11 October 1968.
56. Ibid.
57. *Economist*, 12 October 1968.
58. Ibid.
59. Richard Crossman, *The Diaries of a Cabinet Minister*, vol. 3, London, 1977, p. 187. Wilson's reference to 'twelve Ulster MPs' implied they were all Unionists when in fact one was Gerry Fitt, who sat on the Labour benches and generally supported the Government.
60. Papers of Richard Crossman, Modern Records Centre, University Library, University of Warwick, temporary file X5 (papers not yet catalogued).
61. Flackes, *Northern Ireland*, p. 52.
62. Ibid., p. 186.
63. Paul Rose, The Northern Ireland Problem (2) Breaking the Convention, *Contemporary Review*, vol. 219, 1971, p. 286.
64. *House of Commons Debates*, 5th ser., vol. 770, cols 882–85, 21 October 1968.
65. Ibid., Cols 1088–90, 22 October 1968.
66. See footnote 17, above.
67. *The Times*, 6 August 1968. Mackintosh was that rarity at the time, a Scottish MP who believed in devolution.
68. Crossman, *Diaries*, vol. 3, p. 478.

6 'HISTORY IS AGAINST US', NOVEMBER 1968–APRIL 1969

1. From a 'memorandum' written by a senior civil servant, now retired, who does not wish to be identified.
2. Kenneth Bloomfield, *Stormont in Crisis*, Belfast, 1994, p. 108.
3. Ibid., pp. 100–1.
4. ICBH seminar, London, 14 January 1992 and interview with Sir John Chilcot, Permanent Secretary Northern Ireland Office [retired 1997], 20 July 1994.
5. Interview with Roy Lilley, 12 May 1993.
6. An electricity sub station near Belfast and the main water pipeline between the Mourne Mountains and the city.

7. From the personal archive of Professor Peter Hennessy, Professor of Contemporary History at Queen Mary and Westfield College, University of London. The retired civil servant had put a fictional date on the document: 2 November 1968.
8. Ibid.
9. Ibid.
10. Ibid.
11. Harold Wilson, *The Labour Government 1964–70*, London, 1971, p. 672.
12. Ibid.
13. Ibid.
14. Ibid.
15. For example the political journalist Andrew Roth in 1977 published a biography of Wilson called *Harold Wilson: 'A Yorkshire Walter Mitty'*.
16. Terence O'Neill, *The Autobiography of Terence O'Neill*, London, 1972, p. 105. The contents of the notes referred to by O'Neill are not known. They are not revealed in the autobiographies of either O'Neill or Faulkner.
17. James Callaghan, *A House Divided*, London, 1973, p. 10.
18. Wilson, *Labour Government*, p. 673.
19. Brian Faulkner, *Memoirs of a Statesman*, London, 1978, p. 49.
20. Andrew Gailey, *Crying in the Wilderness,* Belfast, 1995, p. 136.
21. *Belfast Telegraph*, 5 November 1968.
22. Ibid.
23. Ibid., 6 November 1968.
24. Ibid.
25. Ibid.
26. Ibid.
27. Gailey, *Crying*, p. 137.
28. Bloomfield, *Stormont,* p. 100.
29. *Sunday Times* Insight Team, *Ulster*, Harmondsworth , London, 1972, p. 84.
30. Wilson, *Labour Government*, 673.
31. 'Limited companies were entitled to nominate up to six extra voters. These were a good deal more likely to be Protestant than Catholic'. From The *Sunday Times* Insight Team, *Ulster*, Harmondsworth, 1972, p. 35.
32. Wilson, *Labour Government*, p. 673.
33. Jonathan Bardon, *A History of Ulster,* Belfast, 1992, p. 657.
34. Interview with Oliver, 8 February 1995.
35. Gailey, *Crying*, p. 139.
36. Ibid.
37. Insight Team, *Ulster*, p. 59.
38. Paul Bew, Peter Gibbon, Henry Patterson, *Northern Ireland 1921–1996*, London, 1996, p. 178.
39. *Belfast Telegraph,* 29 November 1968.
40. Ibid.
41. *House of Commons Debates*, 5th ser., vol. 774, cols 1038–44, 2 December 1968.

42. *Belfast Telegraph*, 3 December 1968.
43. Bloomfield, *Stormont,* pp. 100–1.
44. Ibid.
45. Gailey, *Crying*, p. 140.
46. *The Times*, 10 December 1968.
47. *Belfast Telegraph*, 10 December 1968.
48. Ibid., 11 December 1968.
49. Bloomfield, *Stormont*, p. 101.
50. Wilson, *Labour Government*, p. 674.
51. Interview with Lilley.
52. ICBH seminar.
53. Ibid. The last sentence was a handwritten addition by Callaghan, to the transcript of his evidence.
54. Ibid.
55. Ibid.
56. Bloomfield, *Stormont,* p. 103.
57. Ibid., pp. 101–2.
58. Ibid. p. 108.
59. Gailey, *Crying*, p. 140.
60. Bob Purdie, *Politics in the Streets*, Belfast, 1990.
61. W.D. Flackes, *Northern Ireland: A Political Directory 1968–79*, Dublin, 1980, p. 108–9.
62. Bloomfield, *Stormont*, p. 102.
63. Gailey, *Crying*, p. 143.
64. Flackes, *Northern Ireland*, pp. 108–9.
65. Paul Arthur, *Government and Politics of Northern Ireland*, Harlow, Essex, 1980, p. 109.
66. *Disturbances in Northern Ireland: Report of the Commission Appointed by the Governor of Northern Ireland,* Belfast, HMSO, Cmd 532, 1969. The Commission was presided over by Lord Cameron and his report is considered in Chapter 7.
67. *Belfast Telegraph*, 6 January 1969.
68. ICBH seminar.
69. Ibid.
70. Telephone interview with Arthur, 4 September 1996.
71. Ibid. In the Northern Ireland General Election the following month, Hume was returned as MP for Foyle.
72. Bloomfield, *Stormont*, p. 102.
73. *Belfast Telegraph*, 9 January 1969; *The Times,* 10 January 1969.
74. *New Statesman*, 10 January, 1969.
75. *The Times,* 10 January 1969.
76. *Belfast Telegraph*, 13 January 1969.
77. *Irish Times*, 21 January 1969.
78. Flackes, *Northern Ireland* p. 56.
79. Faulkner, *Memoirs*, pp. 50–1.
80. O'Neill, *Autobiography*, p. 115.
81. Interview with Lilley.
82. *Spectator*, 31 January 1969.
83. *The Times*, 1 February 1969.

84. Wilson, *Labour Government*, p. 674.
85. Bloomfield, *Stormont*, p. 103–4.
86. *Belfast Telegraph,* 7 February 1969.
87. Ibid.
88. *Spectator*, 7 February 1969.
89. From the unpublished papers of Richard Crossman, Modern Records Centre, University of Warwick, temporary file Y2 (papers not yet catalogued). However, an edited version occurs in the published diary for the entry for 25 February, 1969, after the election when it has become obvious that O'Neill's gamble has failed. Richard Crossman, *The Diaries of a Cabinet Minister*, vol. 3, London, 1997, pp. 381–2. The editor of the published Diaries, Janet Morgan, has combined the material from the two entries presumably for the sake of brevity. [Callaghan's secret take-over plan clearly refers to the work being carried out by a specially appointed civil servant, discussed in the next chapter.]
90. Transcript marked 'Official File Copy *Panorama*' 5319/1007 provided by the BBC.
91. Ibid.
92. Bardon, *Ulster*, p. 663.
93. Flackes, *Northern Ireland*, p. 159.
94. *Sunday Times* Insight Team, *Ulster*, Harmondsworth, 1972, p. 71.
95. A cartoon by Garland in the *Daily Telegraph* on 26 February 1969, showed a snakes and ladders board with O'Neill sliding down a snake with the head of Ian Paisley.
96. *Belfast Telegraph*, 25 February 1969.
97. *The Times*, 25 February 1969.
98. *Daily Mail*, 25 February 1969.
99. *The Times*, 26 February 1969.
100. *Spectator*, 28 February 1969.
101. *Belfast Telegraph*, 28 February 1969. Utley was at the time a leader writer on the *Daily Telegraph*.
102. Ibid.
103. Gailey, *Crying*, 148. Keir was a former Master of Balliol College, Oxford, and an expert on the British Constitution.
104. Wilson, *Labour Government*, p. 674.
105. Crossman, *Diaries* vol. 3, p. 382.
106. Most of the entry for 25 February appears in the unpublished transcript as part of the entry for 9 February. See above.
107. Shanks, an applied economist, had written a powerful critique of Britain's economic and industrial performance in *The Stagnant Society,* Harmondsworth, 1961, a book described by the historian Kenneth Morgan as 'a particularly influential work' which 'made an immense impression on the public mind.' Shanks, who died in 1984, was Industrial Advisor, DEA 1965–6; Industrial Policy Co-ordinator DEA, 1966–7.
108. *The Times*, 6 March 1969.
109. Ibid.
110. *Bloomfield*, Stormont, pp. 105–6.

111. Wilson, *Labour Government*, p. 674.
112. Bloomfield, *Stormont*, p. 107.
113. Interview with Bloomfield, 1 December 1993.
114. Bloomfield, *Stormont*, p. 107.
115. Andrew Whittaker, *Irish Times,* 21 April 1969.
116. *The Times*, 21 April 1969.
117. Ibid. [Bernadette Devlin had defeated the Unionist candidate, Anna Forrest, the widow of George Forrest, the Unionist MP for Mid-Ulster, whose death had caused the by-election.]
118. Ibid.
119. *Belfast Telegraph*, 21 April 1969.
120. Ibid.
121. Flackes, *Northern Ireland*, p. 80.
122. The writer, then a member of the Parliamentary lobby journalists group, was in the Press Gallery for this memorable occasion.
123. *House of Commons Debates*, 5th ser., vol. 782, cols 262–323, 22 April 1969.
124. Jack Lynch, leader of Fianna Fail had succeeded Sean Lemass as Taoiseach in 1966.
125. Wilson, *Labour Government*, pp. 674–5.
126. Crossman, *Diaries*, vol. 3, pp. 450–1.
127. Interview with Paul Rose, 14 August 1992.
128. *Belfast Telegraph*, 25 April 1969.
129. Wilson, *Labour Government*, p. 675.
130. Brown resigned in March 1968 when Wilson and the Chancellor, Roy Jenkins, closed the London Stock Exchange without consulting him. 'One estimate is that George Brown threatened to resign from Harold Wilson's government on 17 different occasions.... On Friday 15 March 1968 his proffered resignation was finally accepted.... No specific issue of policy was cited by Brown as the reason for his departure but it was interpreted by the press as a pointless act of pique'. From Peter Patterson, *Tired and Emotional: The Life of Lord George Brown*, London, 1993, pp. 241–2.
131. George Brown, *In My Way*, London, 1972, p. 190.
132. Ibid., p. 17.
133. Ibid., p. 19.
134. Brown was presumably referring to the type of co-operation Dr John Oliver had instanced (see Chapter 3).
135. *Evening Standard*, 24 April 1969.
136. Entry for 27 April, 1969 taken from both the unpublished transcript (box Y4) and from the published Diaries. Crossman *Diaries*, vol. 3, p. 458. The unpublished material (in italics) has been used because there are several omissions in the published version, the most significant being Crossman's claim that Callaghan had 'kept in careful touch with me' over the Ulster crisis.
137. 'It is perhaps extraordinary that a man who had taught politics should have been so naive. The material was probably in a confidential annexe to the Cabinet Minutes. Crossman should have known about these as he would have encountered several in the past'. Peter Hennessy, in

conversation with the writer, 2 February 1997.
138. Crossman *Diaries*, vol. 3, p. 458.
139. *Sunday Times* Insight Team, *Ulster*, Harmondsworth, 1972, p. 102. The Insight Team wrote that the committee was the most powerful of all Labour's Cabinet Committees – 'and one supposedly so secret that Wilson insisted it be known merely by a number. Everyone promptly forgot which number it was'. Crossman, they claimed, only got on 'because he kept making a nuisance of himself'.
140. Ben Pimlott, *Harold Wilson*, London, 1992, p. 547.
141. Ibid., p. 533.
142. Kenneth Morgan, *The People's Peace*, Oxford, 1990, p. 302.
143. On 2 May David Wood, political editor of *The Times*, speculated on Callaghan succeeding under the front-page headline: 'Attempt to replace Mr Wilson may be imminent'. Joe Haines claimed, 'I was the one who first of all tipped Harold off about the plotting. Because we knew early we were able to nip it in the bud'. (Interview with the writer, 12 September 1996.) In her diary entry for 8 May 1969, Barbara Castle records a ferocious attack by Crossman in Cabinet clearly aimed at Callaghan. Crossman had warned that the plotters had better realise it wouldn't work: 'four of the inner heart of the Cabinet couldn't and wouldn't serve' under the supplanter. (*The Castle Diaries 1964–70*, London, 1984, p. 647.)
144. Peter Hennessy. From 3rd annual CESER lecture, May 1996, 'A question of control: "war cabinets" and limited conflicts since 1945'. Published by CESER Publications, Bristol, 1996.
145. The entry for Terence O'Neill (by Paul Bew). *The Dictionary of National Biography*, Oxford, 1996, pp. 336–7.
146. Gailey, *Crying*, p. 144. Asked to comment on this suggestion Sir Kenneth Bloomfield said that he had written all he wanted to say, 'at this stage,' about his relationship with O'Neill in his own book, *Stormont in Crisis*, Belfast, 1994. Letter to the writer, 14 February 1997.
147. Ibid., p. 146.

7   TO THE TOP OF THE AGENDA, MAY–AUGUST 1969

1. Interview with Sir John Chilcot, Permanent Secretary, Northern Ireland Office, 20 July 1994.
2. Harold Wilson, *The Labour Government 1964–1970*, London, 1971, p. 692.
3. Geoffrey Bell, *Troublesome Business, the Labour Party and the Irish Question*, London, 1982, pp. 108–9.
4. Terence O'Neill, *The Autobiography of Terence O'Neill*, London, 1972, p. 141.
5. The *Sunday Times* Insight Team, *Ulster*, Harmondsworth, 1972, p. 85.
6. James Callaghan, *A House Divided,* London, 1973, p. 23.
7. Barbara Castle, *The Castle Diaries 1964–70*, London, 1984, p. 708.
8. ICBH seminar, London 14 January 1992. In the early 1970s the legality of using servicemen in non-military emergencies was privately

discussed by ministers after the mass picketing at Saltley. From Keith Jeffrey and Peter Hennessy, *States of Emergency*, London, 1983, p. 243.

9. From the undated transcript of *Timewatch*'s interview with Callaghan provided by BBC TV. The interview was carried out sometime in 1992 for the programme, 'The Spark that Lit the Bonfire', which was transmitted on BBC 2 on 27 January 1993.

10. Chilcot had been Private Secretary to the Home Secretary Roy Jenkins. He had already left the department by this time but was recalled to prepare the plan.

11. Interview with Chilcot, 20 July 1994.

12. Ibid.

13. Ibid. A question arises from this revelation: were the Conservatives informed of these preparations, possibly on Privy Council terms? If so it would help to explain the speech made in Belfast by Sir Alec Douglas-Home during the 1970 general election campaign, when he warned Ulster Unionists that there were circumstances in which a Conservative government might have to introduce direct rule. [See Chapter 3 note 10.] However, a retired civil servant who had held a senior Whitehall post at the time, has said that he did not know but if he had to guess 'probably not'. Letter to the writer, 9 February 1997.

14. Ibid.

15. Ibid.

16. Ibid. During the interview with Chilcot, the writer asked him why he thought that Jenkins, with his reputation as a great reforming Home Secretary, had not done more to address Catholic grievances? He replied that Jenkins had only just finished his biography of Asquith [Roy Jenkins, *Asquith*, London, 1964.] when Labour won the general election. Jenkins feared that if the Government became embroiled in the Irish question, 'it would, as it had in the latter part of the 19th Century, so distract and preoccupy political attention at Westminster that it would divert political time, energy and effort from the essential reform programme to which Jenkins himself and the Labour Government of the day were then committed on a United Kingdom-wide scale'.

17. Interview with Wright, 8 September 1992.

18. Sir Frank Cooper, letter to the writer, 19 August 1996. Sir Frank went on to be Permanent Secretary to the Northern Ireland Office 1973–6 and then Permanent Secretary to the Ministry of Defence 1976–82.

19. Interview with Green, 15 July 1996.

20. Bell, *Troublesome Business*, p. 106.

21. Ibid. Benn's own diaries do not bear out his claim. According to his own record there were more than two occasions when Northern Ireland was discussed in full Cabinet. See for example the entry for 4 March 1976. Tony Benn, *Against the Tide. Diaries 1973–76*, London , 1989, p. 526 and the entry for 11 January 1979. Tony Benn, *Conflict of Interests. Diaries 1977–80*, London, 1990, p. 433.

22. Richard Crossman, *The Diaries of a Cabinet Minister*, vol. 3, London, 1977, pp. 477–8. The unpublished diaries: Modern Records Centre, University of Warwick, temporary file Y4 (papers not yet catalogued).

23. Ibid.
24. Ibid.
25. Ibid.
26. Ibid.
27. Wilson, *Labour Government*, p. 675.
28. *House of Commons Debates*, 5th ser., vol. 783, cols. 655–56, 8 May 1969.
29. *The Times*, 12 May 1969.
30. *Belfast Telegraph*, 16 May 1969.
31. *The Times*, 21 May 1969.
32. Ibid., 22 May 1969.
33. *House of Commons Debates*, 5th ser., vol.784, cols. 660–69, 22 May 1969.
34. *Belfast Telegraph*, 23 May 1969.
35. Andrew Gailey, *Crying in the Wilderness*, Belfast, 1995, p. 155.
36. *Belfast Telegraph*, 24 May 1969. Alice Bacon [who had been transferred from the Home Office to the Dept of Education in 1967] was attending the conference as a fraternal delegate from the British Labour Party.
37. 'The ICJ is a non-governmental organisation devoted to promoting throughout the world the understanding and observance of the Rule of Law and the legal protection of human rights ...'. From the *ICJ Review*, June 1994.
38. *The Times*, 19 June 1969.
39. Ibid.
40. Ibid.
41. W.D. Flackes, *Northern Ireland, A Political Directory 1968–79*, Dublin, 1980, p. 82.
42. *Belfast Telegraph*, 19 June 1969.
43. The Orange Order, 'traditionally holds its annual 12th of July demonstrations in more than 20 centres in Northern Ireland to celebrate King William's victory over King James at the Battle of the Boyne'. From: Flackes, *Northern Ireland*, p. 103.
44. Insight, *Ulster*, pp. 101–2.
45. Ibid.
46. Wilson, *Labour Government*, p. 692.
47. BBC *Timewatch* transcript.
48. Interview with McNamara, 25 June 1992.
49. ICBH seminar.
50. Interview with Paul Rose, 14 August 1992. It could be argued, however, that preferring trouble to come from the minority rather than the majority is a rather wise preference!
51. *Belfast Telegraph,* 30 July 1969.
52. Minister of Defence (Administration) 1969–70.
53. Interview with Hattersley, 16 June 1992.
54. Gailey, *Crying*, p. 157.
55. Ibid., pp. 161–2.
56. Callaghan, *House,* p. 19.
57. Ibid., p. 15.
58. *House*, p. 19.
59. Ibid., p. 22.

60. PRO DEFE4/197 MOD Chiefs of Staff Committee, Confidential Annexe to COS 15th Meeting 66, 17 March 1966.
61. *The Times*, 5 August 1969.
62. *Financial Times*, 6 August 1969.
63. Insight, *Ulster*, p. 110.
64. Personal knowledge of the writer who was a lobby journalist at the time.
65. Insight, *Ulster*, p. 110.
66. O'Neill, *Autobiography*, p. 141.
67. ICBH seminar.
68. Interview with Lilley, 12 May 1993.
69. From the unpublished diaries for 10 August, file 154/8/161, two days before the march. Irritatingly, however, much of it appears in the published diaries in the entry for 14 August, vol. 3, p. 618–19, after the march, in the form of Crossman recalling what had been said at the earlier Cabinet meeting. The Editor might have compressed two entries for the sake of brevity. However, presented in this form, Crossman's pre-march thoughts inevitably lose impact.
70. BBC *Timewatch* transcript.
71. Roy Hattersley, *Who Goes Home?*, London, 1995, p. 77.
72. Wilson, *Labour Government*, p. 693.
73. *The Times*, 14 August 1969.
74. Unpublished diaries, entry for 17 August 1969, file MSS/154/8/161; also partly to be found in the published *Diaries*, vol. 3, p. 620.
75. The source for this paragraph is the entry for 14 August in the published *Diaries*, vol. 3, p. 619. The unpublished papers make it clear that it was written on 17 August.
76. *New Statesman*, 15 August 1969.
77. *Spectator*, 16 August 1969.
78. *Economist*, 16 August 1969.
79. Flackes, *Northern Ireland*, p. 155.
80. Interview with Arthur Green, 15 July 1996. Green was Assistant Secretary Northern Ireland Department of Finance, 1972–8 and then Under-Secretary Northern Ireland Office, 1978–9.
81. *Disturbances in Northern Ireland: Report of the Commission Appointed by the Governor of Northern Ireland*, Belfast, HMSO, Cmd 532, 1969. The Scarman Tribunal investigated the August riots but did not report until April, 1972.
82. Bob Purdie, *Politics in the Street*, Belfast, 1990, p. 149.
83. Patrick Riddell, *Fire Over Ulster*, London, 1970, p. 139.
84. Letter to the writer from Green, 16 July 1996.
85. Roy Foster, *Modern Ireland 1600–1972*, London, 1988 p. 589.
86. *House of Commons Debates*, 5th ser., vol. 784, cols 660–69, 22 May 1969.
87. Crossman, *Diaries*, vol. 3, pp. 477–8.
88. Interview with Green, op. cit.
89. ICBH seminar, op. cit.
90. Ibid.
91. Foster, *Modern Ireland*, p. 526.

8 CONCLUSIONS

1. Harold Wilson, *The Labour Government 1964–70*, London, 1971, p. 99.
2. *Daily Herald*, 3 June 1953.
3. James Callaghan, *A House Divided*, London, 1973, p. 15.
4. As Purdie pointed out, 'The CJS and the CDU succeeded in stirring much greater interest in Northern Ireland among British Labour MPs and in giving the impression that Harold Wilson's government might intervene. This simply created hopes that could not be fulfilled on one side and fears that could not be assuaged on the other'. [Bob Purdie, *Politics in the Streets*, Belfast, 1990, pp. 247–8.]
5. Interview with the late Sir Richard Francis, Controller, BBC Northern Ireland 1973–7.
6. *House of Commons Debates*, 5th ser., vol. 768, cols 731–33, 11 July 1968.
7. 20 March 1963. 'On visit of Sean Lemass' (Irish Prime Minister). The Diaries of Harold Macmillan, Dept. of Western Manuscripts, Bodleian Library, Oxford. I am indebted to Dr Peter Catterall for this quotation.

Bibliography

This bibliography contains details of sources found useful, rather than all those consulted.

PRIMARY SOURCES

BBC TV transcripts:
Timewatch, 'The Spark that Lit the Bonfire', broadcast on BBC 2 on 27 January 1993 and *Panorama*, 'The Northern Ireland General Election, 1969', broadcast on 17 February 1969. (Transcripts provided by the *Timewatch* and *Panorama* departments, BBC).

Campaign for Democracy in Ulster papers, Northern Ireland Public Record Office, Belfast.

Diaries of Harold Macmillan. Department of Western Manuscripts, Bodleian Library, Oxford.

Government papers (from 1940 to 1966), Public Record Office, Kew, including the following classes:
CAB128; Cabinet Conclusions
CAB129; Cabinet Papers
CAB21; Cabinet Office, Registered Files from 1916 to 1965
PREM4; Confidential Papers, 1939–46
PREM8; Prime Minister's Office. Correspondence and Papers 1945–51
PREM13; Prime Minister's Office: Correspondence and Papers 1964–70
DEFE4/197, Chiefs of Staff Committee Minutes
House of Commons Debates, Fifth Series vol. 464 to vol. 784.

Institute of Contemporary British History, unpublished transcript of witness seminar on British policy in Northern Ireland, 1964–70, London, 14 January 1992.

Kevin McNamara, MP for Kingston-Upon-Hull North (Labour), private papers, Brynmor Jones Library, the University of Hull.

Labour Party National Executive Committee Minutes, National Museum of Labour History, Manchester.

Richard Crossman's papers, Modern Records Centre, University Library, University of Warwick.

Society of Labour Lawyers papers, British Library of Political and Economic Science, London School of Economics.

Official Publications

Disturbances in Northern Ireland: Report of the Commission appointed by the Governor of Northern Ireland, Belfast, HMSO, Cmd 532, 1969.

Interviews

Archer, Peter, now Lord Archer, formerly Labour MP for Rowley Regis and Tipton, Solicitor General 1974–79. 12 October 1994.

Arthur, Paul, Professor, Faculty of Humanities. History, Philosophy and Politics, University of Ulster, Coleraine. 4 September 1996.

Bloomfield, Sir Kenneth, Assistant and later Deputy Secretary to the Cabinet, Northern Ireland, 1963–72. Head of N.I.C.S., 1984–91. 1 December 1993.

Callaghan, James. Home Secretary 1967–70 [at the ICBH seminar, London], 14 January 1992.

Chilcot, Sir John. Home Office civil servant in the late 1960s. Permanent Secretary, Northern Ireland Office, 1990–98. 20 July 1994.

Cooper, Sir Frank, Permanent Secretary, Northern Ireland Office, 1973–76. 11 January 1994 and 16 December 1996.

Gailey, Andrew, author of *Crying in the Wilderness*, Belfast, 1995. 22 November 1995.

Garrett, John, Belfast solicitor and member of the Northern Ireland branch of the Society of Labour Lawyers. 30 January 1995.

Green, Arthur, Secretary, Cameron Commission, 1969. 15 July 1996.

Griffith, Professor John, Emeritus Professor of Public Law (University of London). 19 December 1995.

Haines, Joe, Press Secretary to Harold Wilson, 1969–76. 12 September 1996.

Hattersley, Roy, MP for Birmingham, Sparkbrook 1964–97, Minister of Defence for Administration 1969–70, later Deputy Leader of the Labour Party. 16 June 1992.

Jenkins, Roy, now Lord Jenkins of Hillhead, Home Secretary, 1965–67, later Chancellor of the Exchequer and Deputy Leader of the Labour Party. 3 October 1992.

Lilley, Roy, Political correspondent (later Editor) of the *Belfast Telegraph*, 12 May 1993.

Longford, Lord, Leader of the House of Lords, 1964–68. 10 October 1995.

McNamara, Kevin, MP for Hull North since 1966. 25 June 1992.

Oliver, Dr John, senior Northern Ireland civil servant. 8 February 1995.

Otton, Sir Geoffrey, Principal Private Secretary to the Home Secretary 1963–65. 24 September 1996.

Rees-Mogg, William, now Lord Rees-Mogg, Editor of *The Times*, 1967–81. 13 November 1995.

Rose, Paul, MP for Manchester, Blackley 1964–79. 14 August 1992.

Thorpe, Jeremy, Leader of the Liberal Party, 1967–76. 10 June 1993.

Waller, Ian, formerly Political Editor, the *Sunday Telegraph*. 15 March 1995.

Whitaker, Ben, MP for Hampstead 1966–70. 27 August 1996.

Wright, Sir Oliver, Private Secretary to the Prime Minister (Harold Wilson) 1964–66, and first UK Government Representative in Northern Ireland, August 1969–March 1970. 8 September 1992.

Newspapers and Periodicals

Belfast Telegraph
Catholic Herald
Contemporary Review
Daily Herald
Daily Mail
Daily Telegraph
Economist
Evening Standard
Guardian
ICJ Review (the journal of the International Commission of Jurists)
International Affairs (the journal of the Royal Institute of International Affairs)
Irish News
Irish Times
New Statesman
Observer
Revue Française de Civilisation Britannique
RSA Journal
Spectator
Sunday Times
The Round Table
The Times

Memoirs, Autobiographies and Published Diaries

Benn, Tony, *Office Without Power: Diaries 1968–72*, London, 1988; *Against the Tide: Diaries 1973–76*, London, 1989; *Conflict of Interests: Diaries 1977–80*, London, 1990.
Bloomfield, Kenneth, *Stormont in Crisis*, Belfast, 1994.
Brett C.E.B., *Long Shadows Cast before Midnight*, Edinburgh, 1978.
Brown, George, *In My Way*, London, 1972.
Callaghan, James, *A House Divided*, London, 1973.
Callaghan, James, *Time and Chance*, London, 1987.
Castle, Barbara, *The Castle Diaries, 1964–70*, London, 1984.
Crossman, Richard, *The Diaries of a Cabinet Minister*, vol.3, London, 1977.
Faulkner, Brian, *Memoirs of a Statesman*, London, 1978.
Hattersley, Roy, *Who Goes Home?*, London 1995.
Jenkins, Roy, *A Life at the Centre*, London, 1991.
King, Cecil, *The Cecil King Diaries 1965–70*, London, 1972.
Longford, Lord, *The Grain of Wheat*, London 1974.
O'Neill, Terence, *The Autobiography of Terence O'Neill*, London 1972.
Rose, Paul, *Backbencher's Dilemma*, London, 1981.
Walker, Patrick Gordon, *Political Diaries, 1932–71*, edited by Robert Pearce, London, 1991.
Wilson, Harold, *The Labour Government: 1964–70*, London, 1971.

SECONDARY SOURCES

Arthur, Paul, *Government and Politics of Northern Ireland*, Harlow, 1980.
Bagehot, Walter, *The Premiership*, in *The Collected Works of Walter Bagehot*, vol. 6, edited by Norman St John-Stevas, London, 1974.
Bardon, Jonathan, *A History of Ulster*, Belfast, 1992.
Bell, Geoffrey, *Troublesome Business, The Labour Party and the Irish Question*, London, 1982.
Bew, Paul and Henry Patterson, *The British State and the Ulster Crisis*, London, 1985.
Bew, Paul, Peter Gibbon, and Henry Patterson, *Northern Ireland 1921–1994*, London, 1995.
Calvert, Harry, *Constitutional Law in Northern Ireland*, London and Belfast, 1968.
Craig, Mary, *Longford*, London, 1978.
Cunningham, Michael, *British Government Policy in Northern Ireland, 1969–89*, Manchester, 1989.
Donoughue, Bernard, and Jones, G.W., *Herbert Morrison*, London, 1973.
Flackes, W.D., *Northern Ireland: A Political Directory*, Dublin, 1983.
Foster, Roy, *Modern Ireland 1600 to 1972*, London, 1989.
Gailey, Andrew, *Crying in the Wilderness*, Belfast, 1995.
Harkness, David, *Northern Ireland since 1920*, Dublin, 1983.
Hyam, Ronald, *The Labour Government and the End of Empire, 1945–51*, London 1992.
Jeffrey, Keith, and Peter Hennessy, *States of Emergency*, London, 1983.

Lyons, F.S.L., *Ireland since the Famine*, London, 1985.
Morgan, Kenneth, *Labour in Power*, Oxford, 1985.
Morgan, Kenneth, *The People's Peace*, Oxford, 1990.
O'Brien, Conor Cruise, *States of Ireland*, London, 1972.
Patterson, Peter, *Tired and Emotional: the Life of Lord George Brown*, London, 1993.
Pimlott, Ben, *Harold Wilson*, London, 1992.
Purdie, Bob, *Politics in the Street*, Belfast, 1990.
Riddell, Patrick, *Fire over Ulster*, London 1970.
Rose, Richard, *Governing without Consensus*, London, 1971.
Stacey, Frank, *The British Ombudsman*, Oxford, 1971.
Sunday Times Insight Team, *Ulster*, London, 1972.
The Dictionary of National Biography, Oxford, 1996.
The Northern Ireland Question in British Politics, edited by Peter Catterall and Sean McDougall, London, 1996.
The Times: Guide to the House of Commons 1966, London, 1966.
Whyte, J. *Interpreting Northern Ireland*, Oxford, 1991.
Wilson, Tom, *Ulster: Conflict and Consent*, Oxford, 1989.

Index

Addison, Lord, 2
Amnesty, 157
Anti-Partition League, 8, 14
Apprentice Boys' March, 68, 150,
    161–3, 165–6, 169
Archer, Peter, 71–2, 78, 83
Armagh, 127
Army, British, 104, 154, 162, 164,
    166
Arthur, Paul, 99, 107–8, 131–2
Astor, David, 94
Atlee, Clement, 9, 16, 172, 177
    and civil rights, 2
    and Ireland Act 1949, xv, 5–7, 9,
        123, 173
    and declaration of Irish Republic,
        3
    and reluctance to interfere in
        Northern Ireland, 3–5

BBC, xiii, 37, 83, 108, 152, 174
    1969 General Election
        (*Panorama*), 134, 136–7
Bacon, Alice, 51–6, 101–2, 160
Bagehot, Walter, 49
Bardon, Jonathan, 15, 48, 126, 137
Battle of the Somme, 39
Belfast, 36, 46, 60, 73–4, 76, 95, 97,
    99, 130, 167, 169, 175
    City Council, 32
    Riots (1964), 14–15, 56, 178
    sectarian violence in early 1920s,
        170
    Trades Council, 66
Belfast Telegraph, xiv, 13, 34, 36–7,
    40, 44, 47, 51, 60–1, 67–8, 76,
    83, 84–7, 89–90, 96, 101, 104–6,
    118, 127–8, 131, 133, 139,
    141–2, 144, 157, 159, 161–2,
    164, 169, 172
    and general election 1969, 135–7
    and Sayers, Jack, 65, 67, 97, 109,
        123, 133

and Society of Labour Lawyers'
    investigation, 70, 82, 105–6
Bell, Ewart, 59
Bell, Geoffrey, 150, 155
Benn, Tony, 155
Bevan, Aneurin, 9
Bevin, Ernest, 1, 5–6, 8–9
Bew, Paul, 2, 8, 20, 26, 41, 64, 80,
    99, 126, 131, 148, 165, 178
Bleakley, David, 12
Bloomfield, Kenneth, 39, 42–4,
    48–9, 63, 65, 68, 97, 99, 109,
    125, 127–8, 130, 132, 135, 140,
    148
Bombings (of installations 1969),
    119, 140, 142, 159
Boyd, Billy, 15
Braddock, Bessie, 37
Bradford, Roy, 41
Brett, Sir Charles, 12
Brooke, Henry, 14
Brooke, John, 105
Brookeborough, Lord, 4, 42, 105
Brockway, Fenner, 158
Brown, George, xiv, 4, 9–10, 96, 143,
    173
    and idea of economic union of
        United Kingdom and Ireland,
        145
Burntollet Bridge riots, 130–1
Bottomley, Arthur, 12, 16
Bourne, John, 164, 169
Bowden, Herbert, 29, 35–6
Byrne, Paddy, 102–4, 106, 158

Cabinet, 3–5, 7, 30, 65, 68, 89, 92,
    94–5, 100, 107, 114, 127, 141,
    145, 148, 150–1, 155, 161, 164,
    165–7, 175–6, 178
    and Northern Ireland Cabinet
        Committee, 146–7, 176–7
Callaghan, James, 12, 38, 42, 52, 71,
    78–80, 92–4, 99, 101–3, 118,

Callaghan, James – *continued*
120–2, 128–9, 132, 143–7, 151,
157, 164, 172, 177–8
and Apprentice Boys' March,
161–4
and intervention plan, 136, 150–3,
155–6, 165–6, 169, 176
and Londonderry riots, 98, 107,
117, 119
and reluctance to intervene in
Northern Ireland, xvi, 10,
98–9, 106, 116, 121, 173–4,
176
Calvert, Harry, 20, 175
Cameron Commission, 69, 131, 134,
151, 167–8, 170
Campaign for Democracy in Ulster
(CDU), xi–xii, 2, 7–8, 20, 25, 28,
31, 35–7, 40, 44–6, 49, 57, 63,
71, 76–7, 80, 86, 89–90, 101,
107, 128, 130, 144, 158–9, 173
and Apprentice Boys' March,
162–4
and debate on Northern Ireland
(1969) called by, 51–3
investigation into civil rights in
Northern Ireland, 58, 65–70,
74, 103
and the media, 60
pessimism over failure to achieve
objectives, 100, 102–4, 174–5
Campaign for Social Justice in
Northern Ireland, 12–13, 27, 74
Casement, Roger, 16, 30, 173
Cassandra (William Conner), 47
Catholic Herald, 29, 61
Castle, Barbara, 146–7, 151, 155,
167
Chamberlain, Neville, 1
Chartres, John, 96–7, 138, 140
Chichester-Clark, James, 140, 145,
148, 155–62, 164–5, 167, 169
Chichester-Clark, Robin, 142
Chilcot, Sir John, 150–5, 176
Civil Service, 76, 100, 167
Northern Ireland Civil Service,
99, 169, 177
Civil servant's 'fictitious' memoran-
dum, 118–21, 148, 176

Clarke, George, 107
Cole, John, 83
Coleraine, 24, 38, 46
Commonwealth, the, 3–4, 6, 9
Connolly Association, 85
Conservative Party, xiv, 29, 60, 76,
112, 116, 176
Cooper, Sir Frank, 104, 154
Copcutt, Professor Geoffrey, 72, 74
Cosgrave, Liam, 9
Costello, John, 3, 6, 9
Craig, William, 51, 108, 111, 115,
121–2, 125, 127–9, 137, 169
Craigavon, 72–3
Craigavon, Lord, 26
Crawshaw, Richard, 24
Crosland, Anthony, 34
Crossman, Richard, diaries of, xv,
86, 95, 100, 114, 117–18, 136,
139, 144–8, 152, 155, 159, 161,
165–6, 169, 176–8
Cunningham, Sir Knox, 28, 37
Cunningham, Michael, 100
Currie, Austin, 108

Daily Herald, 8
Daily Mirror, 47
Daily Telegraph, The, 37, 47
Day, Robin, 136–7
de Gaulle, General, 177
Delargy, Hugh, 14, 24
Department of Economic Affairs
(DEA), 58–9, 145
de Valera, Eamon, 1–2, 4, 9–10, 14,
173
Devlin, Bernadette, 119, 130, 141–6,
166
Diamond, Harry, 15
Diamond, Jack, 114
Diamond, Percy, 36, 44, 47–8, 60,
65, 70, 86, 104, 123, 127–8, 135,
139, 141–2, 144, 162–4
Dungannon, 106

Easter Rising (50th anniversary), 39,
60, 64 *see also* under Northern
Ireland; IRA
Economist, the, 113, 167
Elizabeth II, 31, 40, 45–7

Employment, discrimination in, 38,
    45–6, 54, 66, 74, 81, 87, 120
Evans, Harold, 31, 46–7, 72
Evening Standard, 145

Farrell, Michael, 130, 137
Faulkner, Brian, 43, 109, 121–3,
    134–5, 157
Financial Times, The, 164
Fitt, Gerry, 31, 35, 37, 41, 52–4,
    56–7, 60, 71, 74, 81, 85–6,
    105–6, 108–11, 115–27, 142,
    144, 159, 174
Flackes, W.D., 134, 167
Fletcher, Sir Eric, 52–4
Floud, Bernard, 26
Foley, Maurice, 37–52
Foot, Michael, 8, 127, 173
Foreign Office, 154
Foster, Roy, 41, 108, 169
Francis, Richard, xiii
Freeson, Reg, 55, 85
Friends of Ireland, 2

Gailey, Andrew, 125–6, 130
Gaitskell, Hugh, 12, 95, 134
Garrett, Brian, 71, 83
general elections (1951), 8 (1964),
    8–9, 11, 14–15, 56, 173, (1966),
    11, 32, 56, 173
George VI, 6
Gifford, Lord, 70
Government of Ireland Act 1920, xi,
    9, 21–3, 28, 33–6, 38, 46, 48, 52,
    54–5, 58, 67, 70, 78, 89–90, 92,
    105–6, 110, 112, 115–17, 119,
    121–2, 128, 138, 141, 144, 149,
    167, 171, 175
Government of Northern Ireland
    (Stormont), 38–9, 41, 46–8, 55,
    64,71, 73–8, 84, 86–9, 92, 94–5,
    100, 102, 104–5,109, 111,
    113–18, 120–6, 132–4, 139–43,
    149, 151–3, 155, 159–65, 167–9,
    171, 173–7
    contracts awarded by, 38
    Home Affairs Dept., 129
    and International Commission of
        Jurists (ICJ) report, 150, 160–1

investment in Catholic areas
    discouraged by, 85, 87
and Londonderry riots, 107
and Speaker's Convention, 22–3,
    25, 35, 48–9, 52, 103, 105, 171
Gordon Walker, Patrick, 4, 5, 9–10,
    15, 173
Green, Arthur, 155, 167–9
Griffith, Professor John, 21–3, 92,
    173, 175
Grosvenor Square riot, 174
Guardian, The, 83, 87, 90

Haines, Joe, 13, 56, 78, 172
Hamilton, Dennis, 46–7, 128
Hamilton, William, 28
Hansard, xiv, 62, 175
Hassard, Jack, 67
Hattersley, Roy, 42, 163, 165–6
Healey, Dennis, 156, 159, 161, 163,
    165, 169
Heath, Edward, 60, 77, 101, 111,
    123, 133, 157, 159, 167, 176
Helsby, Laurence, 6
Hennessy, Professor Peter, 23
Hickey, Owen, 80–2
Holland, Mary, 48, 94, 111–12, 174
Home Office, 35, 51–3, 59, 92–4,
    100–2, 119, 129, 131, 139, 142,
    152, 161, 163–4, 167
    contingency plan for Northern
        Ireland take-over, 152–5 *see
        also* Chilcot, Sir John
Housing, discrimination in, 13, 21,
    34, 38–9, 45–6, 66, 73, 81, 87,
    91, 102, 108, 111, 120–1, 125,
    133, 168
Hume, John, 132
Hyam, Ronald, 4

Institute of Contemporary British
    History (ICBH), xiv, 37, 41, 92,
    99, 101, 129, 151, 162
International Commission of Jurists
    (ICJ), 150, 160–1, 170
Internment, 169–70
Ireland, Republic of
    establishment of, xv, 1, 3–4, 9, 26,
        144

Ireland, Republic of *continued*
  and relations with Britain, xiv, 18,
    83, 121
  and return of the Treaty Ports, xv,
    9
  and the Unionists, 47
Irish Association, 9–7
Irish Congress of Trade Unionists,
    64, 97
Irish Free State (Eire)
  attitude of Labour government
    (1945) to, 2, 172
  and Britain, 1, 9
  and campaign to end partition,
    2–3
  and King George VI's concern
    over decision to leave
    Commonwealth, 6
  and Second World War, 1, 26
IRA (Irish Republican Army), 39,
    40, 78–9, 98, 116, 128–9, 161,
    169, 171 *see also* Provisional
    IRA
  and border campaign (1956–62)
    xi, 11, 92
  and threat of bombing campaign
    to mark 50th anniversary of
    Easter Rising, xiii, xvi, 18–19,
    25, 30–1, 35, 39, 56, 60, 64,
    68, 164, 172, 175, 178
Irish Times, 47, 84, 93, 133–4
Irving, Sydney, 86

Jenkins, Roy, xvi, 36, 40, 42, 44–5,
    47–53, 57–8, 63, 65, 67–9, 74,
    79–80, 84 –91, 98, 114, 116, 159,
    174–5, 177–8
Johnson, Paul, 112, 133, 167
Jones, Sir Elwyn, 82
Jones, Tim, 157
Judd, Frank, 123

Kerr, Russell, 163
Kilburn, 103
King, Cecil, 94,
King, Dr Horace, 32, 35, 41
Kilfedder, Jim, 15

Labour Government (1945–51), 28
  attitude to Irish Free State, 2
Labour Government (1964–1970)
  Cameron Commission, attitude
    to, 170
  Catholic leaders, advice to, 169
  and commitment to reform, xv,
    56, 71, 84–6, 90, 153, 171, 173
  Fitt's election, reaction to, 35
  intervention in Northern Ireland,
    possibility of, xvi, 33, 45, 55,
    67, 75, 80–1, 84, 88, 92, 101,
    110–11, 118, 120, 124–5, 127,
    129–30, 132–3, 135, 137–9,
    141, 145, 148, 151, 156,
    158–9, 175–6
  IRA bombing campaign in 1966,
    threat of, *see under* Northern
    Ireland
  reluctance to interfere in
    Northern Ireland, 3, 7, 58, 72,
    91, 98, 112, 122, 125, 151, 169
  sending troops into Northern
    Ireland, xii, xvi, 32, 39, 42, 92,
    117, 120, 142–3, 150–5, 165–6
    171, 174, 176
  subsidies to Northern Ireland,
    possibility of withholding, 3,
    67, 87, 112, 113–15, 118, 122,
    125, 139–40, 143, 149, 157,
    177
  unpopularity of, 80, 178
Labour Party, xiv, 37, 93, 103, 120,
    127, 176, 178
  conferences (1967), 84, 86, 103
    (1968), 106–7
  constituency parties, 84–5, 106–7
  and Northern Ireland Labour
    Party, 11, 13
  and Treaty Ports, 1, 9
Lascelles, Sir Alan, 6
Lawrence, Dr R.J., 133
Lawson, George, 107
Leeds (Ulster Week), 74
Lemass, Sean, 16, 18, 51, 64
Lilley, Roy, 13, 34, 40, 68, 76–7, 96,
    118, 123–4, 128, 134, 157, 165
Lindsey Kerr, David, 139, 160, 163
Local Government Franchise (and
    gerrymandering of boundaries),

xi, 9, 21, 38, 45–6, 59, 66, 71,
73–5, 102, 105–6, 120–1, 125,
127, 130, 134, 140, 144–5,
157–61, 167–8
Londonderry, 46, 66, 73–4, 78, 82,
103, 125–6, 131, 134
Derry Central Labour Party, 131
Londonderry riots (5 October 1968),
xvi, 7, 14, 47–8, 79, 88, 99–100,
105–21, 125, 130, 142, 148, 172,
174–6
further riots, 142, 161
violence in Bogside, 150
Longford, Earl of, 5, 65, 94
Lubbock, Eric, 14, 40–1, 90, 158
Lynch, Jack, 126, 143
Lyons, F.S.L., 3

McAteer, Eddie, 84, 101
MacBride, Sean, 5, 160–1
McClean, Hugh, 39
McCluskey, Pat, 13, 84, 173
McGuire, Michael, 53
McKie, David, 90
Mackintosh, John, 116, 177
McMillan, Liam, 15
Macmillan, Harold, 28, 178–9
McNamara, Kevin, xiii, 28, 36–9,
51–2, 55, 95, 101–3, 115, 129,
158–9, 162
Mahon, Simon, 24
Malvern Street murders, 39, 69
Margach, James, 49
Mayhew, Christopher, 4
Media, the, xiv, 15, 45–6, 69, 72,
80, 100, 108–10, 115–16, 128,
132, 136–8, 142, 166, 172, 174,
176–7
Mellish, Robert, 8, 173
Mid-Ulster by-election, 141–2
Mikardo, Ian, 37
MI5, 19, 100, 129, 164, 169
Miller, Maurice, 65
Mills, Stratton, 88
Ministry of Defence (MOD),
139–41, 163
Morgan, Elystan, 52–4
Morgan, Kenneth, 2, 147
Morrison, Herbert, 1–2, 7, 9–10

Murnaghan, Sheelagh, 90
National Council for Civil Liberties
(NCCL), 84, 85
Nationalists, 48, 51, 64, 83, 101
Newry (riots), 133
New Statesman, 112, 132–3, 167
Noel-Baker, Philip, 4, 6
Northern Ireland, xv, 2, 5–7, 9, 16,
35, 38, 40, 65, 93–4, 123,
172–3
Civil rights (and discrimination)
in, xi–xii, 2, 7–9, 20–5, 28,
31–41, 44–7, 49, 51–3, 55,
57–8, 63, 65–78, 80–4, 86–94,
100–15, 118, 120–1, 125–8,
130–3, 144, 158–64, 170–3,
175, *see also* Employment,
discrimination in; Housing,
discrimination in; Local
Government Franchise;
Public appointments,
discrimination in
deaths from terrorism and sectarian violence in, xii–xiv, 170,
176, 178
direct rule imposed on, possibility
of, 48, 143, 150, 153, 158,
164–5, 167, 169, 176–7
economic policy in, 11, 44, 86, 88,
96–7, 140
financial relations with British
Exchequer, 119
'Five-point programme' of reform
in, 118, 121–3, 125–7, 133,
140, 157–9, 162, 165, 167,
176
general elections (1965), 41, 43;
(1969), 135–41
IRA bombing campaign in 1966
threat of, xiii, xvi, 11, 18–20,
25, 30–1, 35, 56, 68, 100, 164,
172, 175, 178
Parliament of, xi
Republic relations with, 16, 153
sending troops to, *see under*
Labour Government
and subsidies to, 3, 50–3, 67, 87,
112–15, 118, 122, 124–5, 135,
138–40, 149, 157, 177

Northern Ireland Civil Rights
Association (NICRA), xiv, 99, 101,
108, 131–3, 153, 156–7, 159–60,
174–5, 177
and the claim that it was an IRA
puppet, 128–9, 168–9, 171
Northern Ireland Labour Party
(NILP), xiv, 13, 26, 41, 43,
51, 63, 66–7, 71, 83, 131, 148,
160

Observer, 94, 111
Ogden, Eric, 27
Oliver, Dr John, 58–9, 76–8, 99, 126,
177
Ombudsman, 39, 49, 78, 87–8, 112,
121, 125, 175
O'Neill, Terence, xi, 26, 31–2, 39,
48, 54, 63, 67–8, 70, 84, 114,
125–6, 129–30, 132, 138–41,
143, 150, 152, 165, 176, 178
'Crossroads' speech, 118, 127–8,
131–2, 135, 148, 176
and Brian Faulkner, 134–5
Fifth Anniversary optimism of,
xvi, 80, 95–7, 99
and 'Five Point Programme' of
reform, 118, 121–3, 125–7,
133, 140, 144, 148
General Election (1969), calls
sudden, 135–41, 148, 176
Kenneth Bloomfield, letters to,
63, 130
'liberal' policy of, 34–5, 39, 41–3,
46–7, 64, 72, 81, 85–6, 88–90,
93–6, 98, 101–2, 109–11, 113,
153, 160, 163, 171, 178
and Northern Ireland Labour
Party, 41–2
'O'Neillism', collapse of, 118,
147–8, 169
and relations with Harold Wilson,
see under Wilson, Harold
resignation of, 43, 65, 117, 119,
130, 137–8, 140, 145–7,
150–1, 168, 176
and *Times* investigation into
discrimination in Northern
Ireland, 73–5, 78

and threat of IRA bombing
campaign in1966, *see under*
Northern Ireland
subsidy for province, threat of
withholding, *see under*
Northern Ireland
Orange Order, 104, 108, 134, 136,
139, 144, 146, 160–1, 164–5
Orme, Stan, 58, 65, 107, 163
Orr, Lawrence, 24, 32, 34, 61, 77, 116
Otton, Sir Geoffrey, 26
Owen, David, 174

Paisley, Rev. Ian, 15, 39–40, 45–7,
57, 60, 81, 97, 111, 137–9, 144,
157
Parliament, 41, 45, 50, 60, 75, 79,
83–4, 91–2, 104, 112, 121, 127,
142–3, 158, 167
debates on Northern Ireland, 14,
23–8, 32–3, 51–6, 86–9, 142–3
Finance Bill (1966), amendments
to, 37–8
Prices and Incomes Act, (1966),
48, 112, 175
Speakers' Convention on
Northern Ireland, xvi, 11, 14,
20–3, 27–8, 30–2, 34–8, 40,
44, 46, 48, 86, 90, 103–5, 107,
110, 112–13, 115, 137, 142,
144, 171, 173–5
Parliamentary Labour Party, 68,
75–6, 95, 104, 121, 159
backbench MPs; their early
attempts to raise civil rights,
35
rebellion against government over
Ireland Act (1949), 7–8, 173
Partition, 2–6, 8–10, 16, 45, 145,
172–3
Peart, Fred, 115
People's Democracy (PD), xiv, 130,
137
Pimlott, Ben, 147
Police, English,
idea of use of in Northern
Ireland, 120
Provisional Irish Republican Army
(PIRA), xiv, xiii

Public Record Office (PRO), 177
Public appointments, discrimination in, 13, 39, 66, 73
Purdie, Bob, 130

Queen's University Belfast (QUB), 71, 130

Race Relations legislation, 37, 49, 87, 89, 93, 104, 175
Rees, Merlyn, 93, 100, 129, 169–70
Rees-Mogg, William, 72, 80–2, 93, 100, 129, 169–70
Reynolds, Gerry, 35
Richard, Ivor, 70–1, 98
Riddell, Patrick, 168
Robens, Alf, 12
Rose, Paul, 20, 24, 29, 37, 44, 46, 65–8, 83, 85, 107–9, 115–16, 128, 142, 144, 157, 162–3
Rose, Richard, 79–80, 172
Round Table, the, 109
Royal Ulster Constabulary (RUC), 15, 18–19, 68, 100, 108–9, 115, 120, 131, 156, 160–1, 164
  B Specials, 108, 160, 168
  Special Branch, 169–70

St John Stevas, Norman, 61, 143
Sayers, Jack, 65, 97, 109, 123–7, 130–1, 133, 139, 148–9, 159–60, 163
Scotland
  allegations of anti-Catholic bias in Constituency Labour Parties in, 107
Shanks, Michael, 139–40
Shinwell, Manny, 35, 174
Shorts of Belfast, 114
Silkin, Sam, 70, 82
Sinclair, Betty, 66
Social Democratic and Labour Party (SDLP), 32, 66
Society of Labour Lawyers (SLL), xiv, 58, 69–72, 78, 82–3, 100, 105–6
Soskice, Sir Frank, 4, 18, 23, 25–7, 173, 178
South Africa, 160, 170

Special Powers Act (SPA) 38, 78, 102, 120–1, 125–6, 130, 158–9, 160, 168
Spectator, 134–6, 138, 167
Survey into Catholic attitudes (1968), 78–80, 98, 172
Stewart, Michael, xiv, 4
Stonham, Lord, 52, 93, 100–2, 105
Storey, Sir Sam, 24, 26
Sunday Independent, 129–30
Sunday Telegraph, 29, 36, 61
Sunday Times The, 31, 45–7, 49, 72, 125–6, 147
Sunday Times Insight Team, 151, 161, 164
Sunningdale Agreement, 153

Terry, Walter, 138
Thatcher, Margaret, 177
Thomas, George, 27–8
Thomson, Lord, 72, 82
Thornberry, Cedric, 70
Thorpe, Jeremy, 40, 90–1, 101, 104–5, 115, 141, 174
Times, The, 7, 15, 17, 41, 58, 60, 63, 80–2, 95–6, 99–101, 106–7, 110–11, 116, 128, 133, 135, 138–9, 157–8, 160–1, 164, 166, 174
  investigation into civil rights in Northern Ireland, 70, 72–5
Treaty Ports, xv, 1, 9
Trade Unions, 103
Treasury, the,
subsidy to Northern Ireland, allocation of, 114
Trend, Sir Burke, 19
Tyrone, County, 108

Ulster Volunteer Force (UVF), 39–41, 46, 57, 110
Ulster Television (UTV), 108
Underhill, Reg, 107
Unionists, xi, 3, 17, 26–8, 31–4, 41–3, 46, 54, 56, 61, 64, 66–7, 70, 72–4, 78, 82, 84, 86, 89–91, 93–5, 97–8, 113, 115, 125, 127, 129, 133–5, 140–1, 143–4, 150, 155, 160, 162, 171–2, 178

Unionists – *continued*
  anti O'Neill, 51, 60, 63–5, 81, 95,
    97, 122–4, 129, 132, 134–5,
    138, 176
  and general election, 1969, 136–8
  and International Commission of
    Jurists, report of 150, 160–1
  and the media, 45, 47
  and Society of Labour Lawyers,
    69, 82–3, 105–6, 109, 111
  and Westminster, impact at, xiii,
    xiv, 9, 11–2, 24–5, 29–30, 32,
    34, 35–6, 61–3, 76, 96, 104,
    111–12, 115, 121, 124–5, 143,
    174, 177
United Nations, 166–7
United States of America
  Northern Ireland, relationship
    with, 121
Utley, T.E, 139

Walker, Harold, 37
Waller, Ian, 29, 36, 61–2
Wenham, Brian, 69
Whitaker, Ben, 89, 104, 115
Whitley, J.H, 20
Williams, Shirley, 52
Wilson, Harold, xiv, 3, 7–8, 30–3, 40,
    72, 86, 90, 94, 110, 126, 134–5,
    137, 143–4, 146, 148, 150,
    155–7, 160–2, 166, 177
  and civil rights in Northern
    Ireland, xii, 1, 11, 13, 15, 17,
    25, 27–8, 31, 45–7, 56, 58, 65,
    69, 77, 84–5, 88–90, 94,
    103–4, 108, 115, 132–3, 139,
    141, 170, 178–9
  deteriorating situation in
    Northern Ireland, policy on,
    xiii, 99, 101, 105–6, 115,
    121–2, 133–4, 138, 141–2,
    149, 175

  direct rule, threat of, 164–5, 167,
    169, 176–7
  and economic and political crises
    in Britain, implications for
    Northern Ireland policy of,
    49, 56–7, 59–61, 79, 91, 98,
    147, 171, 178; and 'five-point
    programme' of reform, 118,
    121–3, 125–7, 157–9, 168–9;
    and Irish Catholics in Huyton
    constituency of, 12, 44, 104,
    173; and IRA bombing
    campaign in 1966 threat of,
    see under Northern Ireland;
    Irish Republic relations with,
    16, 18, 47, 173; and non-
    intervention in Northern
    Ireland, policy of, 35, 41, 65,
    75, 78–9, 84, 98, 113, 117,
    174–5; and Terence O'Neill,
    25, 35–6, 41–5, 49–51, 56, 58,
    64, 72, 76–7, 80, 96, 105,
    110–11, 115–16, 122–4, 128,
    131–3, 135, 138, 140, 158,
    173, 175
  and sending troops to Northern
    Ireland, xii, 39, 100, 144, 150,
    165–6, 169
  and Speaker's Convention on
    Northern Ireland, 22–3
  subsidy for Northern Ireland,
    threat of withholding, 50–1,
    67, 114–15, 122, 124–5, 135,
    138–9, 149, 177
  and Ulster Unionist MPs at
    Westminster, xiv, 29–30,
    35–6, 58, 61–3, 76–7. 96, 104,
    114, 116, 122, 124–5, 174–7
  United Ireland, belief in, 13,
    61–2, 172.
Wood, David, 72, 138
Wright, Sir Oliver, 17, 30, 154, 167